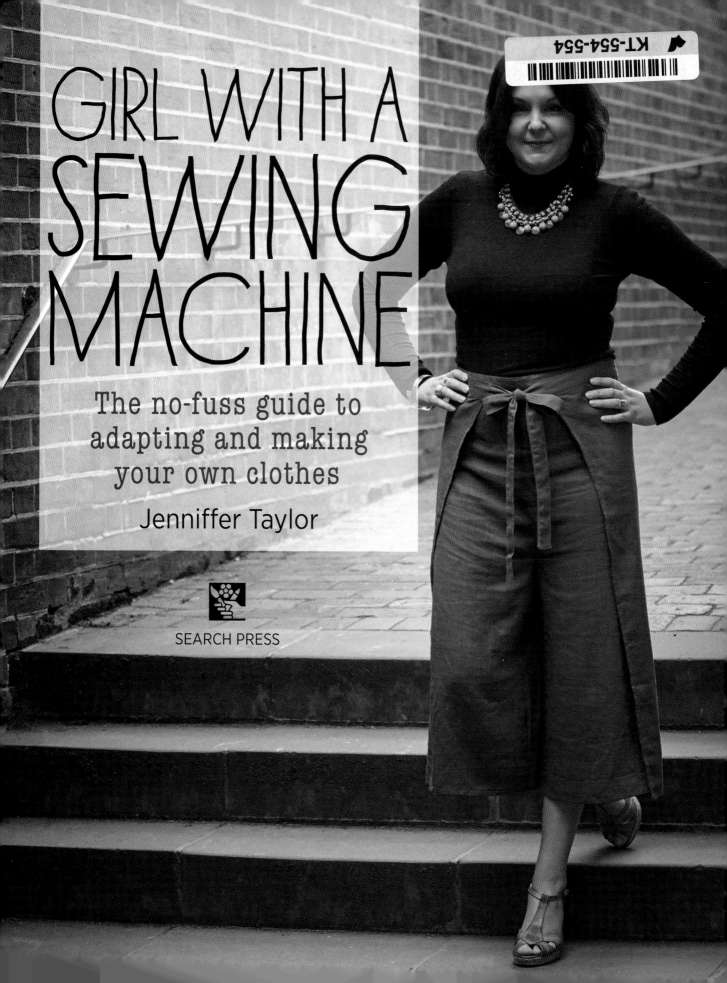

GIRL WITH A SEWING MACHINE

The no-fuss guide to adapting and making your own clothes

Jenniffer Taylor

SEARCH PRESS

GIRL
WITH A
SEWING
MACHINE

First published in 2017

Search Press Limited
Wellwood, North Farm Road,
Tunbridge Wells, Kent TN2 3DR

Reprinted 2017

Photographs by Roddy Paine Photographic Studios

Text copyright © Jenniffer Taylor

Photographs and Design copyright
© Search Press Ltd 2017

ISBN: 978-1-78221-456-4

Suppliers
For details of suppliers, please visit the
Search Press website: www.searchpress.com

Visit Jenniffer's website: www.jenniffertaylor.co.uk
Search for Tailor-Taylor on Facebook
Follow @JenniBobTaylor on Twitter
#sewingrevolution

Printed in China by 1010 Printing International Ltd

Dedication

To Ineke, thank you for inspiring me to make art and
not just a simple wedding dress. Little did we know
what you started in your amazing studio that day!
You are an inspiration!

To Mom (Lain), Dad (Roy) and Bro (Rob) aka the Gardners.
You're always there to brush my knees off when I fall
down and that has been quite a few times. You've always
encouraged me to reach for the sky, while keeping me
grounded. You've always said 'do what makes you happy'.
I'm finally doing it, thanks to your love and support!
Love you all, loads!

To the Taylors aka the in-laws. I struck gold becoming part
of your clan! Your love, support and encouragement has
been amazing.

To my friends and #sewingrevolutionists: thank you so
much for being guinea pigs by attending workshops or
reading my instructions, for following my journey and
inspiring me all the way! Thanks for being the fire in my
belly! Viva la #sewingrevolution!

To my muse, my husband, Kirk. As you said on our
wedding day – life without you is like a pencil – pointless!
I cannot say it in any other way either. Without you, this
would not have been possible. Thank you for believing in
me when I didn't. With all my heart, love you, Punk!

Acknowledgements

Huge thank you to Korbond for your continued support in
providing me with equipment and haberdashery, for not
only the book but for sharing the #sewingrevolution
dream with me!

A special thank you to Jules from Sew Me Something,
Ellie from The Bolt Tree and Brenda from
Inkberrow Design Centre for not only supplying wonderful
fabrics, but for your needed words of support.
Ladies, thank you!

To Abakhan and Craft Cotton Co for supplying beautiful
fabrics, Janome for kindly providing the sewing machine
and overlocker, to Colouricious for fuelling my obsession
with block printing and finally Vilene for providing the
interfacing. Thank you so much for your support.

CONTENTS

INTRODUCTION

Being a self-taught seamstress, I have a no-fuss attitude to sewing. I'm impatient; I want to get started right away and I want to have something to wear as soon as possible. I'm also constantly striving to gain new skills and techniques, as well as perfecting the skills I do have with each new project I sew. This book is full of projects that will give you exactly that: clothes that can be made either with a garment you already own, or by making a garment from scratch with just a few body measurements – which is just how I taught myself to sew. You really don't need to go very far to get started.

For me, sewing is an empowering skill that can transform how you feel as well as how you look. It also comes with a warning: it is addictive! I want to encourage everyone to give it a go and pass my skills on to others, which is what the #sewingrevolution is all about.

Through my #sewingrevolution workshops and my own personal sewing journey I have seen people's confidence flourish and grow with each make. So, to set you on your own #sewingrevolution journey, this book will take you through a few projects that I have made along the way, starting with a sewing-room essential, the vintage teacup pincushion (pages 20–25). I will also share insights into what inspires my makes, such as the tassel top (pages 50–55). I want to prove to you that you don't need to go out fabric or pattern shopping to get started – see my coat made from a blanket (pages 112–121). Although when your confidence and sewing skills begin to grow, I guarantee you won't be able to resist hitting those market stalls or haberdasheries for your next stash of fabric (see pages 14–15). My mantra is: 'creativity is contagious – pass it on'. With that in mind, I want to encourage your individuality and self-confidence with each stitch and prove that a girl with a sewing machine is all it takes!

Join the #sewingrevolution by sharing pictures of your finished makes on social media. Don't forget to include the hashtag. I cannot wait to see them!

Search for Tailor-Taylor on Facebook
Follow @JenniBobTaylor on Twitter
Visit my website: www.jenniffertaylor.co.uk

I love getting to meet my #sewingrevolutionists at events. Getting to hear about what you have been making always makes me feel like I have the best job in the world!

MY SEWING JOURNEY

Me on my second birthday, with my mom (Lain) and Dad (Roy). It's one of my favourite pictures of my mom and dad; they're always there to pick me up. I also love dad's denim shirt so much that I've pinched it for myself... I'm so glad he kept it!

All good stories start with a fairytale setting, and mine started with a wedding dress. That is where my sewing journey really begins...

As I child I always had my fingers in a lot of creative pies, whether it was dance, art, drama or music. I studied Dance and Visual Art at the Northern School of Contemporary Dance before completing my degree at Brighton University. But my creative graduate career didn't appear. Instead, I moved back home to West Bromwich and became a debt collector for the local water board. Ten years passed, and I'd worked my way up to be a Resource Coordinator – a good position but not quite what I had in mind as a career. I still clung onto my creative spark where I could by painting and cooking, but it was when I began singing in a band called Snooty Bobs, that things really began to change.

A muse appeared called Kirk Taylor – he was the guitarist in the band. After only a few months of dating, he popped the question... and as you can probably guess I said YES! We both decided that we didn't want a long engagement, and set a date to get married within a year. My creative sparks were flying thanks to the band, and with a muse to boot I decided I was going to make my own wedding dress. Two-footed, I designed, hacked a pattern and constructed my dress, with a little guidance and equipment from a wonderful friend, Ineke Berlyn, to whom I will always be grateful. This was the first garment I had ever made from scratch and in true tradition, my wedding day was the first time Kirk, along with everyone else, saw my dress and my ability to sew. From then on, sewing has been an addiction that has unlocked my creativity.

For the first time I felt able to express my individual style and empowered to make the clothes I wanted to wear. Cutting up old clothes, bed linen or curtains was and still is my staple way of getting fabric for projects. Being a beginner and, to be honest, skint after the wedding, I needed to sew and this was the cheapest way to do it. It was through cutting up and dissecting clothes and refashioning them that I learned so much about how clothes are made. It filled me with ideas for how I could make my own garments without patterns by simply using existing clothes as base blocks. I then went on to use my own measurements to draft out garments to size. I also liked to use vintage patterns. As these were secondhand, sometimes parts were missing or incorrect, so I learned to figure it out and make it up as I went along. As the saying goes – practice makes perfect!

Kirk recognised my passion for my new-found skill and, as muses do, wanted it to flourish. He secretly submitted a contestant application for *The Great British Sewing Bee* – a programme I had been watching at the time to get more tips to improve my sewing. To say I was surprised to be

Snooty Bobs headlining the Hare and Hounds, Kings Heath, in 2010.

chosen out of hundreds of applications and to get past several audition stages is a HUGE understatement; considering that when I walked on set I had only been sewing for about a year at that point, I can only describe the whole experience as a fairytale. Being a Sewing Bee was a terrifying experience. Don't get me wrong, I love a challenge (as my wedding dress shows!) but this was something else. Not a confident sewer, but a hardworking perfectionist, I wanted to do the best that I possibly could. More importantly, I wanted to learn everything thing I could while surrounded by so many talented sewists. It was an extreme crash course in sewing that I could have killed Kirk for putting me through, yet secretly loved and will never forget.

After the show wrapped, and with the adventure of lights, camera, action well and truly over, I was restless. My creative aspirations were reignited and I was determined to make something of my experience but lacked the confidence to make it happen. Then something changed. People began finding ways of contacting me directly through email and social media, encouraging me with their stories of how I had inspired them to start sewing, and sharing pictures of their makes. I'm just a girl from West Bromwich, doing something that I love, and it's amazing to inspire people to make things for themselves and others. I want you to know that it's YOUR stories of encouragement that propelled me to do what I do now. It is YOU who gave me the confidence to start the #sewingrevolution.

The #sewingrevolution started with small sewing workshops in my local area, after which we would share our makes with each other via social media. I then started writing projects for magazines and doing sewing demonstrations on TV. I now have my very own stand and workshops at sewing events, which thousands of people attend year on year. Four years on, I had the confidence to quit my full-time day job so that I can continue to spread the creative love that makes so many people happy, including myself. The #sewingrevolution is about sharing that gift. I want you to be loud and proud, show off your wonderful makes and most importantly, share your skill by teaching someone else. It is this thought that has inspired me to write this book. I hope it will build your confidence and sewing skills with each new project. I want you to feel like I'm with you every stitch of the way, just as my muse and some of you have been there for me, even if you don't realise it.

Remember, I'm just a girl with a sewing machine but anything is possible...

Jenni x

My wedding day, August 2012 at the Botanical Gardens, Birmingham. Me in my handmade wedding dress with paper and organza lace and pearl flipflops and Kirk in bespoke purple suit with paisley shirt. How rock and roll are we?!

Always there to support me – Kirk and me at my first events stand, sharing the #sewingrevolution love at Sewing For Pleasure, Birmingham NEC, 2016.

SEWING KIT

Sharp things

Rule number one: don't mix up your scissors! Buy a pair of **dressmaking scissors (1)** for your fabric, padlock them and don't let anyone else use them! I'm being totally serious; ask any hairdresser and they will say exactly the same thing about their snips! Your fabric scissors will last a lot longer if you only use them for fabric. Cutting things like paper, sticky tape, food packets, flowers and so on will blunt them and then potentially ruin your fabric when cutting it. I like to have a separate pair of scissors for paper as well as a pair of embroidery scissors for snipping loose threads. I put my **embroidery scissors (2)** onto a piece of long ribbon and wear them like a necklace. It stops me from losing them when in full-on dressmaking mode and also I feel like a proper seamstress with a scissor necklace and my tape measure around my neck! A pair of **pinking shears (1)** are very handy for quickly finishing off your seams. The saw-toothed edge helps to stop your fabrics from fraying as much as a normal straight cut would, meaning your makes will stand up to a lot more washing and wearing.

A seamstress's best friend is an **unpicker** or **quick unpick (3)**. We all dream of sewing without making a mistake, but guys it's just not going to happen! You WILL make a mistake. In fact, I encourage it! Making mistakes is the best way to learn and some of my 'mistakes' have turned out to be awesome in the end so don't be afraid to make them. But when you really do need to unpick, a sharp unpicker is a must. Change your unpicker as soon as you notice it becoming blunt, as you don't want to start damaging your fabric. A sharp unpicker should glide through a seam without much force. The red ball is like a safety ball – it should stop you from cutting the fabric as you cut the threads, so use it ball-side down.

A **rotary cutter (4)** is great if you are making your own bias binding or are cutting slippery fabrics. A rotary cutter looks and works just like a pizza cutter, meaning you can cut your fabric while it is completely flat. When using scissors, you will end up lifting your fabric as the blades cut through it; when dealing with slippy fabric like silk or chiffon, your cutting motion can cause cutting errors as the fabric moves around. Ultimately, this is not an essential tool, but it's something to add to your sewing kit as you get more experienced. Don't forget to buy a cutting mat to go with it, as you will mark your table or cut your flooring to shreds if you don't.

Pins and needles

You can pick up **needles (5)** very easily – even in the supermarket – and they sometimes come in a variety pack or compact. These are perfect as they will include everything you need, from small sharp needles to a wool needle. If you struggle to thread a needle, I would suggest picking up a couple of **needle threaders (6)** too.

When buying **pins (7)**, I always go for glass-headed ones, because they will not melt under a hot iron. I find professional dressmakers' pins (which are the metal ones with no head) really fiddly, but hey, it's a personal preference. When you get more adventurous with different types of fabrics, you may want to invest in some longer and thinner pins, but it's not essential.

Safety pins (8) are the perfect tool to help thread elastic or cord through waistbands. They are also super handy to keep your half-made projects together, so you don't lose any fabric pieces.

A spare pack of **sewing machine needles (9)** is also good to have. There's nothing worse than having to stop and shop because you have broken a sewing machine needle. Trust me it will happen; it happens to all of us. They tend to come in a variety of sizes to cover lightweight to heavier fabrics and include stretch/ballpoint needles, which you will need for stretchy fabrics. A quick tip on sewing machine needles: the lower the number, the finer the needle – great for finer fabrics. The higher the number, the thicker the needle – ideal for thicker fabrics. Try to get into the habit of changing your sewing machine needle after a few projects. Just like your unpicker, your needle will become blunt over time and will start to chew up your fabric. So always do a test sew on a scrap piece of fabric before your start on your project. Better to be safe than sorry.

You can't have pins without a **pincushion (10)**! You don't need to buy one as we are making one together (see pages 20–25), but there are some cute pincushions out there and if you're anything like me you probably won't be able to resist! If you are going to buy a pincushion, it might be worth investing in an emery pincushion. These are filled with a special powder that keeps your pins and needles nice and sharp. Keep an eye out for the **tomato-shaped pincushion (11)** with a little chilli-shaped one attached to it. The chilli part is filled with emery powder. Pass your needle through the chilli a few times and it will sharpen your needle for you, making it last longer – bonus!

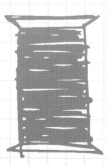

Made to measure

The iconic **measuring tape (1)** is not just for posing purposes but is a sewing kit essential. Even with all my efforts to look cool with it around my neck, I'm always misplacing it, so I have several. Fingers crossed you are a lot tidier than me, so you should only need the one! Your old school ruler will also come in handy, so make sure you dig that out. **Pattern masters** or **tailors' curves (2)** make drawing your own patterns really easy, but before I owned these tools, I just used plates and dishes from the kitchen to get smooth, curved edges.

Making a mark

There are so many different ways to mark your fabric. I sometimes just use a pin, but at other times you need to add a little more information than just mark a point on the fabric. **Tailors' chalk (3)** is a traditional way to mark your fabric and can be easily brushed off when finished with. Chalk wheels and chalk pens are the same material, just packaged differently. What you use will all come down to personal preference. **Water-erasable pens (3)** are also great for when you are adding embroidery detail as you can accurately draw onto the fabric and then remove it with a little water or steam after. The marks tend to stay on a little longer than chalk but cannot be seen so clearly on darker fabric.

Hot things

An **iron (4)** and ironing board are must-haves. The good news is the one you use for your laundry is perfect. Having a hot iron to hand for darts and hems can speed up a sew. A good press can be as good as pinning in place, meaning that sometimes you don't need to pin at all. It's also good to have an **ironing cloth (5)** – something that withstands heat like a clean tea towel will do just fine. When using delicate or manmade fibres you don't want to melt your fabric or ruin your iron, so it's worth having a piece of cloth to hand to place over the top to protect your fabric before you press.

Tailors' hams and **sleeve boards (5)** are indispensable when your sewing becomes more advanced. Tailors' hams come in different shapes and sizes, but all will basically help to create shape when pressing a garment. Check out the tailors' ham tutorial on my blog and make one for yourself. A sleeve board is basically a small ironing board that makes pressing sleeves and cuffs easy. These are tools that make the job so much easier and can make the difference between a good finish and a professional finish.

The unusual suspects

A **lint roller (6)** might not be something you would think to include in your sewing kit, but they are awesome for removing the threads you have had to unpick from your garment quickly. They are also the quickest way to tidy your sewing area. Just run the lint roller over your cut threads and small off-cuts of fabric, remove the used sheet from the roller and pop it in the bin! Quick as a flash! You will quickly notice how messy your area gets with threads and fabric lint, so imagine what it is doing to your sewing machine. **Earbuds (7)** are a quick way to de-fluff your machine without having to become a sewing machine engineer. Before popping your bobbin into your machine, just check for any lint in and around the bobbin case. If there is any, just give it a quick and gentle wipe with an earbud to remove it. Do the same with the needle bar, as lint will collect there too. Doing this little bit of cleaning will help prevent thread snags and keep your machine happy!

Elastic (8) is a must-have item, but not for what you think... Yes, you might need to insert it into garments, but its purpose in your sewing kit is actually to be your fitting buddy. Everything will be revealed later, when we take your body measurements (see page 68).

A leftover piece of **candle wax** is really handy to have in your sewing kit, especially when you are doing a lot of hand sewing. To stop your thread from getting tangled up, run your thread over the candlestick first. The natural wax will lightly coat the thread, making it easier to pass through your fabric. You can buy special tailors' wax but I find my method works just as well.

A pedicure **toe separator (9)** is another handy bit of kit. I use these to store my wound bobbins, so the threads don't come lose while in my sewing kit.

Chopsticks are a perfect poking tool. You can buy point turners very cheaply but as you will probably already have a chopstick in your kitchen, just grab that instead. The chopstick is awesome for poking out corners or pushing out waistbands as the slightly rounded edge won't punch a hole in your fabric.

A **miniature dress form (10)** is a great inexpensive tool for trying out patterns and ideas before you commit to a full-size design and lots of potentially expensive fabric. You may also find a full-size dress form very handy, especially if you plan to make lots of clothes, but most of the time you can use your own body and look in a mirror to test out how garments fit or hang.

A good **chair (11)** and a **mug** are essential! Take it from me – think about how and what you are sitting on. If you end up doing as much sewing as I do, please think about your back. If you have ever worked in an office, you have probably had HR come round and assess your desk and seating at some point, as sitting for long periods is not good for any of us. Try not to slouch, make sure the foot peddle is under your feet so you are not stretching for it and take regular breaks! The #sewingrevolution is built on tea, so make sure you regularly go and make a cup of tea to give yourself and your back a little break.

Where the magic happens: your sewing machine

As long as your **sewing machine (12)** has a few basic stitches such as a straight stitch, zigzag and straight stretch stitch that you can vary in length or width you are more than good to go! My first sewing machine, and the one that is still my workhorse today, only has 30 stitches – other machines have hundreds. If truth be told, I probably only use about five of them on a regular basis: straight, stretch, zigzag, overlock and buttonhole.

A sewing machine with a buttonhole stitch is very handy and quick but not essential, as you can replicate it with a well-practised zigzag stitch. Your machine will generally come with a selection of sewing feet. These will, of course, make the job easier but again are not essential.

I'm going to be honest with you here: an **overlocker/serger (13)** is something you might purchase to reward yourself with later on, but you don't need one. I have only just purchased one for myself as a recent birthday present and because I wanted to include it in my book. (The last part of that sentence is an excuse of course.) You can easily get along

without one, especially as most sewing machines have a mock overlocking stitch. That being said, when you do get one, it's a game-changer. An overlocker (serger) cuts the fabric as it sews; there isn't much room for error, but it makes you a semi-professional seamstress, with your garments finished and sewn to perfection, even if you still feel like you're a beginner.

In short, all you really need to get sewing is a straight stitch. A **vintage hand-cranked machine (14)** will give you that, so check with family and friends if anyone has one in the loft that still works and that you can borrow.

FABRICOLOGY

Sharing the knowledge and love of fabric

Check your wardrobe

When thinking about what kind of fabric I want to sew with, I think about clothes that I already own. Whether you realise it or not, you already have a wealth of fabric knowledge because you wear clothes every day (unless you are a full-time nudist, of course). In the summer months, you reach for dresses or shirts that will probably be made from a light cotton or silk. Likewise, when you are cold, you grab a jumper that may be fleeced or knitted or you wear heavy corduroy or denim trousers to keep you warm. Upcycling old clothes to make new garments helped me to build my fabric knowledge. In cutting up what I no longer wore, I got to handle so many different types of fabric – plus I knew how to care for them because they come with a washing and information label attached to them.

When buying fabric, think about how it feels in your hands. Chances are you have something similar in your wardrobe. What garment is it? When do you wear it? Does the fabric feel right for the project you are making? Check how the fabric flows – is it stiff or does it drape? Is it heavy or light? If it is on a roll, ask if you can unravel a little of it to check this. Put the fabric against you to see if the colour or pattern suits you. You may love looking at it but will you really wear it? Give it a light pull – does it stretch? Fabric is constructed in two different ways – woven or knitted – and these behave very differently to one another. Woven fabrics tend to be more rigid compared to knitted fabrics, which stretch. All these factors need to be considered when using fabric and making a garment.

Keep a fabric diary

I like to keep a fabric diary. I sew little leftover scraps of fabric into a book with a note on what I was making, when and who for, as well as notes on what the fabric is and how to care for it – plus any tips that I came across as I was sewing the project. Building up this kind of resource can help you on future projects.

Where do I get fabric from?

Your home: old blankets or bed sheets are great to use as there is so much fabric in them. Old clothes are a great source of fabric too, as a few of my projects will show. It is also a really cheap way to get started.

Charity or thrift shops: when you have exhausted your home and the homes of your family and friends, the charity shop is a great place to go for a fabric fix. I have come across some amazing retro printed linen and fabric in charity shops, not to mention buttons, lace trims and ribbon. They can be a treasure chest of goodies and you're also giving to a good cause!

Local markets: I'm very lucky to live near Birmingham's notorious Rag Market. It's a vault of fabric delights and if you ever get the chance to go, please do! I also have access to great local fabric stalls in West Bromwich and Walsall, where I grew up. Because of the culturally diverse residents here, you get a wonderful array of fabric choices at very low prices. The fabric used in my Kimono dress (pages 90–95) is from West Bromwich market and was incredibly cheap. You can find some amazing bargains, but be warned – you should always check the quality of the fabric and print. Check for imperfections and marks and always buy an extra half metre or so, in case you need to avoid these areas. Don't be afraid to haggle if buying a few different pieces from the same stall.

Local haberdasheries: it really is worth doing an internet search to find your local haberdashery. Not only will they stock fabric and sewing equipment, but they are also an invaluable source of knowledge. My local haberdashery is super helpful and always willing to give you sewing advice and a slice of cake. I cannot promise you will get cake at every haberdashery, but I'm very sure that you will always find someone who can help – you just need to ask!

I love visiting my home town of West Bromwich and having a look at the fabric markets. Full of colourful and patterned materials, there is always something to be found.

National sewing events: imagine all the haberdashery stores in the world, all under one roof. Yep, it's kinda like that, so bring a trolley. Going to these events can make for a very long day, so go prepared! You will be in fabric and haberdashery heaven with so much to choose from, as well as sewing workshops to take part in – these are places of inspiration.

Online: with technology at your fingertips, you can easily buy fabric from all over the world. If you don't get the chance to dedicate an afternoon to physically go fabric shopping, then online can be a good option. As well as using your search engine, check out Pinterest, Facebook and Instagram too. I have found some wonderful independent online shops though social media, so get browsing. The only downside to online shopping is that you don't get to feel the fabric first, and that's my favourite part.

How much fabric should I buy?

Many factors affect how much material you will need for a project.

1. What are you making?
2. How tall are you?
3. What size are you?
4. Does the fabric have a pattern?
5. What width is the fabric?

Consider how long the garment is. If it is a full-length dress, then a good gauge would be to double your shoulder to floor measurement, as you have a front and a back to the dress, and add a little extra for luck or to pattern match. As a rule, I always buy 3m (10ft) of fabric; this may leave me a little leftover fabric at the end but it will always go into another project. However, my choice of fabric is never really an expensive one – I love an upcycle and a bargain.

If I'm making something really special and I have a more expensive material in mind, I tend to make the garment out of something cheap first. This is known as making a toile. With a toile, you make the garment as normal, make adjustments for the right fit and then use that as a base pattern. To find out how much fabric you need, unpick your toile pieces. Place them on the floor, making sure they stay within your fabric width. Once all of your pattern pieces are laid out as if they were on the fabric, measure the length you require. If your fabric has a very obvious print, you will need to measure the repeat of the print and add that to your fabric measurement to ensure you have enough for pattern matching.

My bargain find from West Bromwich Market, which was perfect for my Kimono Dress (see page 90).

Where do I start?

Washing fabric: the first thing you will need to do is wash your fabric. You don't want to spend time sewing a garment that then shrinks in the wash. Some fabrics will come pre-shrunk and of course upcycled clothes and linen will already have been washed, but it's always best to give them a quick cycle in the washing machine. Vintage or old fabrics will also need to be tested with a quick cycle, as they may not stand up to washing because of their age. Fibres do weaken over time and you don't want to get all excited about a vintage make just to have it fall apart on you.

Ironing versus pressing: once you have washed and dried your fabric you will need to give it a good iron and then a press: there is a difference between the two! Ironing a garment is what you do at home – moving the iron back and forth over the garment until you get the light creases out. Pressing is different. You need to hold the iron over an area like a dart or seam, apply a little pressure and steam and then lift away. You are setting something in place and if pressing is done correctly then it should be still visible after several washes. When ironing, be careful of fabrics that are manmade or have textured surfaces like velvet or corduroy. You don't want to melt or flatten these fabrics, so use a clean tea towel to protect the fabric when pressing, and always iron a test piece of fabric first.

Before storing or making a garment: fold your fabric with the selvedge edges and the wrong sides together and press in a fold. This will make it easier to work with. If you are storing fabric, fold it in half, lengthways first and then again until you get your fabric to the size you need.

Storing fabric: once you have washed, pressed and folded your fabric, try to store it in a dry and dark place, or at least out of direct sunlight. Sunlight, over time, will cause damage to your fabric by fading it.

FABRIC TERMS

Grain line: runs lengthways down the fabric and is created by the vertical warp threads (see right). When you are positioning patterns onto fabric, imagine that the grain line will run from your head to toe down the garment (see page 124 for lining up the grain line).

Cross grain: runs across the fabric and is created by the horizontal weft threads (see right).

Selvedge: the raw edge of the fabric that is created by the ends of the cross grain; it runs parallel to your grain line (see right).

Bias: if you cut at a 45° angle to your cross grain and grain line, this is known as the bias (see right). For a more dramatic or draped garment, patterns will be placed and cut out along the bias because of the stretch and 'give' qualities the bias gives you.

Notches: marks that you make in fabric for points of reference when sewing.

Nap: this is the raised texture of a fabric. Textured fabric such as velvet will need to be handled differently to cottons: you will need to make sure that the direction of the nap is going the same way through all your pattern pieces, otherwise they will look different in colour. You might have noticed this with your carpet at home: if you smooth sections of it in different directions they have a different tone to each other because of the way the pile is sitting. Your fabric will act the same way.

Seam allowance: this is the distance between the edge of the material and your stitch line. Seam allowances can vary from pattern to pattern, so always check the instructions. Generally, I have used a 1.5cm ($^5/_8$in) seam

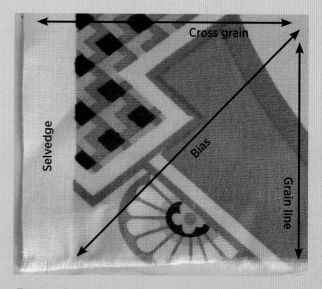

allowance for the projects in this book, but if the project needs a specific seam allowance, I will make you aware of this in the instructions.

Ease: this is the difference between your body measurement and the finished garment's size. Ease is added to your body measurements when making a garment. A tighter garment will have less ease compared to a loose-fitting garment.

Hem: a hem is a way of finishing off your raw edges. Hems can be found at the bottom of trousers, skirts and cuffs. They can be single (folded once) or double (folded twice).

Interfacing: a fusible or sew-in material added to garments to provide support and structure to areas such as collars, facings, cuffs and waistbands.

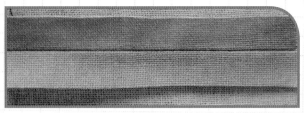
Plain seam

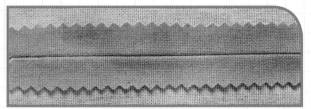
Pinked finish

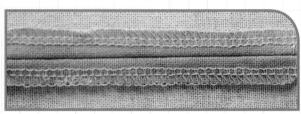
Overlocked finish

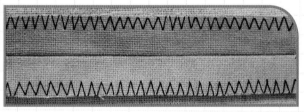
Zigzag finish

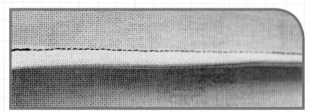
French seam

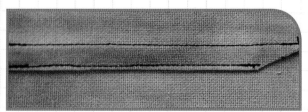
Flat fell seam

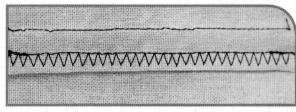
Welt seam

Seam finishings

To construct your garments you will be sewing pieces of fabric together to create seams. There are lots of methods you can use to do this and which seam you use may depend on the fabric you're working with as well as the purpose of the seam.

A **plain seam** is the most common and simple seam. We will be using this method a lot in your projects. It is created by putting the right sides of the fabric together and joining them with a stitched line, leaving you with two seams that will need to be pressed open (as shown) or to one side.

To help your garments last longer, it is always a good idea to finish your seams, especially if the seams are exposed, as with the plain seam. **Pinking**, **overlocking** or **zigzag stitching** are all good ways to finish a seam. If you do not finish your seams, the fabric will begin to fray as you wear and wash it. Over time this may affect the stitches and your garment may fall apart.

A **French seam** is a great one to use if you are sewing fine fabrics that fray. It looks like a plain seam from the front, but the raw seams are enclosed. You do this by placing the wrong sides together first and sewing the seam line. You then refold the fabric so that the right sides are facing and sew again, enclosing all the raw edges inside the seam.

A **flat fell seam** is a very strong seam that you will find on items like jeans. It is created by folding one raw seam under, trapping the other one and is secured with a second line of parallel stitching. This is a great seam finish that can be sewn on all fabrics (see page 115).

A **welt seam** is very similar to a flat fell seam. Instead of tucking one seam under before sewing, with a welt seam you trim one seam allowance and neaten the other one. Press the neatened seam allowance over the trimmed one and then topstitch in place (see page 129).

Enclosed seams can be found on pockets and facings. You won't need to finish the seam but you will need to trim it to reduce bulk; if it is a curved seam, you will need to clip the seams by cutting V-shapes into them. This will allow the curve to lie flat and reduce bulk.

GETTING STARTED

TOP TIP!

Don't wind more than one length of thread onto your bobbin — this is likely to result in your machine getting tangled. Always keep spare empty bobbins or wind off leftover threads before using one again.

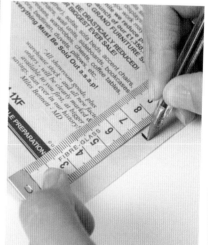

TOP TIP!

If you don't have pattern paper to hand, use baking parchment or old newspaper — simply iron the newspaper on a low heat first, to prevent the ink smudging onto your fabric. Don't forget to give your iron a wipe after with a clean damp cloth.

VINTAGE PINCUSHION

No sewing room is complete without a personalised pincushion. The first pincushion I made was a moustache-shaped one, which I took onto the *Sewing Bee* as a good luck charm. It lasted the *Sewing Bee* but didn't get past Renton, my dog, who chewed it up a few years ago; as you can imagine, I was very upset about this. I now have a collection of pincushions that I use for different things: my wrist pincushion that I wear on TV; a beautiful leather and tweed pincushion that is super posh – I just had to have it; a large square pincushion that I received as a Secret Santa gift – it has pockets on the side for my scissors and tools, which is super handy; and finally, my vintage teacup pincushion.

This teacup pincushion is my sewing-room staple as I use the saucer when I'm sewing at my machine – I quickly throw the pins onto it rather than dropping them all over the floor.

The cup houses the pincushion, which is stuffed with ordinary toy stuffing, but check out the tip on page 24 for a nifty use for wire wool. This is a great beginner project and is a perfect present for your crafty friends.

YOU WILL NEED

MATERIALS
- A cup and saucer
- A fat quarter of fabric
- Newspaper
- Toy stuffing or a pillow

SKILLS GAINED
- Construction techniques
- Drafting a paper pattern
- Hand-sewing techniques

SEAM ALLOWANCE
- 1.5cm ($^5/_8$in)

> Step 1

To start we need to draft our pattern. Place your cup upside down on the newspaper and draw around the rim.

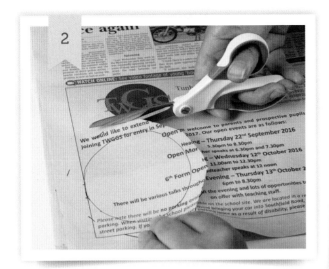

Step 2

You will need to add about 1.5cm (⅝in) extra to this circle for a seam allowance. Once you have drawn this second line in place, cut out the circle and put it to one side.

Step 3

Now, taking your tape measure, place the tip at the bottom of the cup and take a measurement to the rim (cup height). Mine is 7cm (2¾in). You will also need to measure the circumference of the cup by wrapping the tape measure around the outside of the rim. Mine is 27cm (10⅝in).

Step 4

With your two measurements, draw a rectangle onto the newspaper and cut it out. You don't need to add any seam allowances to these measurements as you want the pincushion to sit inside the cup.

Step 5

Place your two pattern pieces onto your chosen fabric; pin in place and cut out. Remove the pins and paper templates from the fabric. Thread your needle with a matching thread so that you have two pieces of thread meeting at the end. You now need to put a knot in the end of your threads (see page 22 for my easy knotting method).

TOP TIP!

The length of the thread should be no longer than your forearm — anything longer and you may start to get tangled up.

HOW TO: KNOT THREAD

A quick way of doing this is to hold the end of the threads between your thumb and forefinger (A), wrap the threads around your forefinger twice (B) and then roll your thumb to the end of your finger (C and D). You should feel a knot form at the bottom of your forefinger. Pinch this knot and pull (E). This will tighten the knot you have created (F). Now you are ready to get sewing!

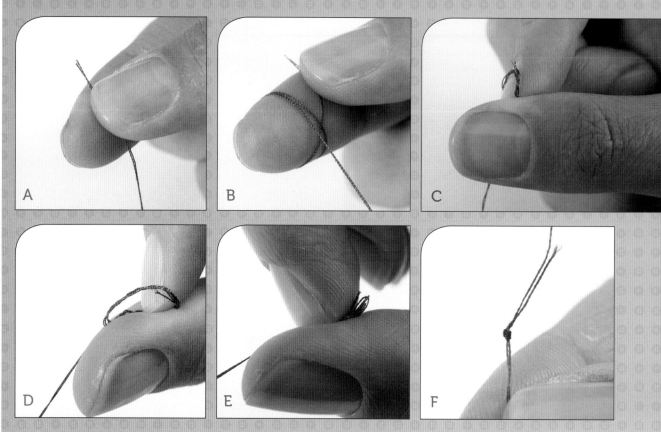

A

B

C

D

E

F

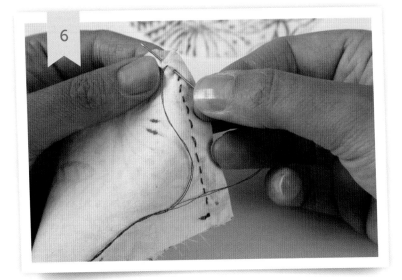

6

➤ Step 6

Fold your rectangle of fabric in half widthways with the right sides (patterned sides) together. Match the corners and pin the fabric in place. Sew together along the short open side to create a tube – use a backstitch about 5mm (¼in) away from the edge.

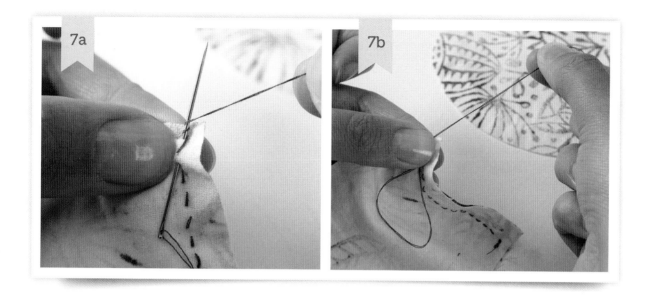

🔖 Step 7

Secure the stitches at the end with a knot. You can do this by putting the needle into the fabric and poking the tip of the needle back through the fabric as if you are about to do a stitch, but before you remove the needle, wrap the thread around the needle twice (7a). Place your finger onto the knot and then pull your thread (7b). This should leave you with a tight knot very close to your fabric.

🔖 Step 8

You now need to make a medium-length running stitch about 2cm (¾in) away from the raw edge of your fabric circle. This needs to go around the full circle of fabric and in a different coloured thread (the reason for using a different colour is because this is a temporary stitch that we will remove later). Once you have sewn around the edge of your circle, don't knot the thread. Gently pull the thread so that the circle begins to gather slightly. We are doing this so we can ease our circle into the tube we have just created.

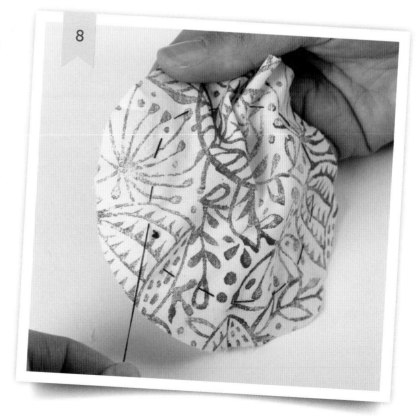

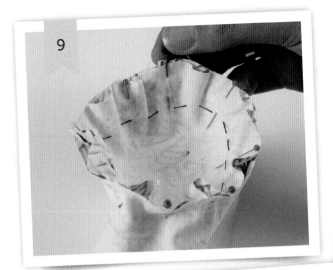

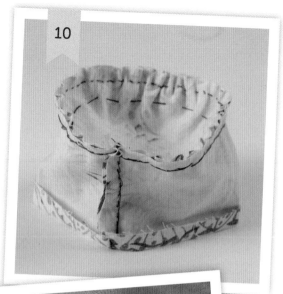

Step 9

Pin the circle into the top of the tube opening with the right sides together. You may need to ease the circle out a little to fit, but your temporary running stitch should help to keep it even.

Step 10

Thread a needle with matching thread and backstitch the two pieces together. When you have done this, you can remove your temporary stitches. Before you turn your pincushion out the right way, you need to fold over the long open edge by 5mm (¼in) to create a small hem and press this in place using an iron.

Step 11

Turn your pincushion out the right way. Before stuffing it, you need to make a running stitch into the crease you have just created with the iron. This time, the running stitch is not a temporary one so will need to be in a matching coloured thread; do not knot the thread at the end – leave the needle and thread attached. You can now stuff your pincushion. Keep in mind that you want a firm pincushion but be careful not to over-stuff it as you need to be able to close the open end without putting pressure on your stitches.

TOP TIP!

To help keep your pins nice and sharp, place a thin layer of wire wool in first before filling with normal stuffing.

Step 12

To close your pincushion you just need to pull the thread with the needle still on it. Pull this as tight as you can to close the gap. Then, while holding the tension on the thread, create a knot to hold it in place.

Step 13

You may want to sew a few more securing stitches by sewing the opposite sides together a few times. Once you have knotted your thread, run the needle into the body of the pincushion until it comes out the other side. Pull the needle out and then trim the thread close to the fabric, leaving a length of thread inside the pincushion. This technique acts like a second knot and it also hides the loose ends. I do this with all my projects for a more professional finish. Pop your pincushion into your cup and you're ready to go!

SCARF TOP

Square scarves are always my staple purchase when I go to a charity shop. I simply cannot get enough of them. Whether they are the real-deal silk kind or the 'don't come near me with a naked flame' kind, they are a great source of luxury fabric that doesn't break the bank. My scarf top is a quick-and-easy make that suits all occasions: a summer evening barbecue, casual drinks with the girls or a holiday essential; it will take up no space in your luggage and you don't need to worry about ironing it either. Just leave it hanging up in the bathroom while you take a shower and the creases will just fall out!

YOU WILL NEED

MATERIALS
- Two square scarves of the same size (approximately 51cm/20in square) or two pieces of fabric 53cm (21in) square

SKILLS GAINED
- Basic fitting techniques
- Construction techniques
- Machine-sewing techniques
- Upcycling

SEAM ALLOWANCE
- Minimal

Step 1

The great thing about using scarves is that they have already been hemmed. But if your scarves are different sizes, or if you are using material instead, you will need to cut fabric to size first. Fold over any raw edges by about 5mm (¼in) and then repeat, giving you a double hem. Secure these folds in place with a straight stitch, known as a topstitch, as it will be visible on the garment.

TOP TIP!

Use the edge of the presser foot as your seam allowance guide to ensure a nice straight stitch line.

Step 2

With right sides together, pin your scarves along the top edge at the top right and left sides, leaving a gap for your head in the centre. Before we start sewing, put the top on carefully to make sure that you can get your head into your top easily and make any necessary adjustments by pinning in place. While standing in front of a mirror, pin where you want your side seams to start. When you are happy with your top, take it off.

Step 3

Leaving it inside out and pinned in place, fold your top in half at the neckline (vertically). Check that your pins are matching at the shoulders and under the arms. Adjust them if need be.

TOP TIP!

Give it one last try on to make sure you are completely happy with the positioning of the seams before you sew. It might save having to unpick it later!

Step 4

Using your sewing machine and a straight stitch, you need to stitch as close as you can to the original hem of the scarves. I would place the scarf hems along the edge of the sewing foot, giving you a constant guide. But if you are feeling more confident on your sewing machine, try to sew into the original topstitching. Start by placing your material under your presser foot, lower the needle into the fabric first and then lower the presser foot.

Step 5

It is really important to secure your threads at the start and end of your stitch line, as you would when hand sewing. When using the sewing machine, you need to create a knot or 'locking stitch' by reverse stitching. Check your sewing machine manual for the reverse function. If your machine does not have one, just make sure you knot your threads by hand instead. When reverse stitching, it is also a good idea to start about 1–2cm (½–¾in) away from the edge. This stops your fabric from being sucked into the machine. Sew about two stitches forward and stop. Then, using the reverse button, stitch back over these stitches and towards the edge of your fabric, then continue forward as normal (5a). Remember to repeat the locking stitch at the end of your seam (5b). Sew your shoulder seams together where your pins are positioned, remembering to do your locking stitch. The golden rule is to remove the pins as you go and definitely before you sew over them – no one wants a broken needle or a broken sewing machine. Now repeat this process with your side seams.

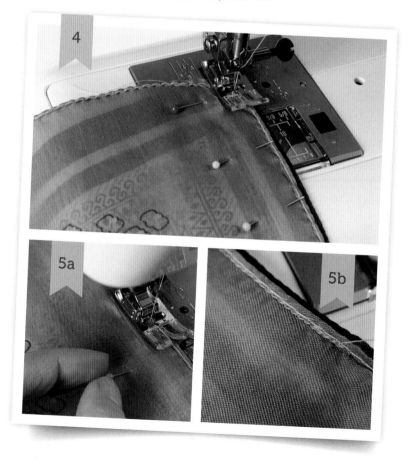

➤ Step 6
Once you have sewn your shoulder and side seams together, snip any of the loose threads away to give you a clean finish.

➤ Step 7
Turn your garment the right way out, as you would a pillowcase, and you are ready to wear it!

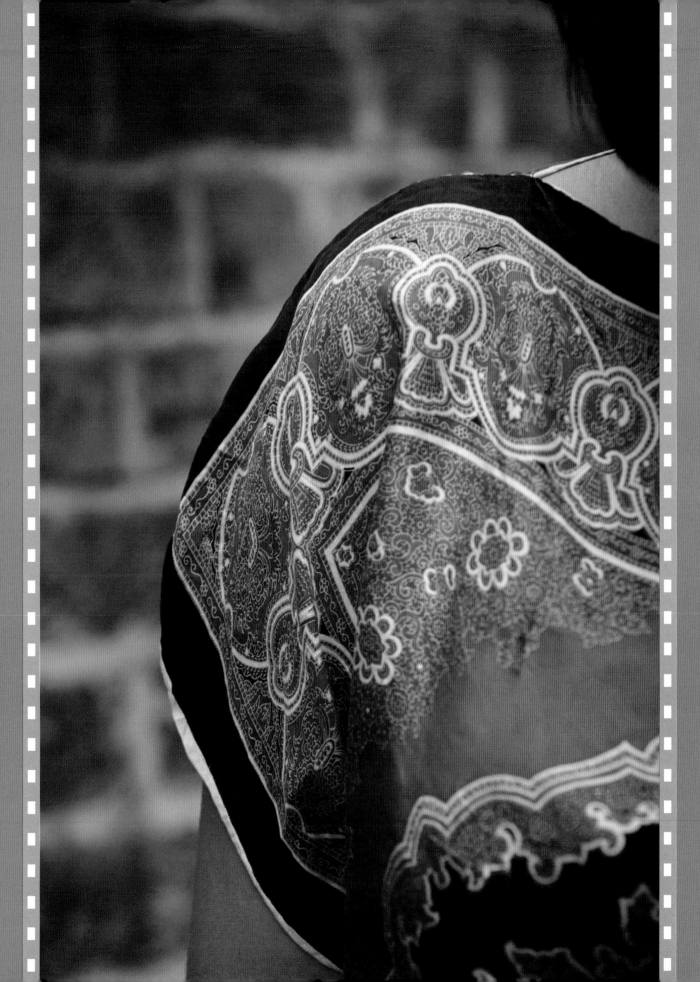

JUMPER MITTENS AND SNOOD

I love upcycling old clothes into something completely different. To be honest, for me, nothing is safe when it comes to upcycling, but a lot of people are surprised and say 'you can't upcycle a jumper as it will unravel'. Well, here is a great project to bring those old, shrunken jumpers back to life! They also make great Christmas or winter birthday gifts.

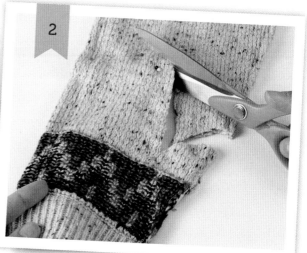

YOU WILL NEED

MATERIALS
- An old woollen jumper
- Embroidery thread (optional)
- Ballpoint sewing machine needle

SKILLS GAINED
- Adapting a garment
- Drafting a pattern direct to fabric
- Hand-sewing techniques
- Machine-sewing techniques
- Construction techniques

BODY MEASUREMENTS
- Your hand

SEAM ALLOWANCE
- 1cm (½in)

➤ Step 1
Firstly, to make the mittens you need to turn your jumper inside out. If you are right-handed put your left hand into the sleeve the wrong way around. The cuff of the jumper is now going to be the cuff of your mitten. Open out your left thumb and keep your fingers together. Carefully pin around the edge of your hand as close as you can, giving you a nice, snug mitten shape. When you are happy with the shape, remove your hand leaving the pins in place.

➤ Step 2
Cut out your mitten shape, 1cm (½in) outside your pins, to provide a seam allowance.

GETTING STARTED

➤ Step 3
Don't forget to change your sewing machine needle to a ballpoint needle. With a zigzag stitch, sew your raw seams together.

➤ Step 4
For a little more reinforcement, run a line of straight stitch in the area where your thumb meets your index finger. Changing your stitch from a zigzag to a straight stitch, sew as close to the edge of the zigzag as you can. Before turning out your mitten, make a small cut (clip) into that section, otherwise it will not turn out properly, it would be bulky and restrict the movement of your thumb. Be careful not to cut your stitches when you do this.

TOP TIP!
Before the next step, give in to temptation and try it on!

➤ Step 5
With the mitten inside out and completely flat, place it onto the other arm at the same place. You are going to use this mitten as a template for the other one. Pin it in place and carefully cut around it. Once you have cut around the shape, remove the pins and stitched mitten. Pop a few pins into the unsewn mitten, keeping everything in place while you repeat the same process to sew it together. Turn both mittens the right way out.

➤ Step 6
To add detail and to make the mittens a little more secure, I have added a little embroidery detail by blanket stitching around the edge, enclosing all the raw edges inside with the blanket stitch. To add even more detail, why not add a few buttons at the outer wrist, for a more elegant finish?

❯ Step 7

Now you have your mittens completed, we are going to use the rest of the jumper to make a snood. Cut across the chest of your jumper from under the armpits, giving you a tube-like shape. Discard the top part of the jumper – unless you can think of anything else to make with it... a hot water bottle cover comes to my mind!

❯ Step 8

Fold the raw edge over by about 1.5cm (^{5}/$_8$in) to the wrong side of the jumper to create a single hem.

❯ Step 9

Bring this single hem to the finished lower edge of the jumper.

Step 10

Pin together, making sure the right sides are facing out and the edges are together. Taking a needle and thread, sew these two hems together using ladder stitch (see below). This is a great invisible stitch and is a must-have skill when making your own clothes. Ta da! You're ready to go!

HOW TO: LADDER STITCH

As you are sewing into knitted fabric, you first need to secure your thread by creating a loop. Start with a double thread. Pass the needle through your fabric but before pulling it all the way, separate the threads at the knot to create a loop. Take your needle back through this loop before pulling to lock it in place (A). Make a small stitch into and along the fold of the fabric (B). Pull the thread through (C). Across from this last stitch, repeat the process on the other layer of fabric. The threads will create a ladder-like stitch between the two layers but when the thread is pulled, the edges come close together and the stitches can no longer be seen. This has been slightly adapted as I have used the original hem of the jumper to pass my needle through rather than create another fold. Finish off with a secure knot.

FESTIVAL POUCH

Inspired by my honeymoon to Morocco, in particular the Marrakesh markets, this pouch is the perfect holiday or festival essential. It's a no-hands pouch that attaches to a belt, leaving your hands free to explore hidden treasures in foreign lands or dance the night away without having to worry about your personal belongings! It has a hidden zip, so it's a great little security bag. You can make this in any material but I decided to use an old pair of denim jeans.

MATERIALS
- An old pair of denim jeans (non-stretch)
- A fat quarter of fabric
- A 20cm (8in) zip and machine zipper foot
- Newspaper to make a template

SKILLS GAINED
- Construction techniques
- Drafting a paper pattern
- Machine-sewing techniques
- Upcycling

SEAM ALLOWANCE
- 1.5cm (⁵⁄₈in)

⚫ Step 1

You can make this pouch any size you like but always make the back piece 3cm (1¼in) longer than the front to allow for your zip insertion; I've given my dimensions here so that you can use them if you want. Start by making your pattern pieces from newspaper. Draw and cut out three rectangle shapes: the first rectangle is the back piece, 20 x 31cm (9 x 12¼in). The second piece will be the front piece, 20 x 28cm (9 x 11in). The third rectangle is for the pouch loops, 8 x 20cm (3¼ x 8in). Taking the back and loop pattern pieces, place them onto your fat quarter of fabric. Pin and cut out. You need to cut out two loop pattern pieces, so to make this easier I have folded the fabric over, to cut two out at the same time.

⚫ Step 2

Taking your front pattern and your old jeans, position your front pattern on an area that fits. I've decided to use my jean back pocket for the front of my pouch. You could also patchwork your denim if you wanted to. When happy with your pattern position, pin and cut out. You also need to pin and cut out two loop pattern pieces from your jeans too.

TOP TIP!

When doing this, be careful not to place your pattern edges close to things like seams, zips or metal details like studs or buttons, as your sewing machine and needle may not be able to handle the bulk. You do not want to damage your needle or your sewing machine.

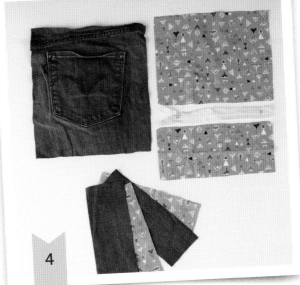

⫸ Step 3

Before removing your pins, take your back pattern piece and mark 10cm (4in) up from the bottom of the pattern with a pen and make a small notch into the side of the fabric at this point; repeat on the other side. Remove the pins and paper pattern then draw a line with tailor's chalk, joining up the two notches before cutting along this line. This is where you will attach your zip.

⫸ Step 4

You should now have one denim front piece, two fabric back pieces, a zip and four loop pieces (two in each fabric).

TOP TIP!

Grab a cup of tea first as we are about to sew in a zip — this is exciting!

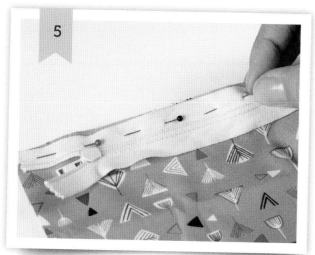

⫸ Step 5

With the right side of your fabric facing up, pin one side of the zip face down to the top edge of the smaller back piece.

USING A ZIPPER FOOT

Zipper feet come in all shapes and sizes depending on your sewing machine model. They make sewing zips so much easier as you can adjust to sew on either the left or the right side of the sewing machine needle. As you can see, the zipper foot is normally a lot thinner than your normal sewing foot, which is why it can stitch a lot closer to your zip.

Step 6

Using a zipper foot, stitch the zip in place. Stitch it in place with the zip open then, when you get close to the end, lower the needle into the fabric, lift the presser foot so the zip can pass under it (6b), close the zip and then lower the presser foot and continue to sew. Doing it this way gives you a clean straight stitch that will be close to the zip edge, otherwise you will have a lump where you have to sew around your zip head.

Step 7

Repeat on other side of the zip with the other piece of fabric. Close the zip when pinning the other side in place, so that you know where to match up your fabric edges. Remember to open the zip again before sewing to make it easier.

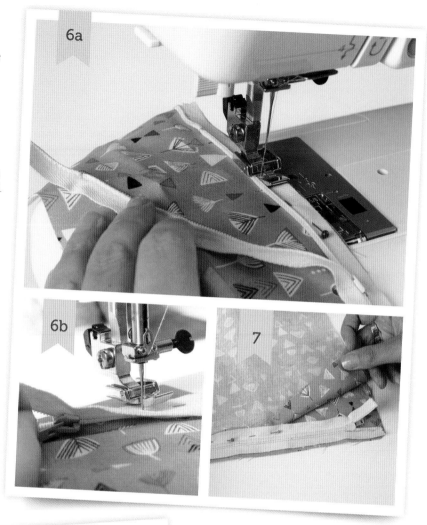

Step 8

Once the zip is stitched in place, remove any remaining pins, unfold your fabric and press the zip seams flat.

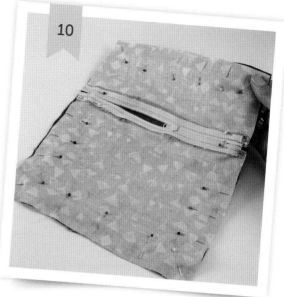

Step 9

Topstitch either side of the zip to give you a clean zip opening. I used the zipper foot to do this bit to get a nice close stitch line.

Step 10

To construct your pouch you need to pin your front and back pieces with the right sides together, making sure your jean pocket opening is facing up and your zip is at the bottom. Pin together and then open the zip slightly – this will make it easier when you have to turn it through later.

Step 11

Change back to your standard sewing foot and stitch around all four sides with a 1.5cm (5/8in) seam allowance. To do this, start at a midpoint on one side and when you get to the corner, leave your needle in your fabric, 1.5cm (5/8in) from the edge. Lift the presser foot and rotate your fabric by 90°, turning anti-clockwise. Lower the presser foot and sew the next three corners in the same way. Continue until you sew over your first stitches by about 1cm (½in). Reverse stitch at this point to secure the thread.

Step 12

Now we need to clip the corners of the pouch, as this helps to reduce bulk when you turn it through. When clipping, you need to take the tips of the corners off as shown, being careful not to cut your stitches.

Step 13

Finish your seams using a zigzag stitch or an overlocker (serger), if you have one.

Step 14

Turn the pouch through then poke out the corners to give you a crisp finish.

TOP TIP!

Use a chopstick or point turner and not your scissors to poke out your corners! Your sharp scissors might make a hole.

Step 15

Press with an iron before finishing your pouch with a topstitch around the edge. I used the edge of the sewing foot as my guide. The topstitch traps all your raw edges inside and makes your pouch look more professional as well as more robust; be careful when stitching over the zip.

Step 16

Now for the pouch loops. I have chosen contrasting fabric pieces: the jean and patterned fabric. With right sides facing, pin and stitch together in pairs, making the corners as in step 11, but this time leave a small opening on the longest side – about three fingers' width will be more than enough. Remember to reverse stitch at the beginning and end of your stitch line.

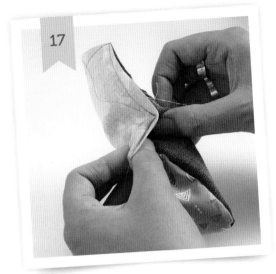

Step 17

Clip the corners as you did in step 12, turn through, press and topstitch. The topstitching will close the small gap you left in step 16.

Step 18

Now comes the difficult part: choosing which side of the strap you want to see! Pin both ends in place at the top of the pouch (the pocket opening is on the front – the zip should be at the bottom on the back). Make sure you can slide your favourite belt through the loops before stitching a box at each strap end to secure in place. To do this you are using the same technique you have learned to make the pouch (step 11) and loops by leaving the needle in the fabric as you turn the corners. Attach your pouch to your favourite belt and off you go on your travels!

CUSTOMISING CLOTHES

▌ TOP TIP!

When making bias binding (see page 61) my two shirt sleeves gave me about 4.5m (15ft) of bias binding — you really do get a lot out of such a small amount of fabric. To store it for future projects, get a wooden peg, wrap the binding around it and secure with a pin to keep it nice and tidy, ready for the next time you need it. You can also buy handy bias-making tools to speed things up when pressing!

▌ TOP TIP!

Keep any unwanted collars — they make great accessories if you add embellishments like embroidery, lace and beads to the tips. Just wear it like a necklace — it will look great with a plain t-shirt!

DOILY DETAILS

I love upcycling! Customising your clothes is a great way to get creative and freshen up your wardrobe at the same time. When in charity shops, I hunt for doilies. Once used in every home to protect furniture from scratches or stains and now discarded as old-fashioned, the doily is great for instantly and easily transforming a garment.

Lace or embroidery details can be added to the elbows of jumpers or incorporated into your makes as cuffs or collars. Why not ask family or friends if they have any doilies hiding in their cupboards and get adding some lace detail to your clothes? If you are able to get hold of a few large embroidered tablecloths and handkerchiefs, why not try to make a blouse? By piecing several cloths together, I was able to create enough fabric to make a cute summer blouse, making sure I made a feature of all the embroidery details.

TOP TIP!

Use your dress form to drape the lace and embroidered cloths to work out how you are going to design your blouse first, before sewing them together.

EMBROIDERY

Adding embroidery to your clothes is another way to make them unique. You can find loads of inspiration and tutorials online. Adding embroidery detail to the edges of pockets is one idea that I like to use and you don't even need to do complicated stitches for your embroidery detail to look impressive.

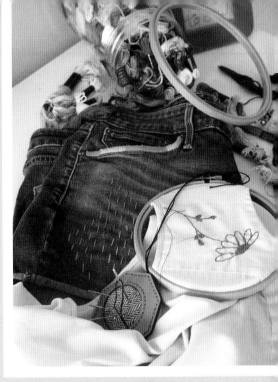

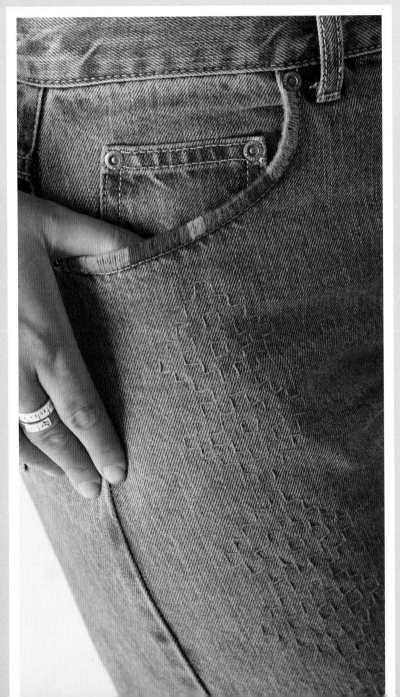

A simple running stitch in different coloured threads or over patchwork jeans to give your mending a unique twist is all it takes. Placing an embroidery hoop onto the area you are going to embellish will help to keep the fabric taut and makes it easier to handle.

47

TOP TIP!
Use a water-erasable pen to work out your designs before you get stitching.

BLOCK PRINTING AND TIE-DYEING

Dyeing and block printing are awesome ways to make your mark on your clothes. Not only do they look great, but you can also use them to disguise laundry disasters or discoloured clothes!

Block printing is an addictive way to customise your clothes. It's great fun and you can even make your own stamps from foam or vegetables. It's a great activity for the kids too, so get them involved (below left is my nephew, Reyer, having a go while we were on holiday). I love using my ever-growing collection of Indian block prints to jazz up a plain blouse or to make my own fabric designs on plain fabrics. Just remember to fix your prints before you wash them, as you don't want them washing out.

48

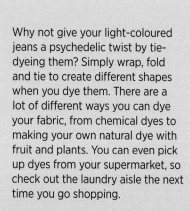

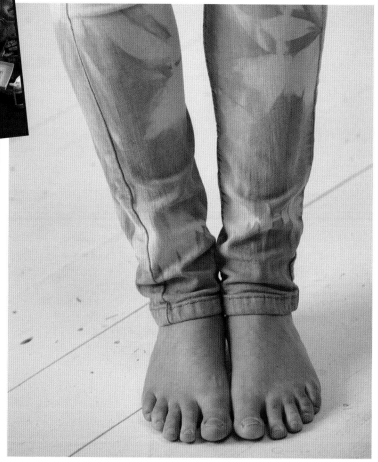

Why not give your light-coloured jeans a psychedelic twist by tie-dyeing them? Simply wrap, fold and tie to create different shapes when you dye them. There are a lot of different ways you can dye your fabric, from chemical dyes to making your own natural dye with fruit and plants. You can even pick up dyes from your supermarket, so check out the laundry aisle the next time you go shopping.

TASSEL TOP

TASSELS! I've only got to hear the word tassel and I do a little dance with excitement. Here is a super-quick upcycle project that I first created as a stage outfit when singing for my band, Snooty Bobs. It's a great garment to wear at music festivals or gigs, especially if you are going for Fleetwood Mac's Stevie Nicks' 70s vibe!

CUSTOMISING CLOTHES

YOU WILL NEED

MATERIALS
- A medium- or long-sleeved stretch top
- An old t-shirt
- Ballpoint or stretch sewing machine needle

SKILLS GAINED
- Adapting a garment
- Construction techniques
- Machine-sewing techniques
- Upcycling

SEAM ALLOWANCE
- Use presser foot as a guide

➤ Step 1
Deconstruct your t-shirt so that you have two large rectangles of material. Do this by removing all the seams and hems from the t-shirt and cut across from armpit to armpit. The great thing about t-shirt (jersey) material is that when you cut it, it doesn't fray, which is why these rectangles are going to be the fabric for your tassels.

➤ Step 2
Turn your long-sleeved top inside out and carefully unpick the arm seams to create a gap. You want this gap to be the same length as the longest part of your rectangle of t-shirt fabric, but you also need to leave no less that 2cm (¾in) of the original sleeve seam at the armpit and the cuff. If your rectangle is too long to fit into the gap, just trim it to size.

TOP TIP!

If you are impatient like me, you can gently cut this part of the seam out, along the stitch line, rather than unpicking, apart from the 2cm (¾in) parts mentioned above. This will make the arms a little smaller when you sew them back together but as this is a stretch material you shouldn't notice it too much.

➤ Step 3

To insert your rectangles of fabric into the sleeve, you need to roll each piece into a cigar shape, lengthways, leaving about 5cm (2in) free to pin into the sleeve. Pin the roll so that it doesn't come loose during the next step.

➤ Step 4

With your sleeves open, place the roll inside the sleeve, with the flat raw edge against the sleeve opening. Then line up all three raw edges like a sandwich to create a new sleeve seam.

➤ Step 5

Pin in place ready to sew.

CUSTOMISING CLOTHES

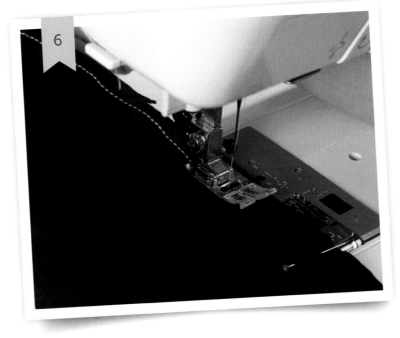

➤ Step 6

Before we begin you will need to replace your sewing machine needle with a stretch or ballpoint needle. If you don't change the needle and use a standard needle it will not sew correctly and may damage the material. With a straight stretch stitch, sew the seam back together again by sewing over the 2cm (¾in) you didn't unpick, along the new seam and sewing over the 2cm (¾in) at the cuff. I have used the edge of the presser foot as a seam allowance guide. If you use a normal straight stitch with this type of material, your stitches may snap as they will not stretch and move with the material.

Step 7

To finish your raw seams, change your stitch to a zigzag stitch or overlocking stitch on your sewing machine and, with the needle very close to the edge, zigzag your raw edges together. By doing this you are mimicking the overlocking stitch you have just removed in order to insert your tassels. Contrast thread is shown in the photographs so that you can see it, but you should use matching thread.

Step 8

Once you have sewn both sleeves back together, you can now turn your garment the right way out and remove the pins that were keeping your cigar rolls in place. We are now going to create the tassels! Lay your garment on a flat surface with the arm and tassel fabric out flat. Starting at the bottom, begin to cut your rectangle up into strips, about 2cm (¾in) in width, being careful not to cut too closely to your sleeve seam. Keep going until you have something that looks like a comb.

Step 9

Gently pull one strand at a time. This will make the strip roll into itself, almost creating a tube-like shape that acts like a hem and hides all the raw edges. Once you have completed these steps on both sides, you are ready to go dancing!

SHIRT REVERSE

Cutting up and refashioning shirts is one of my favourite types of upcycled project. There is so much material to use and you can learn so much about how clothes are made by taking a shirt apart. Collars, cuffs, plackets, yokes, sleeves and pockets, not to mention the different types of seams; there are so many techniques involved in a shirt that I would highly recommend dissecting one just to have a look! This super-quick shirt reverse is a great project for a quick new garment fix – you know, that day you just want to wear something new but don't have the time to make anything completely from scratch. And by adding different embellishments you can completely transform that once-old, now-new shirt.

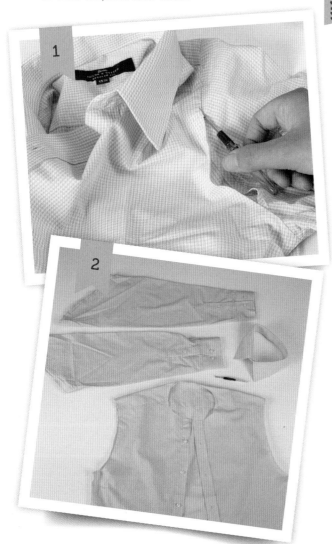

▶ Step 1

If you are using an old shirt with a pocket, check for colour fading inside the pocket. If there is a difference in colour the shirt will not be a good choice for this project. As we will be turning the shirt around so that the front is at the back, we will need to take any pockets off. Here is a little tip for you when removing pockets: use an unpicker and remove it from the right side of the garment – any damage should then only affect the pocket you are removing and not your finished garment. Carefully remove both of the sleeves with an unpicker. Depending on what type of seam has been used there might be two lines of stitching, so don't be tempted to rip them off as you don't want to damage the body of the garment.

TOP TIP!

Don't remove threads individually. Use a lint roller — it's much quicker.

▶ Step 2

Once you have removed your sleeves, keep them to one side for later. You now need to take the collar off the shirt too. Do this by carefully removing the collar stand, which is the part that supports the actual collar. Again, use the unpicker and resist ripping it off.

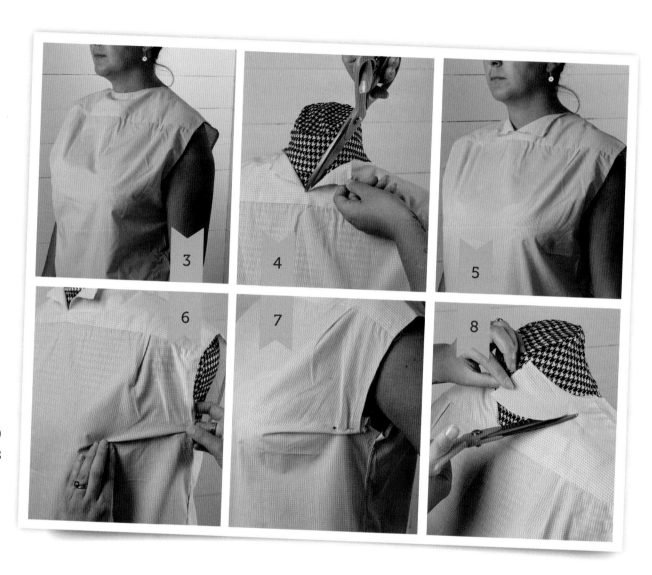

➤ Step 3

Try your shirt on, putting it on backwards, and have a look in a mirror. You may need to make a few adjustments to the neckline and also create a little shaping for the bust. Firstly, check to see if it is tight around the neck.

➤ Step 4

If it is too tight, make a small cut down the centre front (really the back) of the shirt until it sits comfortably around your neck and lies flat against your chest.

➤ Step 5

Secondly, are the armholes gaping? If the answer is yes, then you might want to add a dart from the bust to the armhole to shape and close the gap.

➤ Step 6

With your shirt on and pins at the ready, create a small fold in the fabric along the side of your breast into the armhole on one side of the shirt only.

➤ Step 7

Pin the fold in place. Using a dress form makes this step a lot easier; alternatively, do the same steps but with the garment on inside out and while you are wearing it.

➤ Step 8

Shape your neckline by cutting a curve from the centre front to one shoulder seam, and then continuing around to the centre back if required.

Step 9

Use the off-cut as a template to cut the other half of the neckline. Place the pieces right sides together, matching up the seams, and pin in place. Cut out to give you an even and symmetrical neckline.

Step 10

To make sure your darts are the same on both sides, mark where your pins and folds are with water-soluble pen before removing them.

Step 11

Fold the shirt in half and match up the armhole and side seams. Now you can transfer the tailor's marks to the other side of the shirt knowing that they will be in the same place. To transfer the marks, place pins along the marks – when the shirt is flipped over, you just need to mark where the pins are visible.

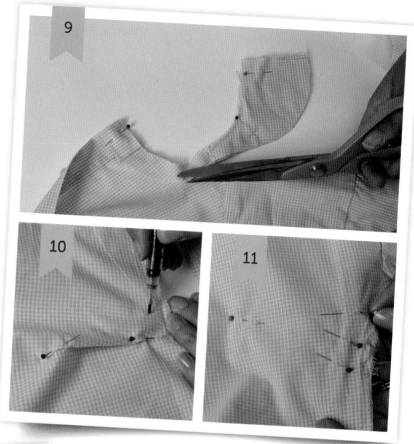

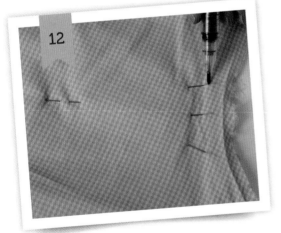

Step 12

Mark the position of the pins with water-soluble pen. To check the fit, pin the darts back in place on both sides and try on the shirt. Once you are happy with the fit, you can now sew in your darts.

Step 13

I like to press the fold of the dart before I sew it in, as I find this makes it easier to handle under the sewing machine. Starting at the armhole, sew towards the point of your dart. Make sure you sew to the very end of your fabric and leave a long length of thread before cutting it from the machine. Taking the tail end of your threads, knot the ends to secure the point. You may want to do this a few times, making sure it is snug against the fabric. Then taking a needle, thread the loose ends back into the dart fold. This acts like a second knot and also hides the thread.

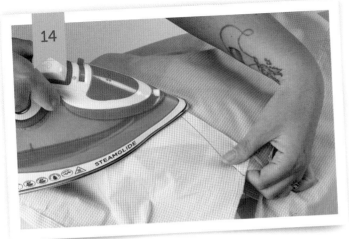

Step 14

Step 14

Press the dart to one side, preferably down the garment rather than upwards, making it nice and flat. Repeat this process with the other dart. For a more professional finish, you may want to use a tailor's ham to help shape your dart while you press. Now we need to make the bias binding from the leftover sleeve fabric, following the instructions below.

HOW TO: MAKE BIAS BINDING

To finish the armholes, we are now going to use the sleeve material to make bias binding. You want to keep as much of this material as possible, so cut out the seam on both sides and remove the cuff of the sleeve. This will give you a flat piece of material to work with. Give your sleeve a good press before cutting it into 5cm (2in) strips on the bias. To find the bias you first need to find the grain line of the material. This should be in the direction of the sleeve length – from shoulder to cuff. If you are struggling to find it, make a small cut into the fabric before ripping it. Your material should rip along the grain line (A). Now you have found the grain line, fold the fabric so the vertical edge now becomes horizontal, giving you a triangle shape (B).

Cut along the diagonal line to give you a starting point. The diagonal line you have just cut along is the bias of the material. Continue to cut your strips using that diagonal line as the reference point for the next strip (C). Once you have several strips of fabric, you will need to join them together at the ends to create a continuous strip. You might need to recut the ends of your strips to get a 45° angle before you place them on top of each other with the right sides together. When placing your strips together make sure you have little triangle overlaps either side of your strips. If you don't, your strip will not line up when you sew them together. Use the very edge of your presser foot as your seam allowance when sewing your strips together with a straight stitch (D). Press out your joining seams and trim the edges (E).

To make traditional bias binding you would normally fold into four lengthways and press, but for this project we are going to use it a little differently. If you've made too much, see my tip on page 45 for how to store it...

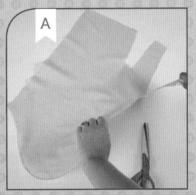

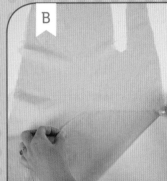

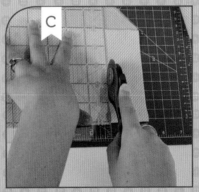

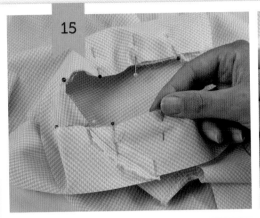

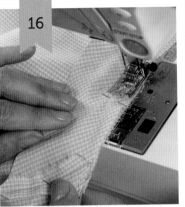

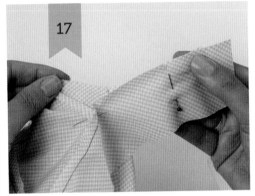

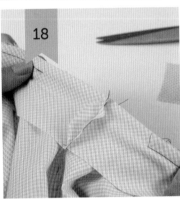

Step 15
Pin your binding around the edge of your shirt armhole with the right sides together. Leave at least 2.5cm (1in) excess fabric at each end of the underarm seam – this will ensure a perfect fit. (You will then pin the binding together at the end, to make sure the bias seam and side seam match up).

Step 16
Machine stitch the binding in place but do not sew over the side seam area. Leave a gap either side of about 2.5cm (1in), ready for the next step.

Step 17
Pin the two 2.5cm (1in) excess lengths of binding together, making sure the bias seam and side seam match up before pulling the binding away to make it easier to sew together.

Step 18
Sew your binding ends together with a straight stitch. Trim off the excess binding to reduce bulk.

CUSTOMISING CLOTHES

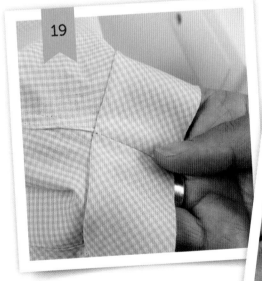

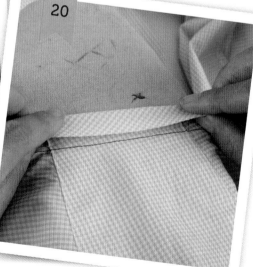

Step 19
Complete the armhole stitch by sewing over where you left off, opening out your binding seam as you go over it and sewing over where you started to complete the seam.

Step 20
Press the seam towards the binding first and then fold your binding edge until it meets the stitch line and press.

Step 21

Fold the binding again at the stitch line. This fold should be on the inside of the garment, creating a facing for your armhole.

Step 22

To finish your binding, we are going to pin and stitch in place with a straight stitch. To make this easier for you, rather than topstitching with the right side facing up, sew with the binding facing you instead (the wrong side, which is the inside of the garment). Carefully stitch along the edge of the binding. Continue along this edge until you sew over where you have started by about 1cm (½in), then secure with a reverse stitch. As you get more experienced you will be able to sew from the right side and feel your way along.

Step 23

We are going to repeat this binding process along the neckline, but this time with a slight difference. Pin the binding to the neckline with the right sides together, this time leaving a small overhang of about 2cm (¾in) on both sides of the neck opening. With a straight stitch, secure in place using the edge of the foot as a seam allowance guide. Clip the curve of the neckline by making V-shape cuts into your seam allowance. This is to help reduce bulk and also make your neckline lie nice and flat. Press the seam allowance towards the binding.

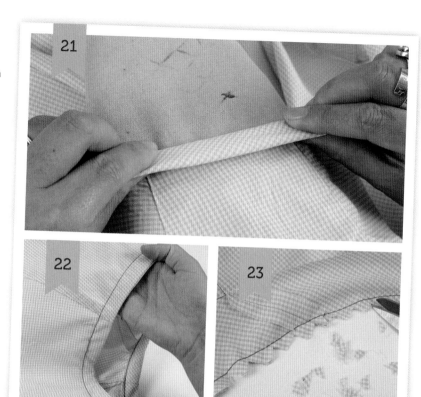

TOP TIP!

Clipping corners and curves is the ultimate sewing rule, especially if you want professional looking results.

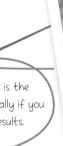

Step 24

To tidy the raw edges of your button plackets you will need to fold the raw edge into the fold of the bias before stitching, not forgetting to clip the corner of the binding to reduce bulk.

Step 25

Fold over the binding to meet your raw edge first, before folding the binding again at the stitch line, to the wrong side of the fabric. However, instead of machine stitching in place, this time we are going to hand sew using a slip stitch.

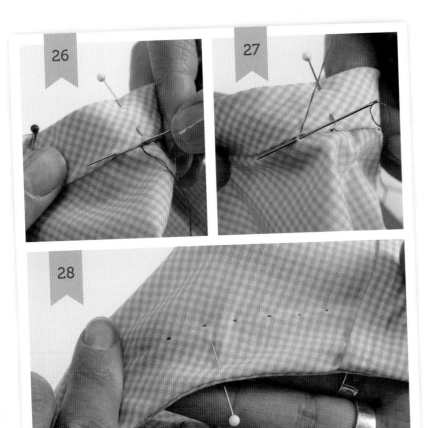

Step 26

Thread a needle with matching thread (I used a contrast thread here so that the stitches would show clearly) and tie a knot in the end. Starting at the neckline opening and in the fold of the binding, bring your needle out through the fold.

Step 27

Go in and out of the main fabric with a very small stitch. You want it to look like a very small dot rather than an actual stitch. Then go into the fold of the binding and along the fold by about 5mm (¼in) and come back out again. Repeat by going back into the main fabric to create your dot-like stitch.

Step 28

Try to keep the stitches well-spaced and even for a great hand-finished look. Give your garment one final press, especially around the neck and arm areas.

Step 29

For extra detail why not add some embellishments to your neckline or yoke? Things like studs, embroidery or lace would really add that extra feature and make your shirt reverse even more special.

MAKING CLOTHES FROM SCRATCH

█ TOP TIP!

I find having a miniature dress form handy for trying out patterns and ideas before committing to a full-scale version and lots of fabric! This was one was very cheap — it is one you normally hang jewellery on.

█ TOP TIP!

If you are going to use a dress form to make clothes for yourself, put one of your bras on it — this will give you a more accurate shape of your chest.

TAKING MEASUREMENTS

Using clothes as a template

Using clothes that you know fit you well is a quick way to make a base pattern and to ensure your new garment is going to fit you. Unless you are making a garment from stretch fabric, avoid using clothes made from stretch fabric as a base, as they will not be a true reflection of your size. A shirt or linen top is a great item to use for this method. Before you start, make a few notes first while wearing it in front of the mirror. Things like: where does the shoulder start and finish on your shoulders? Do you want to lengthen or shorten any part of it? Where does the top finish on your body? Is the top close or loose fitting around your body? All these types of questions will help you to draft, alter and make your new garments. When tracing around your garment remember to add a seam allowance, otherwise when you come to sew your new garment together it will be too small (see also pages 80 and 96).

Measuring yourself

Making clothes from just your own measurements is so exciting, but it can be a little daunting. Here, I'm going to show you that you don't need many measurements to get started and you can take them on your own. No one needs to know your measurements – so be honest and write your true measurements down.

Before we start, you need your fitting buddy – elastic. Tie a length of elastic around your waist and leave it – over time, it will slowly wiggle towards your true waist, so resist the temptation to adjust it while we take the other measurements. Most people don't know where their true waist is. It is actually about 5cm (2in) above your belly button. Do you ever feel like you are constantly pulling down tops or dresses? That's your garment trying to find your waist. It is worth finding out where is it, as most fit problems occur when the waist of a garment doesn't align with your body. In addition to this, we will also need to measure your *waistband*. This is where you want your garment to sit on your body. It can be positioned anywhere from your hips to your high waist. This will be down to your personal preference.

A few tips to get you started

• Avoid wearing several layers when measuring yourself – a t-shirt and trousers will be fine – you don't need to strip down to your underwear, thank goodness! While I do believe that size is nothing but a number, you don't want to add extra inches on either.

• When measuring yourself, try to make sure your tape measure is parallel to the floor at the front and the back by checking in the mirror.

• Try to stand up straight and look in the mirror to get your measurement rather than looking down, as this can alter your size as you bend and twist.

• You want the tape measure to wrap closely to the body, but not too tightly. Breathe properly. There is no point sucking your tummy in or holding your breath. I want you to feel comfortable and confident in your new clothes – so be you! Take a deep breath in and out and then breathe easily, before taking each of the measurements.

• A body measurements list is given at the start of each relevant project so you know which measurements you require. Keep your calculator to hand as you may need to add several together as well as do other mathematical equations to draft your patterns. Don't worry, I'm rubbish at maths, which is why I have the calculator.

• You will need a pen and paper, tape measure, elastic, a mirror and a calculator.

1. Bust: measure right around the fullest part of your body, and don't forget to breathe.

2. Front bust: with your fingertips at the front of your armpits, measure from finger to finger.

3. Upper bust: the same position as the front bust but the whole way around your body.

4. Shoulder to front bust: ignoring the shoulder seam on your garment (as this might not be in the right place), measure from the very top of your shoulder to the position of your front bust.

5. Shoulder to bust: from the top of your shoulder, measure to the fullest part of your bust.

6. Shoulder to under bust: from the top of your shoulder to under your bust, making sure the tape measure goes through the centre of your bust, measuring where your bra strap would sit.

7. Waist: measure where your elastic is – this is your true waist.

8. Waistband: this is lower than your true waist and where your clothes are likely to sit. You might want to think about a favourite pair of trousers. Where do they sit? Pop them on and take a measurement.

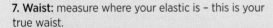

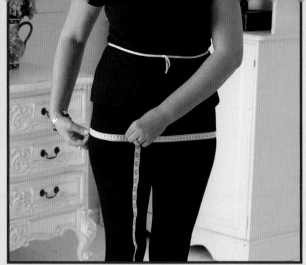

9. Shoulder to waist: measure from the tip of your shoulder down over the bust, along the body until you get to your elastic marker. Don't look down to get the measurement – look in the mirror.

10. Hip: this is not where your hip bone is. You need to measure around the fullest part of your bottom. Remember to keep your tape measure parallel to the floor by checking in the mirror.

11. Waist to hip: measure from your elastic waist marker to where you have just taken your hip measurement. Look in the mirror to get the measurement.

12. Shoulder to shoulder: ignore any seams on your garment – you want to measure where your arm meets your shoulder. Imagine the perpendicular lines of your arm and shoulders meeting – the point they cross over is where you will be measuring from. Go across the back of the neck to the other shoulder point.

13. Shoulder to neck: from the same shoulder point measure to where your shoulder meets your neck.

14. Shoulder to wrist: stand with your hand on your hip. From your shoulder point, measure down your bent arm, across your elbow and take the measurement at your wrist bone.

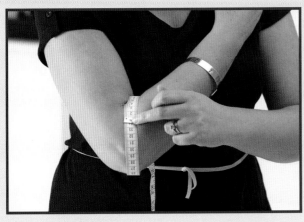

15. Elbow circumference: wrap the tape measure around your elbow and then bend it. This is to make sure your sleeves are not too tight at this point.

16. Crotch: depending on where your waistband will sit, you will need to measure from the back to the front in between your legs. Hold the measurement in place and do a sitting motion. If it is too tight then loosen the measuring tape off until you are able to sit comfortably.

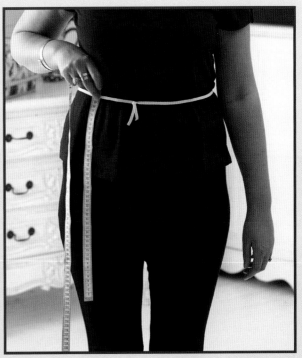

17. Shoulder to length: this will depend on what garment you are making. With the start of the tape measure pointing towards the floor, at the length you want your garment to be, place the other end at the tip of your shoulder. Lay the tape measure against your chest so that it hangs down; adjust if necessary and take the measurement from your shoulder point. Keep your finger on the measurement you want so you can move it away from the body to look at it more easily. Remember to stand up straight.

18. Waist to length: with the start of the tape measure pointing towards the floor, adjust the tape measure to the length you want, depending on where your waistband is. Keeping your finger on the tape measure at the waist point, move it away from the body and take note of your reading.

CAROUSEL SKIRT

This project takes me right back to my childhood as these types of skirt always remind me of my mom, Lain. When I was a child, she always wore what I called 'gypsy skirts': brightly coloured, full and flowing skirts that swished as she walked bare-footed or in flip flops, in all weathers. If asked, she would describe herself as a heavy-rock chick but she will always be a wild child hippy in my eyes, even if she doesn't wear the skirts as often now. In the original project, I used a circular tablecloth as I loved the print and it was already hemmed, but for the instructions I have used normal fabric. You could always use a square tablecloth for a pointed and unusual hemline if you prefer...

MAKING CLOTHES FROM SCRATCH

YOU WILL NEED

MATERIALS

▮ A large tablecloth or medium- to lightweight fabric (see below for dimension calculations)

▮ Interfacing: your waist measurement in length by 4cm (1½in) in width

▮ 20cm (8in) zip with plastic teeth, not metal, and a zipper foot

▮ A button

▮ Extra fabric for a waistband if using a tablecloth: waistband measurement + 5cm (2in) in length by 8cm (3¼in) width

SKILLS GAINED

● Construction techniques

● Drafting a pattern direct to fabric

● Machine-sewing techniques

BODY MEASUREMENTS

🖐 Waist (or where you want the skirt to sit on the body) + seam allowance of 3cm (1¼in) for zip

🖐 Waist measurement ÷ 3.14 (pi) = your diameter

🖐 Diameter ÷ 2 = your radius

🖐 Waist to length of skirt + 3.5cm (1½in) for hem and seam allowance

🖐 The skirt is made from a square piece of fabric: (waist to length of skirt + 3.5cm/1½in) x 2, + diameter calculation. Depending on how long you want your skirt you may need to sew two lengths of fabric together, so you have the same measurements on all sides

SEAM ALLOWANCE

▬▬▬ 1.5cm (⅝in)

» Step 1

Calculate your waist and radius measurements (see Body Measurements, above right); make a note so you don't forget. Fold your fabric in half and then half again to give you a folded quarter of fabric. If using a tablecloth, make sure that the hemmed edges are together by pinning them in place. To make these steps easier, I would press your fabric at the half and quarter folds and pin them into position before marking and cutting out your waist. At the corner which is at the fabric centre, place the tip of your tape measure. Measure from here along one edge by your radius measurement and mark with tailor's chalk.

Repeat at intervals to create an arc, by keeping the end of the tape measure at the tip of the fold and moving the tape measure along until it reaches the other folded edge. If you are using fabric rather than a pre-hemmed tablecloth, then repeat this process but this time with your waist to length measurements to give you a symmetrical curved edge by placing the tip of your tape measure along your radius marks as you follow it round to mark the length. You can now cut along your marked line, creating a hole in the centre of your fabric.

Step 2

Now we need to insert the zip. Partially unfold your fabric so that it is now folded in half. Choose one of the pressed folds in the fabric. Place the tip of the zip at the raw edge and along the pressed fold. With a pin or tailors' chalk, mark approximately 2cm (¾in) before the end of the zip tape. Cut along the fold of the fabric, up to this marked position.

Step 3

Using your sewing machine and a straight stitch, sew a V-like shape, starting at the raw edge, approximately 1.5cm (⅝in) away from the crease line and down to the zip length mark. Keeping the needle down in the fabric, lift the presser foot and rotate the fabric around so that you can now sew towards the opposite side of the fold. After two or three stitches, sew towards the raw edge, completing your V-shape.

Step 4

With your iron, press over the fabric at the stitch lines onto the wrong side. At the opening, place your zip against the wrong side of the fabric, and pin in place. You want to get the zip opening as close together as possible. The easiest way to do this is by turning over your fabric, so the right side is now showing and it will be how you will see it on the skirt. Close the opening by pinning the remaining side in place. Before sewing you might want to hand-sew the zip in place with a quick running stitch, so that you do not have to worry about removing the pins as you go. This is known as a tacking/basting stitch; you will remove it later so it doesn't matter what colour you use – I would use something that you can see easily later.

Step 5

Change your regular sewing foot to a zipper foot. Carefully, stitch down the length of the zip until you get to the marked position. Leaving the needle in the fabric and lifting the presser foot, rotate the fabric until you are in a position to sew. Now sew across the zip. Carefully do this by manually working the sewing machine until you have completed four to six stitches or until you get over the zip and roughly the same distance as the topstitching on the other side. Leaving the needle in the fabric, rotate the fabric again so that you can complete the parallel topstitch along the other side of the zip. You should have completed a nice boxed shape to secure your zip in place. You can now remove all the tacking/basting stitches.

≫ Step 6

To keep the waist of your skirt in shape, sew a line of 'stay stitching' along the raw edge, using the edge of the foot as a guide. Stay stitching is a construction technique used to support curved edges like waists or necklines. It is just a straight stitch that helps to stop the fabric from stretching out of shape. You will not be removing this stitch, so make sure you keep it within your seam allowance guide.

≫ Step 7

Next, you need to add a waistband. The length of your waistband will need to be your waist measurement plus 5cm (2in). Taking a separate piece of material, cut out an 8cm (3¼in) wide strip of this length. The interfacing needs to be the same length but 4cm (1½in) wide. Iron your interfacing to the wrong side of the waistband fabric, aligning three edges.

≫ Step 8

Pin the interfaced edge of the waistband to the skirt, right sides together.

≫ Step 9

Once you have pinned all the way around, attach the waistband along the long edge with a straight stitch. Then with the wrong side facing up, press all the seams into the waistband. To make the next steps easier, press a 1.5cm (⁵⁄₈in) seam allowance along the long free edge of the waistband and then fold your waistband in half with the right sides facing each other. Press lightly, ready for step 10. You will now need to make a button loop, as shown on page 76.

MAKING CLOTHES FROM SCRATCH

Carousel skirt inspiration – a day at the beach for my mom and me, in Looe, Cornwall. Check out the fabric – it's almost a match!

HOW TO: MAKE A QUICK BUTTON LOOP

With the leftover circle of fabric we are going to make a quick button loop. Cut a strip of fabric about 4cm (1½in) wide and no more than 8–10cm (3¼–4in) long (you may need to make it a bit longer if your button is a lot larger than mine). Fold and press the strip in half lengthways. Then fold the raw edges to the centre fold and press (A). Now fold in half again for the final press. Sew a line of topstitching in the centre of the folded fabric so that all layers are caught (B).

A

B

10

➤ Step 10

With the interfaced side facing down, open out the waistband. Place the loop on the right-hand side of the waistband, with the raw ends out, and adjust until your loop fits your button and includes the 1.5cm (⅝in) seam allowance. Pin in place.

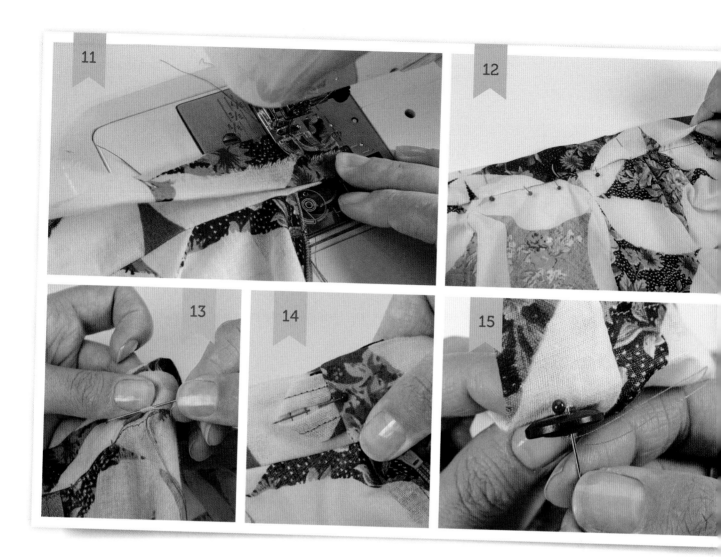

Step 11

Secure the button loop with a straight stitch. Use the edge of the foot as a guide for the seam allowance as we don't want to see this stitch later. To finish your waistband and create crisp corners, we need to fold the band back on itself so the right sides are together. Pin and stitch at both ends of the waistband with the right sides together and the seam allowances turned up.

Step 12

Clip away the seam allowances at the corners and turn out the waistband, making sure the tips of the corners are nice and crisp by poking out the corners. Remember to use your chopstick and not your scissors! Now pin the rest of the waistband in place with seam allowances tucked under.

Step 13

With a needle and matching thread, hand stitch the waistband in place using a ladder stitch (see page 64).

Step 14

Now to sew on the button. You might want to try your skirt on to check where the button needs to go first. You can do this by putting the skirt on backwards and looking in the mirror; place a pin where your button needs to be sewn.

Step 15

While sewing the button on, keep the pin in the fabric. This helps to ensure that the button is not sewn on too tightly. I have also double threaded my needle to make the button more secure.

Step 16

Before finishing your button with a knot, wrap the thread around the back of the button, enclosing all the threads and creating a shank. Once you have done this a few times, pass the needle through the centre of the shank, wrap the thread around the needle twice and pull the needle out to create a knot.

Step 17

To finish your skirt you need to press a narrow double hem into the bottom edge (unless you are using a ready-hemmed tablecloth). Fold over 1cm (½in) of the raw edge towards the wrong side of the fabric. Either pin or press in place as you go along the length of your hem circumference. When you have come back to where you started, repeat the process by folding the fabric again to conceal the raw edge. Repin as you go.

Step 18

Pin or press the hem in place and then secure with a topstitch. Now go give your skirt a twirl!

BATWING DRESS

I love retro-style clothes and the batwing sleeve is something that looks great whatever era or style you prefer. The deep armhole makes it a very comfortable and cool item to wear as it falls loosely around your body. It's also very easy to make! You can make it as either a dress or a top, so look out for step 8 to see how.

YOU WILL NEED

MATERIALS
- Approximately 2m (2¼yd) of lightweight, floaty material
- Approximately 25cm (10in) of interfacing for your collar
- A t-shirt to use as a pattern base
- Elastic

SKILLS GAINED
- Alternative necklines
- Construction techniques
- Drafting a pattern direct to fabric
- Machine-sewing techniques
- Using a garment to draft a pattern

BODY MEASUREMENTS
- Shoulder to waist (A)
- Waist to hip (B)
- Shoulder to length + 3cm (1¼in) for hem (C)
- Shoulder to elbow (D)
- Elbow circumference ÷ 2, + 2.5cm (1in) for seam allowance and ease (E)
- Hips ÷ 4, + 5cm (2in) for seam allowance and ease (F)
- Waist minus 5cm (2in) for elastic length (G)

SEAM ALLOWANCE
- 1.5cm (⁵/₈in)

➤ Step 1
I have used a non-directional print so that I can fold my fabric in half widthways without it looking upside down on the opposite side (the fold in the fabric sits along the shoulders). If you do want to use a directional print you will need to sew front and back pieces together first, with the print positioned correctly (in this case the seam will run across the shoulders). Make sure the selvedge edges meet and are in line, then pin in place so that they are secure while you begin to draft the outline of the garment. Find the centre of the folded fabric by using your tape measure to calculate it by dividing the selvedge to selvedge measurement in half. Mark the centre with pins along the length of the fabric.

➤ Step 2
Now, fold your t-shirt in half, matching up the underarms and neck edges so that you find the centre of the t-shirt; mark with pins all down the centre. Place the centre of the t-shirt at the same point on the fabric and match up the shoulder seams with the fold in the fabric. Make sure the bottom of the t-shirt is central by measuring from the pin to the selvedge edge and making sure that the measurement is the same on both sides. To stop it from moving, pin the t-shirt to the fabric as you would a paper pattern.

Step 3

On one side of your t-shirt, place the tip of your tape measure on the top fold and measure down your shoulder to waist measurement (A); mark with a pin.

Step 4

We are going to add 4cm (1½in) to the side of the garment at this point to allow for ease and a seam allowance. Mark with a pin. This is going to be the reference point of where your batwing shape will begin.

Step 5

Now go back to the folded shoulder edge. Measure from the shoulder point on the t-shirt along the fold as far as your shoulder to elbow measurement (D) and mark with a pin.

Step 6

To make sure your sleeve fits you, measure down from this elbow point using your elbow circumference calculation (E) and mark it with another pin. You should have two points of reference now, one at the waist and one at the elbow.

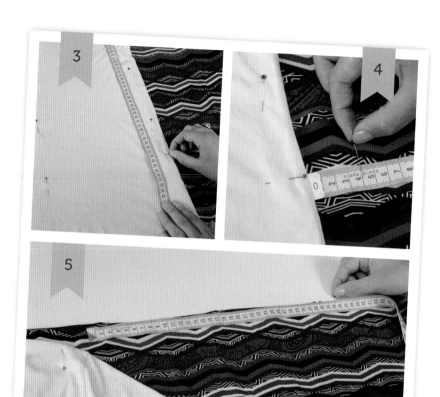

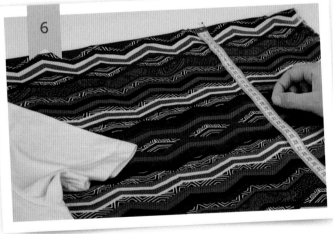

Step 7

With tailor's chalk, make a gentle curve connecting these two points together. You can do this free hand or with a tailors' curve. Continue the curved shape up and out until you get to the selvedge edge. You need to make this extending line either the same size as your elbow measurement or you can taper it slightly, but remember you need to be able to get your lower arm and hand through it.

Step 8

Now depending on whether you are making a dress or a top, this step will be different. For a top: measure 4cm (1½in) down the remaining length of the t-shirt and mark with either pins or tailors' chalk for your hem, then skip to step 21. If you want to lengthen your top to be a little longer than your t-shirt, then just add this onto your hem measurement. For a dress: using your waist reference point, measure and mark with a pin where your hips are by using your waist to hip measurement (B).

Step 9

We are going to need to add a little more ease in this area, as generally your hips will be bigger that your bust. So, from the centre front pin along the hip-pin line, measure and mark your hip calculation (F). Then with your shoulder to length calculation (C) mark how long you want your dress.

Step 10

Draw a gentle curve from your waist to hip measurement and then continue with a straighter line from the hip to the desired dress length.

Step 11

With these marks made, cut out one side of the garment carefully, from sleeve end to hem.

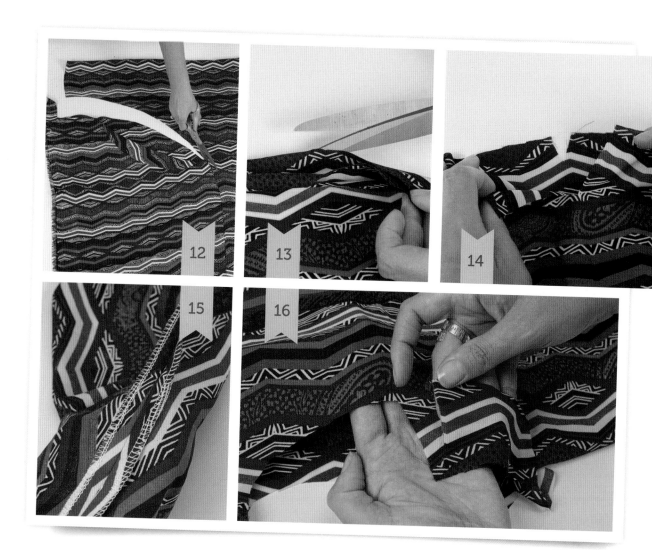

Step 12

Remove the t-shirt carefully, replacing the pins in the fabric as you go so that the fabric stays in place. Fold the cut-out side over, along the centre-front marker pins so that it becomes a template for the other side. Pin in place and then cut out, so you have two symmetrical sides.

Step 13

To make the neckline, make a small cut into the fold at the centre point, then cut along the fold about 10cm (4in) either side.

Step 14

At the centre front, cut down into the front of the fabric by about 5cm (2in) and do the same on the back but by about 2.5cm (1in). This should be enough for you to get your head through to make personal adjustments. But before you do, let's sew the side seams.

Step 15

With a straight stitch, sew both side seams from cuff to hem. Finish the seams with a zigzag stitch or using an overlocker (serger).

Step 16

Once you have done this, try the garment on in front of the mirror to adjust the neckline. Remember, the smaller cut line is the centre back. Take off the garment and cut a curve from the centre front to the shoulder point and then shoulder to centre back. Keep the off-cuts; use these as a pattern for the other side of the neckline. Pin them in place and then cut around them to get a symmetrical shape. To make sure the neckline stays in shape, sew a line of straight stitch around the circumference of the neckline using the edge of your presser foot as a guide. This is called a stay stitch.

Step 17

To draft your roll collar, you will need to measure the circumference of the neckline roughly with your tape measure. I would then add about 5cm (2in) to this, to account for a seam allowance and any misjudgement in neckline size. Take this measurement and cut out a strip with a width of at least 13cm (5in) or bigger if you prefer. If you want to provide a little structure to the collar, apply interfacing on the wrong side of the fabric: it will need to be the same length and half the width of your fabric strip (I haven't interfaced my collar as I want it to be a more relaxed shape). Pin your collar in place with the right sides together and keeping the ends of the collar loose. As you did in the shirt reverse project (see page 62), you need to mark where your collar seam needs to be and then join the ends with a straight stitch.

Step 18

Now that your collar fits your neckline; secure it with a straight stitch, using a 1.5cm (⁵⁄₈in) seam allowance.

Step 19

Fold your collar back on itself and tuck under a 1.5cm (⁵⁄₈in) hem; position this in line with the stitching you have just done, press, and pin in place.

Step 20

You can now hand stitch this in place using a ladder stitch or alternatively for speed, when pinning your hemmed edge, place the hem slightly over the original stitching line by about 2mm (¹⁄₁₆in), then topstitch in place by 'stitching in the ditch'. You can sew from the wrong side (as shown) or the right side to do this. If you sew from the right side, it is really important to take your time, as the overlap will make all the difference on whether you catch or miss your collar on the other side. Sew into the crease, where the two fabrics are sewn together, so that the stitches become almost invisible but catch the hemmed edge on the other side.

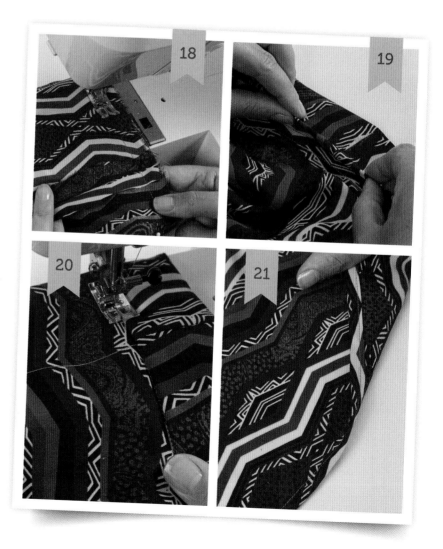

Step 21

All you need to do now is hem the bottom of your garment and sleeves. At the ironing board, press a double hem of about 1.5cm (⁵⁄₈in) and pin in place. Topstitch in place using a 1cm (½in) seam allowance.

HOW TO: MAKE AN ELASTICATED WAIST

If you have made the dress and want to give it a little more shape around the waist you can sew a line of elastic into the waistline. I like to wear my dress with a thin belt but you could also make a fabric sash by cutting out a length of fabric at least 2m (6½ft) long and 15cm (6in) wide. Follow the same instructions for the kimono belt (see page 94).

Measure out a length of elastic – your waist measurement minus 5cm (2in). Sew the two ends together by overlapping them and securing with a zigzag stitch. I would go forward and then reverse stitch, so you sew it twice to be extra secure (A). Taking a water-erasable pen, divide the elastic into quarters. First mark the two folded ends with the pen then bring these two points together and mark the new folds to give you an evenly quartered elastic (B).

To find where you want the elastic to sit I would advise trying the garment on, inside out in front of the mirror. Place the elastic on over the dress and adjust until you are happy that the hem is roughly even and the top part looks good. Then on one of the side seams, pin the elastic in place before taking the dress off. To make the waistband even, take a measurement from the hem to the pin in the side seam and transfer this to the other side and mark with a pin. Bring the two side seams together and mark the fold just as you did with the elastic to create four evenly spaced marks. Check that the hem to waist measurements you took on the side seams are the same for the centre front and back.

Now that you have four reference points on the dress and four on the elastic, match these up and pin in place. Secure the elastic in place with a zigzag stitch. Starting at the side seam, place the needle into the fabric and then pull the fabric and elastic at the pinned point until they match. Keeping this tension, stitch until you get to the pin (C). Continue this process until you complete all four quarters. When meeting your first line of stitching again, sew over it by 2cm (¾in) to secure it in place (D). You are all ready for that night on the town!

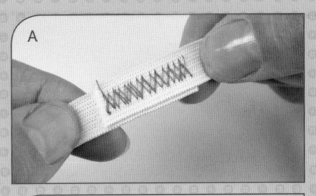

A

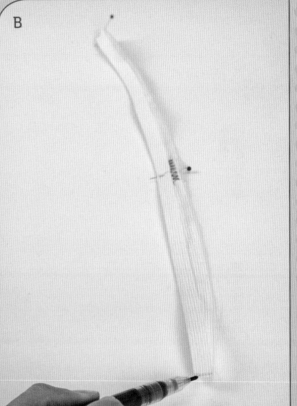

B

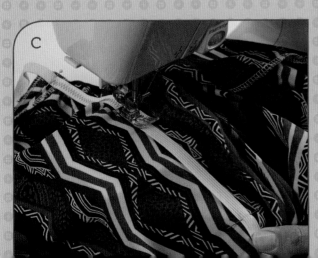

C

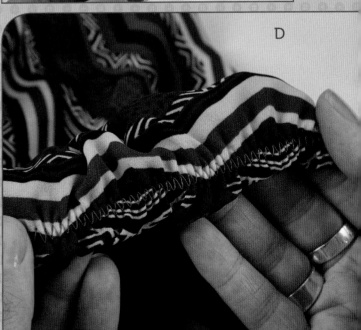

D

HOW TO: MAKE AN ALTERNATIVE NECKLINE

By facing a neckline, you can make any shape you like. Here, I have gone for a split neckline, which is a little 'V' opening down the centre of a curved neckline.

After cutting your neckline shape (A), you need to create a facing. This needs to be bigger that your neckline area and has to be interfaced. I have finished the raw edge by overlocking it. The neckline shape is the same as the main fabric. Pin it in place with the right sides together (B). Sew around your neckline shape and then clip all the curved and pointed edges, being careful not to cut your stitches (C). Turn out your neckline, poking out any corners and press to give you a clean finish (D). To stop your facing from turning back out, sew a line of topstitching around your neckline (E).

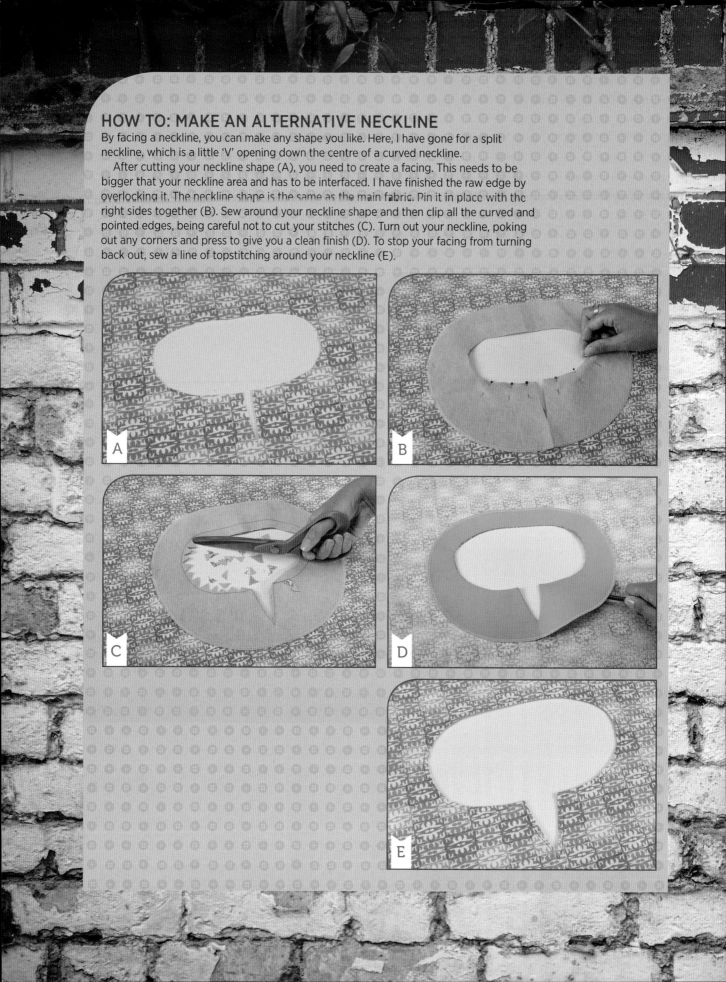

KIMONO DRESS

I first made this dress when I was lucky enough to play at the O2 Birmingham music venue with my band Snooty Bobs. I was faced with the situation we have all been in – a wardrobe full of clothes... nothing to wear. Based loosely on the Japanese kimono, this is a super-quick project that looks great but is really easy to make. The basic shape is a rectangle that wraps around the body and is secured with an obi-style sash.

➤ Step 1

Cut two pieces of fabric using your shoulder to shoulder (width) and the shoulder to length (length) calculations (A and B), giving you two large rectangles of fabric. Pin them right sides together along one short side – this will become the top. Using a straight stitch, begin to sew in from the side of the fabric by about 20cm (8in) and using a large seam allowance of about 2.5cm (1in); don't forget your reverse stitch at the the beginning and end of your stitching line. Repeat the process on the other side of the fabric to give you two shoulder seams. Once you have done this you should have a large enough hole for your head to get through. Try the garment on to check this and that it sits on your shoulders properly. Adjust as needed by marking the position with pins. If you have made adjustments, remember to do a quick fold check to make sure the neckline is even on both sides, before sewing in place.

YOU WILL NEED

MATERIALS

- 1–2m (1–2¼yd) of medium to lightweight fabric: anything that has a nice drape
- 25cm (10in) of interfacing

SKILLS GAINED

- Construction techniques
- Drafting a pattern direct to fabric
- Machine-sewing techniques

BODY MEASUREMENTS

- Shoulder to shoulder + approximately 20cm (8in) (make sure this measurement is more than half your largest measurement – bust, hips or waist – by more than 10cm/4in), then add 5cm (2in) for seam allowances (A)
- Shoulder to length + 5cm (2in) for seam allowances and hem (B)
- Shoulder to waist = belt position (C)
- Shoulder to front bust = armhole measurement

SEAM ALLOWANCE

- Variable seam allowances

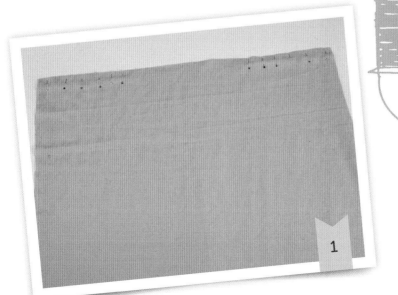

1

TOP TIP!

The kimono dress has quite a sharp boat neckline, so if this is too close to the neck for you, feel free to adjust the neckline (see the shirt reverse or batwing dress for alternative necklines).

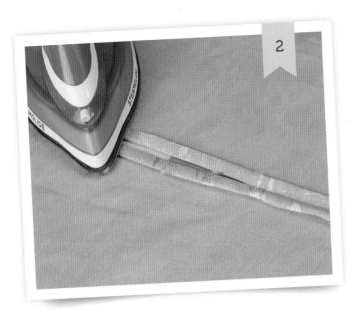

Step 2

With the wrong sides of the fabric facing you, press over a double hem on one side of the raw seam and pin in place. Then repeat the process with the other seam allowance. Even if you have only slightly curved your neckline, you will need to clip the seam so that it lies nice and flat against the body, but only do this 1cm (½in) into the seam as we don't want any visible cuts on the back of the hem.

Step 3

With a straight stitch, secure the double hem, finishing your shoulder seams as well as your neckline in one long stitch. (I used contrast thread here to make it clear!) You may want to match up your seam with the edge of the presser foot to give you a clean and straight topstitch.

Step 4

Now you need to sew the side seams together. You might want to try your garment on again to find your armhole position by pinning it in place first and adjusting it. Alternatively, use your shoulder to front bust measurement by placing the tape measure tip on the shoulder seam and marking the measurement with a pin. With the right sides together, pin along the side seam edge from the armhole position to your bottom hem. Sew along this length using a 2.5cm (1in) seam allowance.

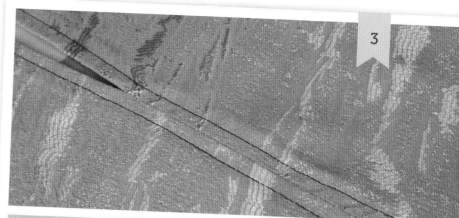

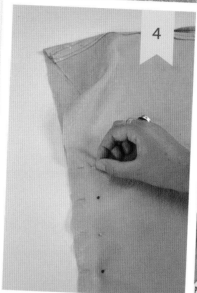

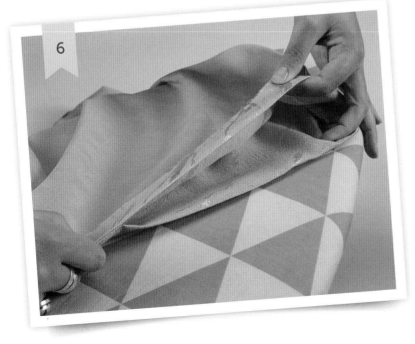

Step 5

Taking your garment to the ironing board, press open your seams and continue to press over a 2.5cm (1in) single hem around your armhole.

Step 6

Repeating the same process as in step 2, press the fabric under to make a double hem along the entire side seams and armhole. Pin in place if you find this easier.

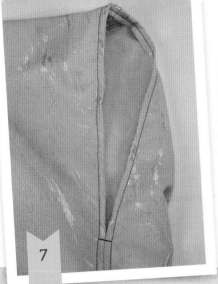

Step 7

Secure the double hem with a straight stitch. Again, use the edge of the presser foot as your seam allowance guide. To ensure your underarm and neckline stitches do not become weak over time, sew a line of stitching between the two lines of parallel stitching, close to the opening of the armhole. Sew over this line a few times by using the reverse stitch. Now make the belt as described below.

HOW TO: MAKE A BELT

To make your obi-style belt you are going to need a strip of fabric approximately twice your waist measurement and 10–15cm (4–6in) in width depending on how wide you want it to be. You will also need to cut a piece of interfacing. This will need to be the same length as the fabric strip but only half the width. Iron the interfacing to the wrong side of the belt (A).

Fold the belt back on itself so the right sides are together and all edges are matching before pinning in place. Starting at one end, on the folded side, sew a straight stitch towards the corner. You can make this edge tapered (as shown) by sewing at an angle if you prefer. Leaving your needle in the fabric, rotate and continue along the belt for 10cm (4in) or so then secure with a backstitch. Repeat at the other end, but this time stop sewing about 10cm (4in) from your previous stitches so you can turn your belt through later. Clip away the bulk in the corners (B) and turn through, making sure the tips of the corners are nice and crisp (C).

To give a little more structure to your belt and to close the gap you left to pull your belt through, sew a continuous line of topstitching around the edge of the belt until you get back to where you started (D). Continue to sew over the original stitching for a little while before reverse stitching to finish. With a hand sewing needle, thread the loose threads back into the belt so they cannot be seen.

For a closer topstitch, use the edge of the presser foot to line up your fabric edge. Then, while on a straight stitch, adjust your sewing machine's stitch width so it moves the needle closer to the edge of the fabric. This way the machine is doing all the hard work – you just need to keep the edge of the fabric in line with the edge of the presser foot. Remember to reset your machine when you have finished topstitching, otherwise your seam allowances will be out for the rest of the make.

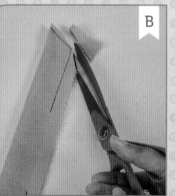

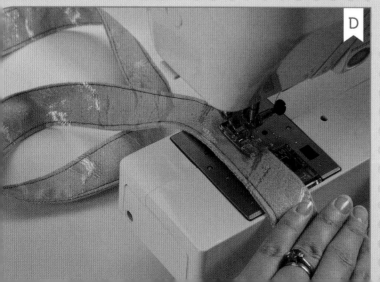

Step 8

Before pinning the belt on the garment, find the centre point of the belt by folding it in half lengthways and marking it with a pin. Taking your garment, we are going to do a similar thing by folding the side seams together and marking the fold with a pin: this will be your centre back. Remember, if you have shaped your neckline, make sure you are doing this to the back of your dress. Next, find your waistline position by using your shoulder to waist measurement (C). Using the tape measure and the centre-back pin as a guide, mark the correct position with another pin. Mark the side seams with the same shoulder to waist measurement so it makes the next step easier. You now need to match up the centre of the belt with the centre back of the garment first then align the belt with the points you have marked on the side seams. Pin it in place.

Step 9

Secure the belt to the back of the dress with a straight stitch – try to sew over the original topstitching on the belt. When you get to the side seam, sew in line with it by placing the needle into the fabric and rotating it first, then continue stitching until you meet the other side of the belt's topstitching. Continue stitching and rotating until you have reached where you started. You may not be able to see where this position is but if you quickly check on the wrong side of the garment, without removing it from the sewing machine, you'll be able to see.

Step 10

Make sure you go over the original stitching a little bit before doing a reverse stitch to finish. All you need to do now is hem your dress and you're ready to go! To create your double hem, press over a 1.5cm (⁵⁄₈in) strip of fabric all the way around. Repeat this process again to create a double hem. Secure with a topstitch.

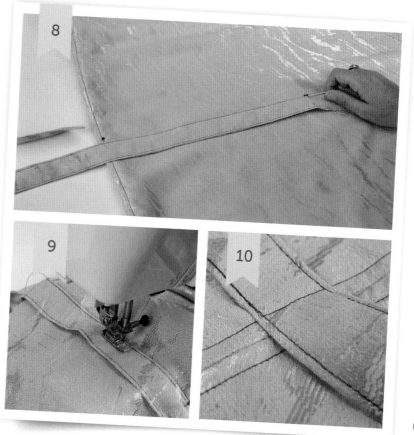

CROSS-BACK TOP

YOU WILL NEED

MATERIALS
- 1–1.5m (1–1¾yd) of lightweight cotton or rayon
- Pattern drafting paper or newspaper
- A t-shirt or top to use as a pattern base

SKILLS GAINED
- Altering your pattern
- Construction techniques
- Machine-sewing techniques
- Using a garment to draft a pattern

SEAM ALLOWANCE
- 1.5cm (⅝in)

When I worked in an office, I used to get bored of wearing the standard office top or blouse every day and wanted to make something that was smart but also reflected my individual style. I decided to make this cross-back top. From the front, it has a smart and clean finished look but when you turn around, the cross-back detail adds a little bit of chic: wave goodbye to the boring office top! I love this pattern as it's a great base for other variations. By simply changing your fabric you can make this into an evening top by using viscose or silk, or sports or casual wear by using stretch knits. You can also reverse it, to have it cross your heart instead, or alter the depth of the crossing curves.

▶ Step 1

Take your base garment and fold it in half, making sure that you are matching the side and arm seams together as well as the neck and shoulder areas. Secure these in place with pins. Lay the garment onto the paper with the fold in line with the straight edge of the paper. This is the centre front of your pattern. Pin in place and trace around it; don't worry about tracing the sleeves if using a t-shirt. Once you have done this you can remove your base garment.

Step 2

As the pattern will be placed on the fold of the fabric, you will not need to add a seam allowance to the centre front. However, you will need to add a 1.5cm (⁵/₈in) seam allowance to the majority of the sides apart from the bottom edge.

Step 3

You will need to add 3–4cm (1¼–1½in) to the bottom edge to allow for a double hem here.

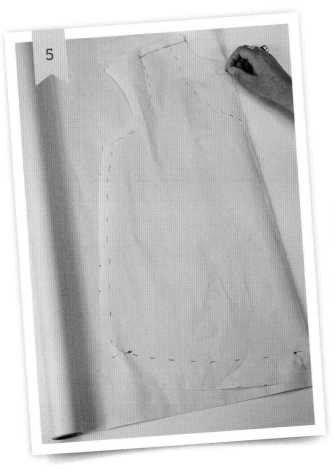

Step 4

As this garment was only the basis for your new pattern, you might want to make adjustments to the shape. In my project, I lengthened my shoulder seam and adjusted the neckline from a V-neck to a round neck. I did this by wearing my base garment and using the shoulder straps as reference points for my new neckline by taking new measurements while I was wearing it. I also wanted to create a cap sleeve look by extending the shoulder seam and redrawing my armhole using the tailors' curve.

Step 5

Fold another piece of paper in half. Place the centre front on the fold of your new paper and trace around this. You may want to pin in place.

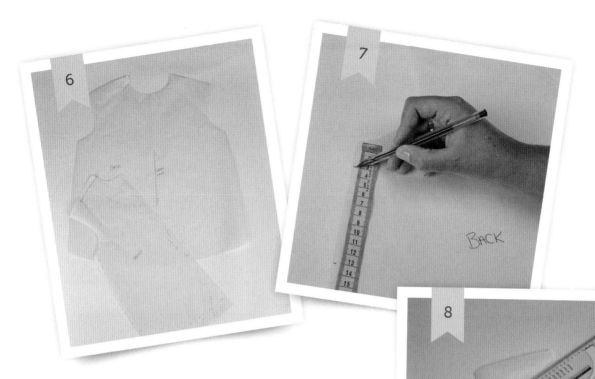

Step 6

Remove your front pattern and cut out your back piece; open it out to reveal the full back shape. So you can keep the pattern for another time, make notes on it so you know what the pieces are for. On your back piece, where you folded the paper will become your grain line. Draw along this line so it becomes more visible. Remember, your front pattern will be placed on the fold, so make a note of that also.

Step 7

To make the cross-back shape, you will need to make two marks on the left side seam. These are at 3cm (1¼in) down from the underarm (point A) and 13cm (5in) down from the underarm (point B).

Step 8

Now, starting at the right side of the neckline, draw a gentle curve connecting to point A on the left underarm.

Step 9

Then from point B, draw a curve to the bottom right hem. Fold your paper back along the original fold line and mark points A and B on the other side seam, giving you a point of reference later for your fabric notches. Once you have made all your marks, cut out your back pattern. You will not need to add seam allowances as this has already been done on the front pattern, which you copied as a base.

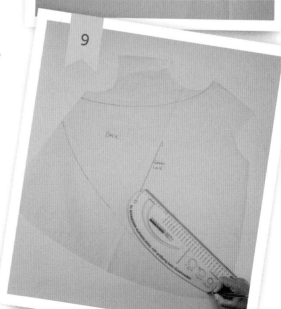

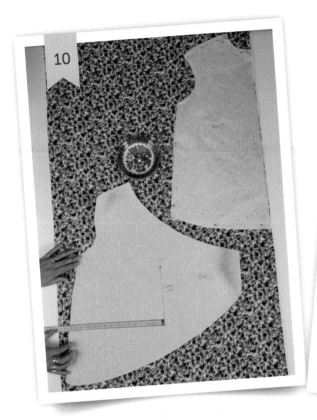

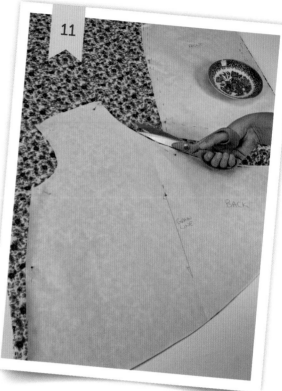

Step 10

Now place your patterns onto your fabric. Remember your centre front needs to be placed on the fold and you will need to cut out two back pieces. Depending on how wide your fabric is, you may be able to do this while your fabric is on the fold with right sides facing together and cutting your pattern out once. Remember to check the position of the pattern's grain line to the fabric's grain line by measuring at the top and bottom of the line you created earlier and adjusting it until they are the same measurement from the selvedge edge. If your pattern is bigger than the fabric while on the fold, you will have to cut your back pieces out separately. Remember to turn your paper pattern over so you have a mirror image – you don't want to have two pieces for the same side. You will also have to allow extra material for this, especially if it is patterned fabric. Pin in place, making sure your grain line and centre front are in the right positions.

Step 11

Cut out your fabric pieces. Before removing your paper patterns, transfer the side seam position marks on your pattern by making small notches into the fabric with your scissors. Make sure these notches are smaller than the seam allowance of 1.5cm (⁵/₈in).

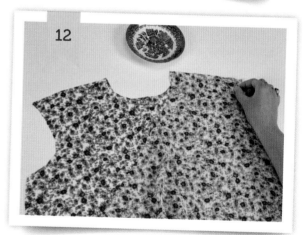

Step 12

Join the back shoulder seams to the front shoulder seam, with the right sides together. Pin and then sew in place using a straight stitch. Do this on both the shoulders. Press and finish the seams.

❯❯ Step 13

You might want to try your garment on quickly to check the neckline, especially if you have made any manual adjustments to the original base pattern. Check out the shirt reverse project for tips on adjusting a neckline (page 58). Before you move onto your next step, you need to add a row of stay stitching to the front of your neckline to help keep it in shape. The stitches need to be quite close to the edge of the raw seam, about 5mm (¼in) away, as we don't want to see them later.

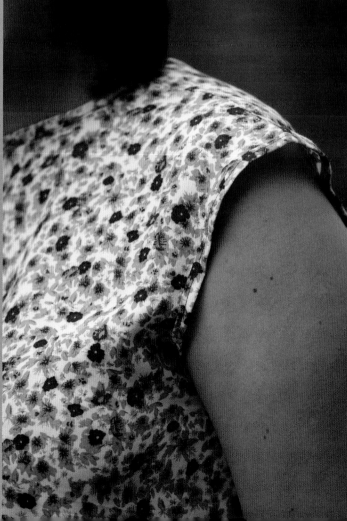

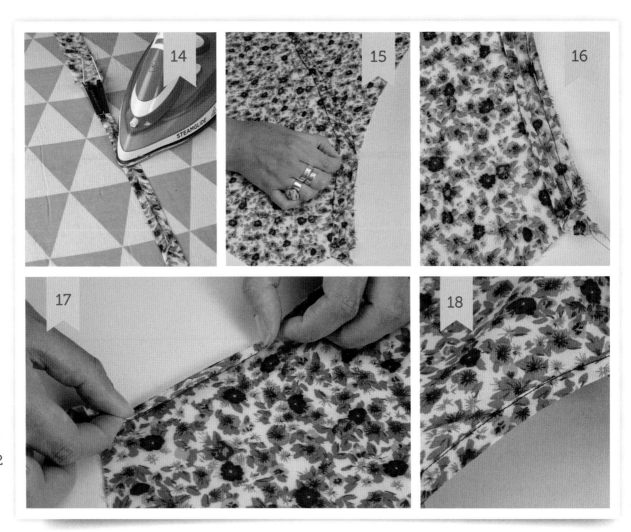

Step 14

Before you can sew the side seams together you need to attach your bias binding and complete the hem. You should have enough leftover material to make your own matching bias binding, so you will need to prepare that first. You don't want a thick binding, so it needs to be made from strips around 3.5–4cm (1¼–1½in) wide. For help on how to make bias binding, see page 61. You can also buy bias-making tools to help speed things up for you, as pictured above.

Step 15

Starting at the top of your short back side edge seam (point A), take your bias binding, place the right side of the binding to the wrong side of your fabric and pin in place. Continue all round the neckline until you reach the other back side edge, being careful not to stretch your binding.

Step 16

Using a straight stitch sew along the crease of the binding to secure it in place.

Step 17

Turn your fabric the right side up and press your binding away from the fabric, being careful not to press out the other fold on the bias binding. I find doing this next step on the ironing board a lot easier than on the table. Starting at one end, bring the remaining folded edge of the bias binding just slightly over the stitch line you have just created. Pin in place and continue along until you get to the other end.

Step 18

Secure your binding with a straight stitch about 3mm (⅛in) away from the edge of the binding, where it meets the fabric.

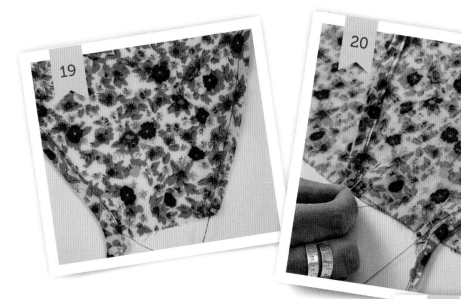

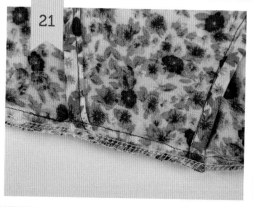

Step 19

To create your double hem, starting at the bottom of one short back side edge, press over a 1.5cm (⁵/₈in) strip of fabric all the way around until you get to the other side edge. You will now need to repeat this process again to create a double hem. A good press should keep this in place, without having to pin, but pin in place if you prefer. Secure with topstitch.

Step 20

With your binding and double hem finished, we can pin the side seams together. Making sure the garment is inside out with the right sides facing each other, pin the side seams together, making sure that you are also pinning the smaller back side section in as well. Check you have everything pinned together correctly before sewing. Sew, starting from the hem up to your armhole and secure with a backstitch.

Step 21

Stitch your remaining side seam together using a straight stitch. Press and finish your seams.

Step 22

All that needs to be done now is to finish your armholes. A quick and easy way to do this is by using the bias binding you have already made and the same technique we used for the neckline binding. With your tape measure, take a rough measurement of the armhole circumference and add about 6cm (2½in) to cover any misjudgements and seam allowances. Using the technique we used in the shirt reverse project (page 62), pin the binding in place, leaving about 3cm (1¼in) of binding before you start and finish. Pin the binding together at the underarm seam to give you a close finish. With a straight stitch, sew into the crease of the binding, remembering to leave a gap. Open out the binding and sew along where you placed your marker pin, being careful not to sew this section of your binding to your garment just yet. Trim and clip the binding before continuing to stitch along the fold line as before, pressing the seams open as you go over them. To finish your binding, press and fold it over the same way as you did with the neckline binding. Topstitch to finish. Job well done!

103

SUMMER TOP

Summer is my favourite time of the year, and most of the clothes I make are inspired by the warmer months: whether it is bright and colourful prints or light floaty fabrics, I'm drawn to the sun! This summer top is smock inspired, with a box pleat for detail at the chest, attached to a yoke neckline. It's a loose-fitting, simple summer top to keep you nice and cool in the summer sun.

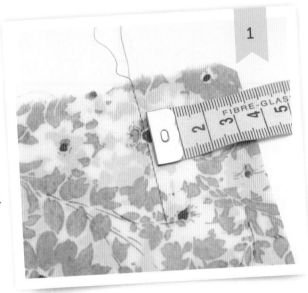

1

➤ Step 1

Cut out a rectangle of material using your hip calculation (A) as the width and upper bust to length calculation (B) as the length. Fold your material in half widthways with the right sides together and make sure that all raw edges are in line. Make a small notch in the top fold, so you know where your centre front is and press the centre fold with an iron. Before opening your fabric back out, sew a 5cm (2in) line of straight stitching straight down, 3.5cm (1½in) from the centre fold – this is your pleat.

YOU WILL NEED

MATERIALS

- 1–1.5m (1–1¾yd) of fabric
- 50cm (½yd) interfacing
- Elastic
- Pattern drafting paper or newspaper
- Buttons (optional)

SKILLS GAINED

- Basic fitting techniques
- Construction techniques
- Drafting a pattern direct to fabric
- Hand-sewing techniques
- Machine-sewing techniques

BODY MEASUREMENTS

- Hip + 10cm (4in) for ease and seam allowances (A)
- Upper bust to length + 5cm (2in) for seam allowance and hem (B)
- Front bust + 3cm (1¼in) for seam allowances (C)
- Upper bust minus front bust minus approximately 5cm (2in) = elastic measurement (D)
- Shoulder to front bust + 2cm (¾in) for seam allowance (E)
- Shoulder strap width (suggest 5cm/2in) + 3cm (1¼in) for seam allowance (F)

SEAM ALLOWANCE

- 1.5cm (⅝in)

TOP TIP!

To make sewing the pleat easier, increase your stitch length to maximum, giving you a tacking/basting stitch. Sew a line of stitching as explained in step 1, but sew down the full length of the fabric. Create your box pleat as instructed but when you have finished making your top, take these tacking/basting stitches out; leaving only the permanent stitching at the top.

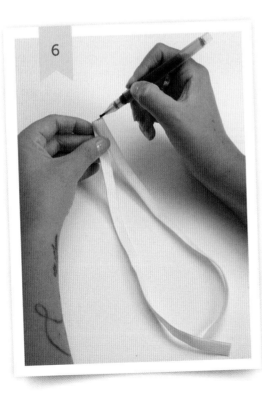

Step 2

Open out the fabric and match your centre-front notch to the line of stitching you have just completed. This should give you two equal folds either side of your centre-front notch, known as a box pleat. Press the pleat with an iron and continue to press the box pleat shape down the length of the garment.

Step 3

To reinforce your box pleat, sew a line of straight stitch across the folded area of fabric. Use the edge of presser foot as your seam allowance so that it will not be visible later.

Step 4

Divide your upper bust calculation by two. Place the tip of your measuring tape at the centre front (your box pleat opening), measure along the raw edge by your half-upper-bust length and mark the point with either tailors' chalk, erasable pen or a small notch. Repeat on the other side.

Step 5

We can now sew the centre-back seam. With right sides together, pin and sew the side edges together to make a tube. Press and neaten the seam.

Step 6

Cut your elastic to size using your elastic measurement (D). To make sure you put your elastic in evenly, we need three reference points. You already have three reference points on your top – the two upper bust notches or marks and the centre-back seam. Start by folding your elastic in half to find the centre and mark this with a pen or a pin.

Step 7

This halfway point needs to match your centre-back seam. The ends of the elastic need to match up with the front bust notches or marks with a little overhang of about 1cm (½in). Pin the elastic to the right side of the fabric at the top edge and to these reference points only before going to your sewing machine.

Step 8

Adjust your sewing machine to a zigzag stitch. A three-step zigzag is best but a normal zigzag will also work. Starting at one of the front bust points, place your needle into the fabric first, then pull until the elastic and fabric are now the same size. While keeping that tension, begin to sew your elastic in place by sewing over the elastic until you get to your centre-back seam. Pause to adjust yourself ready for the final section of elastic then complete the stitching.

Step 9

To finish your elastic, fold over once to the back and pin in place. Secure with the same zigzag stitch, creating a single hem. Remember to pull the fabric like you did earlier, but this time try to catch the edge of the elastic and raw edge in between the zigzag stitches, so it overlocks the raw edge while sewing the two layers of fabric together.

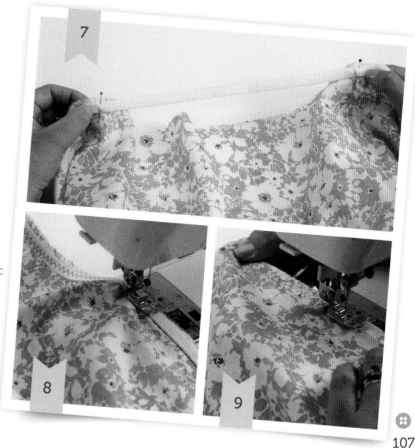

Step 10

Now to create the yoke for your summer top. Cut two rectangles of fabric and one piece of interfacing, the width of your front bust calculation (C) and approximately 50cm (20in) in length. These are going to be your yoke pieces. Taking one of your yokes, fuse the interfacing to the wrong side of the fabric with an iron. Making sure that everything matches up, fold in half lengthways and make a small notch to indicate the centre front at the edge of the fabric. From this point, measure approximately 10cm (4in) up the fold. This will be the lowest point of your neckline. You can adjust this measurement by placing the tape measure against your front bust point and measure upwards to check where it will finish. Take your shoulder to front bust calculation (E) and mark with erasable pen on the left-hand open edge of your folded fabric. At this point, measure your shoulder strap width calculation (F) and mark again with the pen. Continue to mark the same measurement along the length of the fabric, up to the top of your fabric. At the shoulder point, create a curved line towards your neckline point in the centre of the fabric, creating a shape for your yoke neckline.

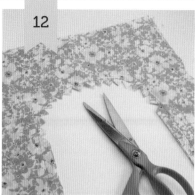

Step 11

While the fabric is still folded, cut along your marks to create your yoke neckline. Use this off-cut as a template to cut out the second yoke piece, remembering to match up the edges before you pin in place and cut.

Step 12

Bring the two yokes together, right sides facing and with all edges matching. Pin along the 'U' shape of the yoke. Using a straight stitch, sew around the 'U' of the neckline. To reduce bulk and give your neckline a nice smooth shape you need to clip around the curved edges, making sure that you do not cut into your stitch line.

Step 13

To keep a smooth neckline shape and to stop the underside of the yoke from rolling forward, you need to understitch the seam allowance to the curve of the facing. You do this by pressing all the seams to the yoke lining – the one you have not interfaced. Then with a straight stitch, sew very close to your original stitch line – about 3mm ($\frac{1}{8}$in) away. Starting at the shoulder point, secure both the seam allowance and the yoke lining together until you reach the other shoulder point. When you turn your yoke back the correct way, you should not be able to see this stitch at all, so don't worry if it is a little wobbly. You will get better with practice.

Step 14

Now we can attach your yoke. Start by matching up your centre-front notch in your interfaced yoke to the centre front of your top with the right sides together. Pin in place.

Step 15

Secure with a line of straight stitch. This time we are going to be using a 2cm (¾in) seam allowance. To make this step a little easier, clip into the seam allowance about 1cm (½in) away from the end of the single hemmed elastic to give you a nice flat edge to work with. Start and finish your straight stitch about 1.5cm ($\frac{5}{8}$in) away from the edge of your yoke, as you will need to turn this under later. Remember to secure your stitches with a reverse stitch.

➤ Step 16
Trim and press this seam towards your yoke.

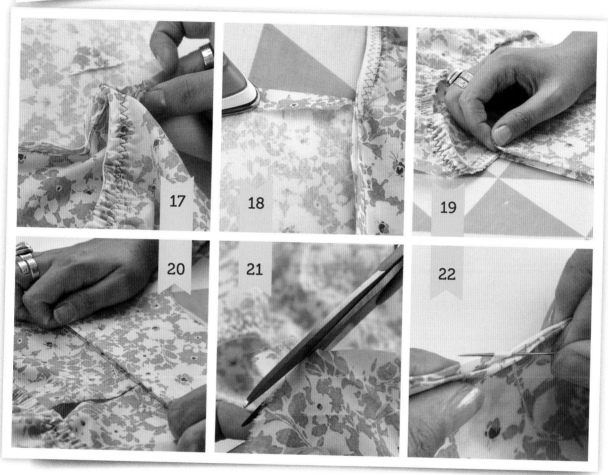

➤ Step 17
While you are at the ironing board, clip the corners where you have not quite sewn to the edge.

➤ Step 18
Press the 1.5cm (⅝in) allowance to the wrong side along the long side edges of the interfaced yoke.

➤ Step 19
Repeat on the yoke lining: press a 1.5cm (⅝in) allowance to the wrong side along the long side edges, so that when you bring them together in the next few steps, they match with no raw edges showing.

➤ Step 20
Now press under the bottom edge of the yoke lining in the same way.

➤ Step 21
Clip the corners as you did before.

➤ Step 22
Pin your yokes together, matching up the seams. Handstitch the turned edges together using a ladder stitch for a great professional finish or, for a speedier finish, topstitch in place with your sewing machine.

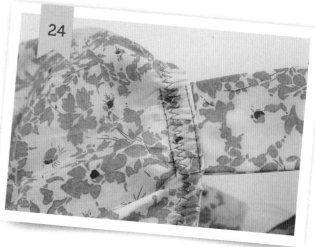

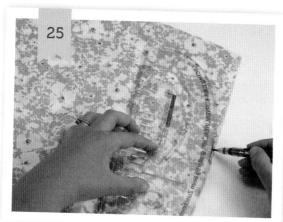

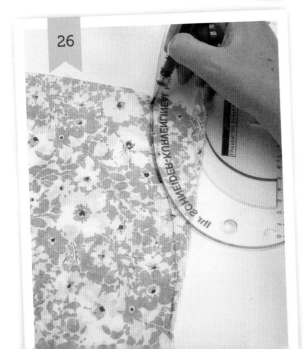

Step 23

To sew your straps in place I would suggest getting someone to help you; if this is not possible your dress form will be just as good. Put an old bra that fits you comfortably onto your dress form. Then put your garment over the top. This way you can make sure that you position your straps in the right place for you and so that your bra cannot be seen when you wear your finished garment later. Pin the straps in place while the top is on the dress form.

Step 24

Secure the straps to the inside of the summer top with two lines of straight stitch, one at the very edge of the garment and the other just under the elastic. Once you have done that you can remove the excess strap with a pair of scissors, but leave 2cm (¾in), then finish the raw edge of the straps.

Step 25

To add a little more detail you are going to scoop your hemline. You can do this by creating a gentle curve at the side seams by using your tailors' curve or a large round plate. Start by matching up your centre-front notch with the back seam. Press with an iron giving you a clean crease at the sides to make it easier to work with. Taking your tailor's curve, draw a gentle slope upwards from the bottom hem and towards the crease you have just created.

Step 26

To smooth the curve, turn the ruler around and continue to the side of the garment, trying to keep this line as straight as possible. Try not to make this shape too sharp or it will be difficult to hem later.

⫸ Step 27

Simply cut this shape out while the fabric is still folded and use the off-cut to transfer the shape to the other side of the top.

⫸ Step 28

All you need to do now is hem the bottom of your summer top with a double hem. Press over 1.5cm (⁵/₈in) of fabric all the way around. You will now need to repeat this process again to create a double hem and secure it with topstitch. If it is not lying flat you may need to clip into the first fold to allow the fabric to curve with the hemline shape. Try not to clip into the second fold as you don't really want to see the clipping on the back side of the hem. Why not add more detail to the yoke by attaching a few buttons?

BLANKET COAT

This was one of the first garments I created without using a pattern and with just a few body measurements. It was a blanket that I found in a charity shop – I just loved the colours and the wool is super soft. It's a perfect garment for an autumnal walk or a late summer's evening when you get a little chilly after a barbecue. If you see a blanket you like, bear in mind that it needs to be quite large – at least 2m (6½ft) square so that you can get sleeves and pockets out of it as well; you need to make sure that you can wrap it loosely around your body when checking the size. Alternatively, a boiled or felted wool would be perfect for this project; you can see the blanket version in the finished shot (right), and the boiled felt version in the following steps. The blanket version has less drape at the front, as I was limited to the amount of fabric I had to work with; in the boiled felt version I allowed a larger amount of fabric at the front to give a lovely flowing drape. Work with what you've got!

YOU WILL NEED

MATERIALS

- A large blanket or boiled wool, 2–3m (2¼–3¼yd)
- Embroidery thread (optional)
- Large buttons (optional)
- Walking foot and buttonhole foot (optional)
- Dress form adjusted to your size (optional)

SKILLS GAINED

- Construction techniques
- Drafting a pattern direct to fabric
- Draping techniques
- Hand-sewing techniques
- Machine-sewing techniques

BODY MEASUREMENTS

- Bust + front bust for maximum fabric width required (A)
- Shoulder to desired length + collar depth, + 3cm (1¼in) for seam allowances (B)
- Shoulder to shoulder + 3cm (1¼in) for seam allowances, ÷ 2 (C)
- Shoulder to front bust + collar depth, + 3cm (1¼in) for seam allowances (D)
- Collar depth + 1.5cm (⁵⁄₈in) for allowances (E)
- Shoulder to neck + 1.5cm (⁵⁄₈in) for seam allowances (F)
- Arm length + 3cm (1¼in) for allowances (G)
- Shoulder to front bust x 2, + 10cm (4in) for allowances (H)
- Cuff size + 3cm (1¼in) for seam allowance ÷ 2

SEAM ALLOWANCE

- 1.5cm (⁵⁄₈in)

>> **Step 1**

You need to cut a fabric rectangle the width of your bust calculation (A). The length of your rectangle is your shoulder to desired length calculation (B). If you are using a blanket, you might need to consider not having it too long, as you'll need leftover material to make the sleeves – around 50cm (20in) in length, depending on how long your arms are.

Step 2
Fold the fabric in half widthways with right sides together and place a pin into the fold. This will be the centre back.

Step 3
Along the top edge of your fabric, measure across and mark out your shoulder to shoulder calculation (C) with a pin through both layers.

Step 4
From this point, measure down the length of your material by your shoulder to front bust calculation (D), and mark this point with another pin.

Step 5
Doublecheck that the half shoulder to shoulder calculation is the same at the two pinned marks and make adjustments if you need to.

Step 6
Now cut into the fabric, starting at the first point and then finishing at the second point. This cut is the beginning of your armscye or armhole.

7

8

these flaps will form your collar

shoulder to shoulder (C)

shoulder to neck (F)

centre back

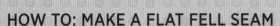

⟫ Step 7
Measure down the fabric using your collar plus seam allowance calculation (E). Pin the two layers of fabric across this measurement as far as your shoulder to shoulder calculation plus your neck to shoulder calculation (C + F) (you will pin across the cut).

⟫ Step 8
Cut across the folded fabric to the end of your neck to shoulder (F) point. Remove the offcut section to leave you with a flap that will form your collar. Follow the steps for making a flat fell seam below to sew the two short ends together to create your collar.

USING A WALKING FOOT
For this project, I would change your normal sewing foot to a walking foot. A walking foot is a great tool for sewing multiple or thick layers of fabric as well as fabrics that are slippery or have a nap. A sewing machine only has one set on feed dogs, which means that sometimes the top layer of fabric may not move at the same rate as the bottom layer, causing fabric to shift apart when sewing. A walking foot helps to equalise this by pulling your fabric layers through at the same time. You may want to increase your stitch length if your fabric is particularly thick as we don't want to over strain the thread. If you haven't got a walking foot, pin or hand tack/baste like mad to keep those layers in place.

HOW TO: MAKE A FLAT FELL SEAM
With the wrong sides of your two collar flaps together (A), pin and sew the collar together at the ends, using a straight stitch. To finish your raw visible seams, you are going to make a flat fell seam. Firstly, trim one of the seams very close to your stitch line (B). Then with the other seam, turn under the raw edge and then lay it over the trimmed seam (C). Pin in place and then secure the new seam with a straight stitch along the folded edge (D).

A

B

C

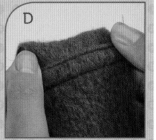

D

Step 9

Now you can pin your shoulders together for a fitting. With the wrong sides together, line up the centre-back pin with the seam of your collar first then continue to pin along the seam until you get to the shoulder edge. Repeat this process with the other shoulder. Standing in front of a mirror, try the coat on. Does it sit nicely on the shoulders? If not, you may need to angle your shoulder seams a little so it looks like a wedge when you pin it, with the larger section at the shoulder and getting thinner as it gets to the neck area. Is it too tight on the underarm? Don't forget that you have seam allowances here, so you may want to tuck or pin about 1.5cm (⁵⁄₈in) of the fabric over to get a real sense of how it will feel on you.

Step 10

Secure the whole shoulder section with a flat fell seam, as you did with the collar.

Step 11
To ensure a good fit, you might have to make adjustments to the armholes. Place your coat on a dress form.

Step 12
Carefully cut around the arm shape using the dress form arm shape as a guide, starting at your underarm. Remember that you want to include a seam allowance, so make sure you cut 1.5cm ($^5/_8$in) away from where you want it to be. Keep the off-cut to one side. If you are not confident enough to get cutting straight away, mark out the arm shape with tailors' chalk first, imagining this is the stitch line. Then add the seam allowance by using the 'stitch line' as a point of reference, then cut out.

Step 13
Make adjustments to other side of the coat by using the off-cut fabric as a pattern piece. This makes the adjustments symmetrical and quick!

Step 14
For a gilet coat (see page 121), simply stop at this point and don't add any sleeves! You may want to add a decorative blanket stitch around the armholes and the edges of the coat.

Step 15
Placing the coat flat on the table, you are going to start drafting your sleeves. Your sleeve fabric will need to be the length of your arm calculation (G) wide and twice your shoulder to front bust calculation (H) long for each arm. To make life easy, make sure that your fabric is at least this size; then fold the fabric in half widthways, with wrong sides together. Place it under the shoulder and armhole of the coat, allowing at least 3cm (1¼in) to sit behind the edge of the armhole, as well as 7.5cm (3in) down. Mark out the sleeve to size while the fabric is in this position.

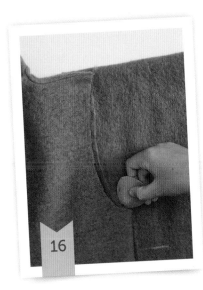

➤ Step 16

Keep the line of the shoulder the same as the fold in the fabric you are using for the sleeve. Taking your tailors' chalk, draw around the shape of the armscye until you get to the end. Then measure down 5cm (2in) along the side of the coat. If the front and back of the sleeves are very different shapes you will need to repeat on the other side of the fabric. Make sure you line up the coat in the same position. You will also need to make a note of which is the front of the sleeve. You can do this by making a mark with tailors' chalk into the fabric. Now you can remove the body of the coat and just work on the arm shape.

➤ Step 17

With a tape measure, mark 5cm (2in) up along the curve. You already made the other mark (5cm/2in down the coat side) earlier. With your tailors' chalk, join these two points together with a curved shape. Repeat on the other side, if the armscye is different.

➤ Step 18

Now you just need to draw the rest of the sleeve. Measure the length of your arm and make a mark with tailors' chalk or a pin. In line with this point you will need to mark out your cuff size. Take your tape measure, make a loop and place it on your wrist. Loosen and tighten the tape measure until you have the size cuff you would like and make a note of this measurement. Add 3cm (1¼in) to this for your seam allowance, then divide the number by two to get your cuff calculation. At the edge of the fabric and down from the fold, mark your cuff calculation. Join that mark with the one at the end of the curve, giving you a sleeve shape. Repeat on the other side, if your armscyes are different. Before cutting out, add 3cm (1¼in) for seam allowances onto the head of the sleeve only. To make the other sleeve, place the sleeve you have just created onto the fabric with the right sides together. Pin the sleeve in place and cut around it carefully. Before removing the pins, you might want to make a quick tailors' mark to show which side of the sleeve is the front. You will know this because of the mark you made earlier.

➤ Step 19

To create your sleeve, fold the sleeve in half with the right sides of the fabric together and pin along the straight edge. Secure in place using a straight stitch and repeat this step with the other sleeve.

Step 20

To insert the sleeve head smoothly into the bodice of the coat, you are going to sew an ease stitch and also make a notch, so you have a reference point for later. With the sleeve nice and flat, where the fabric is folded at the head of the sleeve, make a small notch. This is so you know that this point needs to match up with your shoulder seam. Then about 8–10cm (3¼–4in) away from the arm seam, place a pin either side. This is going to be where you start and end your ease stitch. An ease stitch is an extended straight stitch that when pulled, gently gathers the fabric to reduce fullness and creates shape, so that you can fit it into the armhole.

Step 21

Extend your straight stitch to the maximum the machine will let you. Starting at the first pin you are going to sew around the curve of the sleeve head, passing the notch you created and stopping at the other pin. If you are going across the seam, then you are going the wrong way. Don't do a reverse stitch. If your material is particularly thick then you may need to do this by hand by sewing a small running stitch instead but don't knot it at the end. To sew your sleeve to the body of your coat, you will need to ease your fabric by gently pulling the thread until you start to gather your material. You won't need to gather it too much but you will need to distribute your gathers along the curve of the sleeve so that it is even. Pin your sleeve into the armhole of the coat by matching up the shoulder seam with the notch in the head of the sleeve and the seam with the side of the coat first, making sure the right sides are together. You will also need to check that the front of the sleeve is on the same side as the front of the coat by checking your chalk marks. Place your pins into the fabric at right angles to the raw edge rather than parallel. I find it easier to see where things need adjusting and it's easier when you come to sew the sleeve.

Step 22

Remove your sewing machine table to leave the small sewing machine arm. It makes sewing cuffs and arms easier as it is smaller and your garment can fit around it! Keeping your sewing machine on the longest straight stitch, sew your sleeve in place using a 1.5cm (⅝in) seam allowance and without reverse stitching at the beginning or the end.

23

⟫ Step 23

When finished, turn your sleeve out and check for any nips or tucks. If there are, then you can remove the stitches quickly as they are only a tacking/basting stitch and try again. However, if your sleeve is looking good, then just go over your line of stitching with the normal stitch length you used at the beginning of the project to secure the sleeve in place properly. Repeat this process with the other sleeve. The great thing about boiled or felted wool is that you do not need to hem your edges as the fibres are so tightly woven that they do not fray. But if you want to add buttons or a little more detail to your coat then I would suggest using an embroidery stitch, and the blanket stitch just seems so fitting as it is a blanket coat!

TOP TIP!

If you have a little extra fabric left over why not add some patch pockets? Check out page 130 for pocket instructions and see page 116 for a close-up. Ta da! You now have your blanket coat!

HOW TO: SEW BUTTONHOLES BY HAND

Find out where you want to put your buttons by trying the coat on and popping a pin into the fabric as a marker. Take the coat off and place the button back on top of the pin. With two pins, mark either side of your button so you know what size you need (A).

Sew a small thin box, using the pin as guides (B). If you have been using an extended stitch you will need to reduce this down as you are only going through one layer of fabric now. With the pins at the beginning and end of the buttonhole, use an unpicker to cut open your buttonhole. The pins will stop you from cutting your stitches (C). With a needle and embroidery thread, finish the buttonhole with a buttonhole stitch (D).

Here is a little verse for you to remember which way your buttonhole goes. Girls are always right! So, boys are left... sorry boys. Meaning the right-hand side of the garment should be on top of the left-hand side for girls. This applies to fly zips and waistband overlaps too.

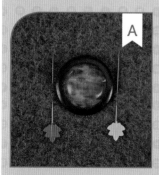

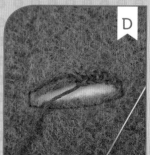

DUNGA DRESS

I get as excited by dungarees as I do tassels! I cannot get enough of them. Dungarees and pinafores are my favourite garments, so I just had to include a dunga project in the book! My dunga dress is a simple pattern that can be adapted by either changing the neckline or pockets. Here I have two options for you: patch or inseam pockets, and tunic or buttoned strap variation. Either way, I hope you enjoy wearing them as much as I do!

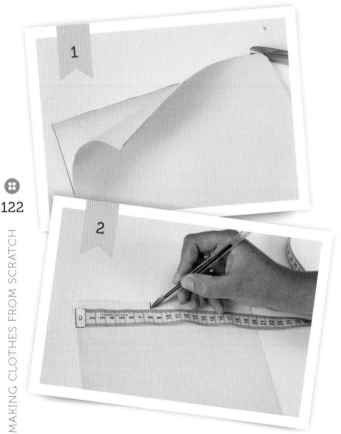

➤ Step 1
To create the front and back panels (the main panels) of your dunga dress you need to draw out a rectangle shape using your front bust calculation (A) for the width and your shoulder to desired length calculation (B) for the length. Once you have drawn this, cut it out. Fold your rectangle in half lengthways to find the centre point and cut out a small notch in the fold. (The side panels will provide the remaining width of the dress.)

➤ Step 2
On the open corner of the folded rectangle, you are going to mark out the size of your strap. I decided I wanted my strap to be 5cm (2in) wide so, using the strap calculation, I have marked out 8cm (3¼in) across.

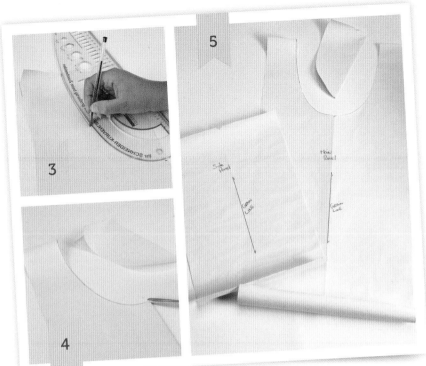

➤ Step 3

You now need to think about your neckline shape: I wanted mine to be quite deep, so I measured 23cm (9in) down from the centre notch. If you are undecided, place the paper pattern on your shoulder and look in the mirror to see roughly where you want it to be. Once you have these two reference points, use the tailors' curve to draw your neckline on your folded paper.

➤ Step 4

When you are happy with your neckline shape, cut this out while the paper is still folded in half. This will ensure an even and symmetrical shape. Recut your centre notch in the fold.

➤ Step 5

To create your side panel, draw a rectangle using the side panel width (D) and length (E) calculations and cut it out. Fold in half lengthways and make a small notch at the folded edge so you know where the centre point is. Now you have your two pattern pieces drawn out, you need to make a few notes on them. First, label the main and side panels pieces, then draw along the fold lines you created: these mark your grain lines. Mark it in pen, so you can see it easily.

MAKING CLOTHES FROM SCRATCH

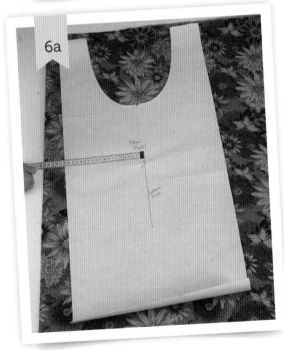

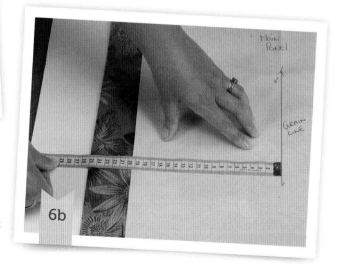

➤ Step 6

Fold your fabric so that the opposite selvedge edges are together first, then pin your pattern pieces onto the fabric, ensuring the length of your rectangles are along the grain line of the fabric. Using your tape measure, take measurements from the selvedge edge to the grain line mark on each pattern; make sure the two are parallel to each other and adjust the pattern if not. Pin the patterns in place.

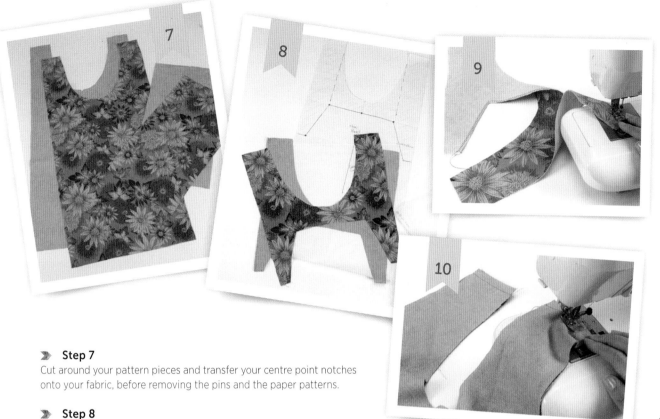

Step 7

Cut around your pattern pieces and transfer your centre point notches onto your fabric, before removing the pins and the paper patterns.

Step 8

Now to cut out your neckline facings. To do this I used the main panel pattern again, but only the top section: place the pattern onto the fabric in exactly the same way as in step 6, but this time you only need to cut down as far as your shoulder to under bust calculation (F) to get the facing length. (I folded my original paper pattern back at this point, so that I didn't cut the pattern while I was cutting my facing out.) Remember to transfer your centre notches before removing the pins and paper pattern. You will also need to cut the same shape out of a single piece of interfacing. Fuse the interfacing to the wrong side of one of the fabric pieces. Fold the fabric in half, matching up the neckline and the raw edges and pin in place. With your tailor's chalk, mark 5cm (2in) down from the centre point. Continue to draw across horizontally until you are in line with your shoulder straps. Draw down to the end of the fabric towards the corner. Square off about 2cm (¾in) towards the edge to allow for a seam allowance along the side. Now cut this section out. Use this amended facing as a template to cut out the other facing fabric.

Step 9

Finish the lower shaped edge of each facing piece with either a zigzag stitch or an overlocker (serger). The other raw edges will be enclosed seams so you don't need to finish these.

Step 10

Now to get making these dungas! Place your main pieces together with the right sides facing. Pin at the shoulder seams and sew across each with a line of straight stitching. Press out your seams.

Step 11

While you are at the ironing board, grab your side panels. Fold each side panel in half, lengthways, with the right sides facing. Make sure your raw edges match first before pressing a centre crease into the fabric. This will make more sense later on. Now pin your side panel to your main front panel, matching up the hem edges first, with the right sides together.

Step 12

With a straight stitch, sew these edges together. Because you are going to make some adjustments, increase your stitch length to the longest on the machine, giving you a tacking/basting stitch. Start at the hem and stop about 10cm (4in) before you get to the top of the fabric; secure with a reverse stitch. Now attach the other side panel to the main front panel in the same way, then sew the back panel in place.

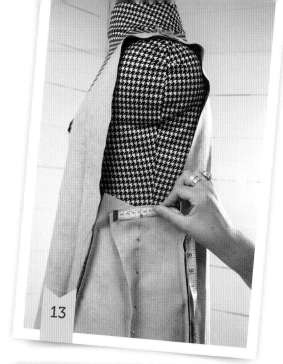

13

14

15

16

Step 13

Try your garment on inside out in front of the mirror, with your pins to hand. Alternatively, you can do this on your dress form. Remember the centre crease you pressed into the side panels? Well, you are going to pinch the fabric at this point until it fits you better – pin it in place to create a dart. By pressing in the crease in step 11 you guarantee that your darts are straight. The dart needs to be wider at the top and thinner at the bottom. If you are doing this on the dress form, try the dress on again after you have pinned in the darts to check it fits before sewing.

Step 14

If your darts seem very large – over 3cm (1¼in) from the fold of the dart to the pin – then you need to make some adjustments to your side panel pattern before you continue. Measure the dart depth first then remove the pins and unpick the side panel stitches. On the top edge of the side panel, mark half the dart depth measurement in from each edge. With a ruler, draw a straight line from these points to each bottom corner. Cut along the lines carefully making sure both sides of the fabric are the same. Why not make this adjustment to your paper pattern as well, so you don't have to do it again? With the adjustment made, pin and sew your side seams back onto your main panels and repeat the fitting process. Remember to reset your stitch length as you do not want this to be a tacking/basting stitch any more.

Step 15

Sew your first dart in place, starting at the raw edge. Angle your fabric so that your needle is in line with the last pin, which will be the point of your dart. Remember to secure the start of your stitch with a backstitch first and then sew towards your last pin. As you get to the last pin, sew right towards the edge of your fabric. You can secure this dart with a knot like you did with the shirt reverse (see page 59) or why not try the reverse stitch but along the fold of the fabric to keep it in place. Before sewing the other dart, I like to check that they are even first. Place the sewn dart on top of the pinned dart and check that the pins are in the same place as your stitch line. You may need to adjust these very slightly. Sew the other dart in place. You are now ready to hem your side panels. At the ironing board, press your first dart to one side. Whichever side you chose will become the back. Press the other dart towards the back of the garment too.

Step 16

Now press over a narrow double hem of about 1.5cm (⅝in) at the top of each side panel and secure with a pin. The reason you didn't sew along the full length of the side seam was to make this step easier. With a straight stitch, secure your double hem using the edge of your presser foot as the seam allowance guide. Once you have completed this step on both sides, you can now sew up the remaining unsewn parts of your side seams: start your stitches on top of your original stitches.

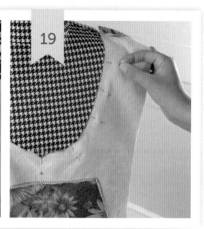

Step 17
Now you're almost ready to attach your facing. Sew the shoulder seams of the facings together like you did in step 10 with your main panels, and press the seams out. For the next bit, I find it easier to place my garment onto the dress form and pin the facing to the garment. Place your facing on top of the main panel with the right sides together. Match the shoulder seams and pin together.

Step 18
Next pin the centre points.

Step 19
Continue to pin the rest of the neckline in place.

Step 20
Sew your facing in place around the neckline using a straight stitch, then clip and trim the neckline so it will sit nicely on the body when you turn it the right way around.

Step 21
Press your neckline down, making sure you have a crisp edge where you have just stitched so that the facing and main panel are in line and not rolling forward. To stop the facing from rolling out of the garment, and to also give it a little more detail, sew a line of topstitching around the neckline, using the presser foot as your seam allowance guide. Next, press over a 1.5cm (⁵⁄₈in) single hem, along the raw side edges of both the main panel and facings, ready to pin in place. Follow the instructions in the box opposite to prepare the welt seams on the vertical side-panel seams.

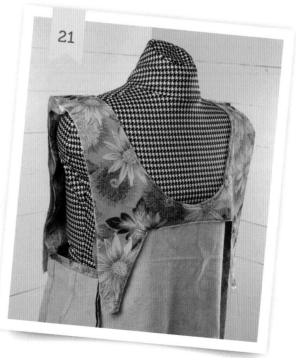

MAKING CLOTHES FROM SCRATCH

HOW TO: MAKE A WELT SEAM

You are now going to prepare your main panel seams to become a welt seam. You need to press all these seams to one side and towards the main panel (A). Trim the underside seam to half the size, being careful not to cut your main fabric, your stitching or the other seam. You only need to trim this up to the point your side panel stops (B). Then, with your pinking shears, trim away the very edge of the top seam, until you get to where your side panel finishes (C). If you don't have pinking shears then a zigzag stitch will be just as good to finish your top seam. You should now have two seams of different widths; press the wider one over the trimmed one. Repeat on the other three side seams.

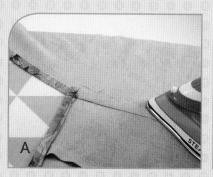
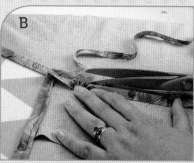
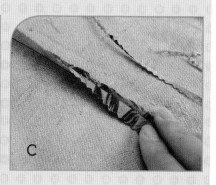

Step 22

Welt seams are usually topstitched in place. However, you are going to pin and secure your facing first, making sure the fabric lies nice and flat, and that your folded edges are in line with each other.

Step 23

Sewing a topstitch, you are going to start at the bottom hem, along the side welt seam – making sure you are sewing all your raw seams down – continuing along the facing until you sew down the other side's welt seam to the end of the opposite hem. I used the edge of the presser foot as my seam allowance for this topstitch. Repeat this on the other seam. That was multitasking at its best: you've definitely earned a nice cup of tea!

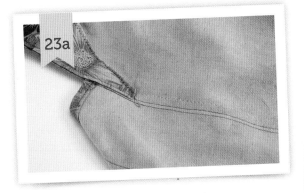

Step 24

No garment is complete without a pocket, so although this step is optional, it just has to be done! To cheat and save fabric, I used the 'U' shapes left over from my neckline. On the straight edge, fold and press under a double hem of about 1.5cm ($^5/_8$in) and secure with topstitch. Then, extend your straight stitch to the longest length on your machine. Starting at where you have just hemmed, sew along the curved shape of the pocket, using the edge of the presser foot as a guide. Continue all the way around until you get to the other side of the hem. Gently pull your bobbin thread so the fabric begins to gather. You won't need to gather very much to do this but you need to distribute this gather to the bend of your pocket. As you do this, your raw edges should start to curve towards you, especially if you press your fingertips towards your stitch line.

Step 25

Once you have a nice curved edge, use your iron to press the raw edges down. This technique will ensure that you have a nice curved edge for your pocket. Now, quickly fold the pocket in half and press a light crease. Repeat these steps with the other pocket. Place your garment on and stand in front of a mirror. If you are right-handed, place your left hand where you roughly want your pockets to sit and with your right hand, place a pin where your fingertips end. Take the garment off and place on the edge of the ironing board. Line up the bottom of the pocket with the pin and then match up the light centre crease of the pocket with the centre fold and dart on the side panel. Pin in place then repeat with the other pocket.

Step 26

With a topstitch, secure the pockets to your garment.

TOP TIP!

You may want to remove the extension table on your machine — this way you can manoeuvre your garment more easily and it can also stop you from sewing your garment together accidentally.

Step 27
All you need to do now is press under a double hem at the bottom of your garment and secure with a topstitch.

DUNGA DRESS VARIATION

If you don't want a tunic-style dress and want it to be more dunga-style, fold your pattern over at the base of the neckline, giving you a square shape.

HOW TO: MAKE A STRAPPED DUNGA

Square off your neckline. Continue with the instructions for the dunga dress as far as step 16. Before you attach your facings, you will need to make some straps. The width of the straps is completely up to you, but I find that 3cm (1¼in) is a good size; add 3cm (1¼in) to your chosen width for seam allowances. If you want a contrasting lining, as on mine, you will need four straps, two from each fabric, and they will need to be twice the length of your tunic straps (from the shoulder to the fold you created at the neckline) plus 10cm (4in).

Place the strap pieces right sides together in pairs, and sew along the length of each strap, across the top and back down the other side, leaving a small gap so you can turn it right side out. Clip your corners to reduce bulk and turn through. Press and finish your straps with topstitch. Before attaching your facing you need to sew your straps to the back main panel first, with the raw open ends trapped in the seam (A). Then continue the steps as normal to attach your facing (B).

On the front of your main panel, you will need to sew two buttonholes using your sewing machine – one in each corner. Try your garment on in front of the mirror. With a pin, mark where your button needs to go by pushing the pin through your buttonhole and into the strap underneath, and transfer this position to the other strap as well to make it symmetrical. Sew the buttons in place, and you're ready to go (C)!

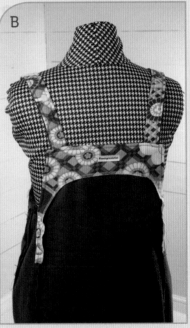

MAKING CLOTHES FROM SCRATCH

HOW TO: MAKE AN INSEAM POCKET

You will need to insert the inseam pocket between the front panel and side panels before sewing them together. Using your hand as a template, draw around it to create a pocket shape. Make sure you have a straight edge where your hand would enter the pocket (A). With your pocket fabric folded, pin and cut out two pocket shapes, so you end up with four pieces.

Find out where you want your pockets to go by marking the position onto the main panel first with a notch, then transfer this notch to the side panel by matching up the hemline first. With the right sides together, pin your pockets to both your panels, using the notches as guides. Secure with a straight stitch (B). Press over the pocket and then secure with an under stitch close to the edge of the pocket seam. This will stop your pocket from sticking out. Repeat on the other pocket (C).

Then, with right sides together, join your side and front panel together, as explained in the main instructions. However, this time you need to sew around the pocket as well (D). Leave your needle in the fabric when rotating the fabric to get to your pocket seam and again to get back to your normal seam. Finish the raw edge with pinking shears or a zigzag stitch. Repeat with the other pocket.

A

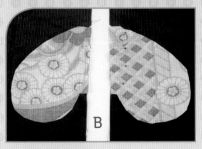

B

C

D

WRAP TROUSERS

These trousers send me right back to when I studied dance and visual art at Brighton University. I had bought a pair of wrap trousers at a festival and I literally lived in them. They were really simple in design but could easily be dressed up or down depending on the occasion. They are also a pair of trousers that you can adjust to size – simply move the button and snap fastener when your size fluctuates a little too much, as mine does. Unfortunately, time and over-washing saw the last of my favourite trousers... so this was the perfect excuse to bring them back to life!

⟫ Step 1

Depending on the selvedge to selvedge size of your fabric and your waist size, you might need to sew two pieces of fabric together as it may not fit (if you are able to wrap the fabric around the fullest part of your bottom or waist with about 23cm/9in to spare, it will work). If you need to stitch two pieces together, use the stitch line as your fold line and continue as below. Start by folding your fabric in half, parallel to your selvedge edges, and press a central crease. This gives you a starting point to work from. Open out your fabric with the wrong side facing up. We are going to make a mark either side of the fold line with tailors' chalk. Starting to the left of centre, mark 5cm (2in) from the fold line and mark it in some way, so you know it is the front. I have just marked it with a simple 'F'. Then mark 8cm (3¼in) to the right of the fold line and mark it as the back; you guessed it, with a 'B'.

YOU WILL NEED

MATERIALS

▮ 2–3m (2¼–3¼yd) of lightweight polyester mix or linen, depending on the length

▮ 50cm (20in) of interfacing

▮ A button and buttonhole foot

▮ A snap fastener

SKILLS GAINED

● Basic fitting techniques

● Construction techniques

● Drafting a pattern direct to fabric

● Machine-sewing techniques

BODY MEASUREMENTS

⌒ Waistband ÷ 2 plus 4.5cm (1¾in) for seam allowances and hem (A)

⌒ Crotch + 3cm (1¼in) for seam allowances (B)

⌒ Waist to length + 4.5cm (1¾in) for hem and seam allowance (C)

SEAM ALLOWANCE

▰▰▰ 1.5cm (⅝in)

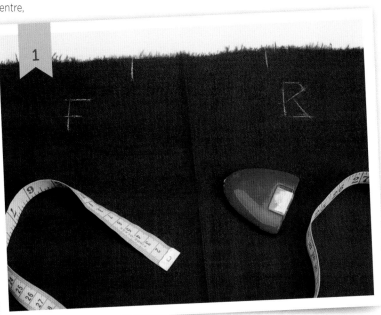

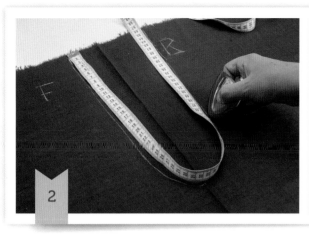

Step 2

Taking your crotch calculation (B), place the tip of the tape measure at the left point and the measurement at the right point. With the tape measure on its side, you want to create a 'U' shape. Once you are happy with the shape, mark using tailors' chalk, then cut the 'U' away. This curved line is your centre front and centre back in a continuous 'U' shape.

Step 3

Now we can draw out the leg shapes. Starting at the right-hand edge of your 'U' shape, you need to measure and mark out your waist calculation (A). Repeat on the other side. All you need to do now is to make a decision on the length of your trousers. I have gone for a culottes-style trouser, but you can make these trousers to any length you wish, whether full-length trousers or shorts. Mark the length of your trousers (C) with tailors' chalk on both the left and right side edges: to make sure the length of your leg is straight, take a measurement from the selvedge edge to your waist calculation point. Then repeat this distance along the length of the selvedge edge until you reach your desired leg length calculation. Join all the lines together to give you a rectangle shape with a 'U' shape in the top. Cut out your fabric carefully, following your tailors' chalk. Use this as a template to cut out the other 'side' of the trousers, making sure that the right sides of the fabric are pinned together, so that you have a left and right piece. I would avoid trying to cut two legs out at the same time – as it is such a big pattern piece, we are likely to make mistakes.

Step 4

To construct your trousers, pin and stitch the crotch area with the fabric right sides together, making sure that centre front and back are matching. Press and finish the raw edges. Believe it or not you pretty much have your pair of trousers now – you just need to hem and make a waistband!

Step 5

Press over and pin in place a double hem on all four side edges, approximately 1.5cm (⁵⁄₈in), and stitch in place using a straight stitch.

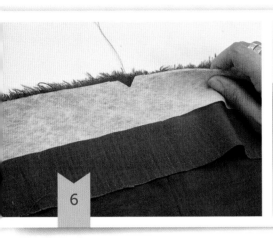

Step 6

For your waistband you will need two strips of fabric: one approximately twice your waistband measurement by 10cm (4in) in width; the second waistband needs to be your waistband measurement plus 20cm (8in), with the same width of 10cm (4in). You will also need to cut two pieces of interfacing. These will need to be the same lengths as the waistbands but only 5cm (2in) wide. Iron on the interfacing to half of the wrong side of each waistband. Find the centre point of each waistband by folding in half lengthways and making a small notch with scissors or tailors' chalk. Taking the longer waistband, match the centre of the band to the centre back of the trousers with the right sides together.

Step 7

Pin in place then secure with a straight stitch.

Step 8

Fold the waistband back on itself so the right sides are together and pin in place. At the ends of the waistband, still with the right sides together, start at the folded edge and sew towards the corner. Leaving your needle in the fabric, rotate 90° and continue along the waistband until you almost meet where the trouser leg is attached.

Step 9

Clip away the bulk and turn through, making sure the tips of the corners are nice and crisp. Repeat on the other side of the waistband. Don't forget to use your chopstick to push out your corners!

Step 10

With the whole waistband turned through, pin the rest of the waistband in place with seam allowances tucked under. Secure with topstitch around the whole waistband. Not only will this secure your waistband but it helps to keep it in shape and it also looks great.

➤ **Step 11**

Repeat steps 6–10 to attach the other, shorter waistband to the front of the trousers.

USING A BUTTONHOLE FOOT

Using a buttonhole foot is the quickest and most accurate way to sew buttonholes in my opinion. It is an awesome gadget that measures your button as it sews. Check your sewing machine manual for details, as the foot may differ depending on the sewing machine model. If you don't have a buttonhole foot, use the method on page 120 but instead of hand stitching them, practise using a zigzag stitch instead.

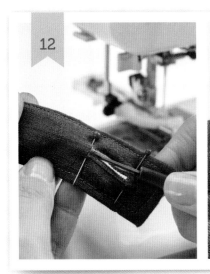

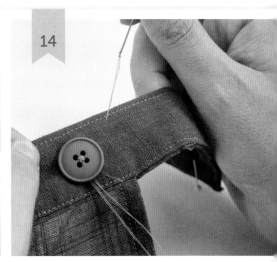

» Step 12

Concentrating on the smaller straps of the front waistband, and with the right side of the fabric facing you, sew a buttonhole at the tip of the left belt. Follow your sewing machine instructions for how to sew your buttonhole in place. To open the buttonhole, place a pin at each end of the buttonhole just before the stitches. Taking a sharp unpicker, cut open the buttonhole. The pins will help to ensure that you do not cut through your stitches.

» Step 13

Now put the trousers on back to front, so the buttonhole is on your front. Overlap the button tab until it feels comfortable on your tummy and, taking a pin, mark where the buttonhole tab ends. You can now remove the trousers. Placing the tab back to the mark you just made, place a pin into the buttonhole to mark where your button needs to be sewn.

» Step 14

Sew the button in place with a double-threaded needle and place a pin under the button. This helps to ensure that the button is not sewn on too tightly. Take the thread behind the button and wrap it around the threads, binding them together to give the button a shank. Create a knot by wrapping the thread around the needle and pulling it. Then pass the needle from under the button shank and out somewhere in the waistband, before trimming the thread away. I love this professional finish and it acts like a second knot too!

⋙ Step 15

To secure the other side of the same tab, sew a snap fastener to the other end. It will just stop the remaining tab from being visible. Your button is doing all the work.

⋙ Step 16

Now press and pin in place a double hem at the bottom of the trousers. Before stitching in place, clip away the corner edges to reduce bulk. Refold the hem and secure with a topstitch.

⋙ Step 17

You are now ready to wear your wrap trousers; remember the buttons are on the back and need to be fastened first...

⋙ Step 18

....then the back wraps around to the front with the ties. I hope you enjoy the trousers as much as I do!

INDEX

the liquid. *Wine must taste a lot like this,* she thought, swirling the sugary drink in her mouth. This was what it would be like when she was a lady. She would pile her hair high atop her head in curls and wear deliciously tight dresses, her shoulders draped in mink. Just like Marilyn Monroe.

"Ha, ha, Dary's drinking wi-ine. Dary's drinking wi-ine," Kevin sang as he raced back and forth across the kitchen floor.

"It's not either wine," she said, more embarrassed then frightened at being caught by her little brother.

"If it's not wine then prove it," he said, snatching the glass from her hand. He held it tightly in his fist, one pinky shooting straight out into the air, mocking her already exaggerated grip. He sipped it, then made a face, eyes bugged and whirling. "Ugh, it is wine," he said, looking at her impishly. "I must be drunk." He began to stagger about, flinging himself around the room. Daria saw it coming. She wanted to cry out and stop him, or at least to cover her eyes so that she couldn't see the disaster, but it happened before she could do any of those things. Kevin tripped over the leg of a chair and went down in a crash of shattered crystal.

Her first thought was for the glass. That was one of the things that she hated herself for later. All she could think about was how it was Kevin's fault that the glass was broken, but she would be the one who got the spanking for it. Especially the way he was howling. Then she saw the blood all over her brother's arm. Already there was a small puddle on the floor. She knew that she should get a bandage, or call the emergency number that her mother always kept near the phone, or at the very least, run and get a neighbor, but she couldn't move. She couldn't take her eyes off of the bright-red stain. It was not as if she had never seen blood before, but suddenly she was drawn to it as she had never been drawn to anything before. Without knowing what she was doing, she found herself walking toward her brother, taking his arm in her hands and pulling it slowly toward her face. And then she could taste the salt and copper taste as she sucked at her brother's wound, filling a need that she hadn't even known existed. It was a hunger so all-consuming that she could not be distracted even by Kevin's fists flailing away at her back, or the sound of her mother's scream when she entered the room.

Daria realizes that she has wedged her face too tightly between the bars and the cold metal is bruising her cheeks. She withdraws into the dimness. There is a metal shelf bolted to the wall. It has a raised edge running around its sides and was obviously designed to hold a mattress that is long since gone. There are cookie-sized holes in the metal, placed with no discernible pattern along its length. Words have been scratched into this cot frame with nail files, hair pins, paper clips—mostly names like Barbara and Mike, and Gloria S. There are many expletives and an occasional statement about the "pigs," but no poems or limericks to occupy her attention for even a brief time. The metal itself is studded with rock-hard lumps of used chewing gum, wadded bits of paper and who knows what else. It is uncomfortable to sit on even without these things—too wide. Her skirt is too tight for her to sit cross-legged, and so if she sits back far enough to lean against the wall, the metal lip cuts sharply into the back of her calves. Already, there are bright red welts on her legs, and so she lies on her side with her knees drawn up and her head pedestaled on her arm, the holes in the metal leaving rings along the length of her body. She pulls a crumpled package of cigarettes out of her pocket and stares at them longingly. Only three left. With a sigh, she puts them back. It is going to be a long night.

The doctor's name was printed in thick black letters on the frosted glass. Who knew what horrors waited for her on the other side. She knew that she had promised her mother that she would behave, but it was all too much for her. With tears streaming down her cheeks, she tried to pull free from her mother's grasp.

"No! Please. No, Mommy! I'll be a good girl, I promise."

Her mother grabbed her by both shoulders and stooped down until she could look into her daughter's eyes. With trembling fingers she brushed the child's hair. "Dary, honey, the doctor won't hurt you. All he wants to do is have a little talk with you. That's all. You can talk with the nice doctor, can't you?"

Daria sniffed and wiped her eyes with the backs of her hands. She knew what kind of people went to see psychiatrists. Crazy people. And crazy people got "put away" in the nuthouse. She allowed her mother to lead her into the doctor's office, a queen walking bravely to the gallows.

The waiting room was supposed to look inviting. One whole side was set up as a playroom, with a child-sized table and two little chairs, an open toybox with dolls and blocks spilling out of the top. A lady in starched white greeted them at the door and pointed Daria toward the corner, but she was not the least interested in playing. Instead, she hoisted herself onto a large wooden chair and sat there in perfect stillness, her hands folded across her lap. There she could hear some of the words that passed between her mother and the nurse. Their voices were hushed and they were quite far away, but she could hear enough to tell that her mother was ashamed to tell the white lady what Daria had done. She could hear the word "crazy" pass back and forth between them just as she had heard it pass between her father and mother all the last week. And she could tell, even though she could only see the back of her head, that her mother was crying.

Suddenly, the door opened up behind the nurse's desk and Daria's mother disappeared through it. The nurse tried to talk to the sullen little girl, but Daria remained motionless, knowing that she would wait there forever, if necessary, but she would not move from that spot until her mother returned.

Then, like a miracle, her mother was back. Daria forgot all about her resolve to stay in the seat. She rushed to her mother's side. She would go anywhere, even inside the doctor's room if only her mother wouldn't leave her again. When her mother opened the door to the doctor's office and waved Daria through, the child went without hesitation, but then, her mother shut the door without following, and Daria was more frightened than ever.

"You must be Daria," Doctor Wells said without moving from his desk. He reminded Daria of the stuffed walrus in the museum, and he smelled of tobacco and Sen-Sen and mustache wax. He smiled, and it was a pleasant smile. "Your mother tells me that you're very smart and that you like to do puzzles. I have a puzzle here that's very hard. Would you like to try and do my puzzle?"

Daria nodded, but she did not move from her place near the door. Dr. Wells got up and walked over to a shelf and removed a large wooden puzzle. It was a cow. A three-dimensional puzzle. Daria had never seen anything like it before. He placed the puzzle on a little table that was a twin to the one in the waiting room and went back behind his desk.

"Well, you don't have to do it if you don't want to," he said after a minute, and then began to look through some papers on his desk, ignoring her. Soon, Daria's curiosity got the better of her and she found herself standing at the table looking at the puzzle, taking it apart.

Daria had expected the doctor would talk to her, but he didn't really seem interested in talking. He seemed content to watch her play with the puzzles and toys and he asked her very few questions. By the time she left his office, Daria had decided that she liked Dr. Wells very much.

She wakes slowly, unsure whether minutes or hours have passed. Her eyes are weeping from the cold of the metal where her head has been resting, and her muscles ache with stiffness. Her neck and chest, still covered with crusted blood that the arresting officers had refused to let her wash away, have begun to itch unmercifully. She sits up and realizes that her bladder is full. There is a toilet in the cell. It is a filthy affair with no seat, no paper, no sink, and no privacy from the eyes of the policemen who occasionally stroll up and down the corridor. She will live with the pain a while longer.

Suddenly, she realizes what it is that has woken her up. Silence. It is a silence as profound as the noise had been earlier. No singing, no taunting voices, nobody howling in pain. It is so quiet that she can hear the rustling newspaper of the guard at the end of the hall. She feels that she ought to be grateful not to have to listen to the racket, but instead, she finds the silence frightening.

Once again, she pulls the crumpled pack of cigarettes from her pocket. This time she cannot resist. She pulls one from the pack and straightens its bent form, then holds it between her lips for a long time before she begins the finalizing act of lighting it. She lets out the smoke in a long plume, pleased by the hominess of its smell. A familiar scent in this alien world.

"Can you spare one . . . please?" a soft voice calls from the next cell. "Please?" it asks again. The noise acts like a trigger as the tiny gospel singer starts in once more. A hand pokes through the bars in the corner of the cell. It is black and scarred and shaking with the strain of the reach. It is easily the largest hand she has ever seen. Large even for a man. Daria stares at the two cigarettes remaining in her pack. What the hell, she figures, they'll be gone soon anyway. She removes one and places it in the hand. It squeezes her own gently and withdraws.

"So, it has happened again, Daria?" Dr. Wells asked. The child nodded, looking down at her feet. "After three years we had great hope that it wouldn't happen again. But now that you are a little older, perhaps you can tell me what went on in your mind. What were you thinking when it happened? Do you have any idea why you did it?"

"I don't remember thinking anything. I don't even remember doing it. It was like a dream. They had us all lined up outside for gym. We were going to play field hockey. Tanya and Melinda were playing and Tanya hit her with her stick. I only wanted to help, but there was blood all over everything. I remember being afraid. I remember doing it, but it was almost more like watching television, when the camera's supposed to be you. The next thing I knew, Mrs. Rollie was holding me down and there were people everywhere." There was a long pause. "None of the other girls will talk to me now. They call me . . ." The child burst into tears. "They call me a vampire," she said.

"And how do you feel about that?" Dr. Wells goaded her.

"I don't know. Maybe it's true. It must be true, else why would I do what I do?" Tears streamed down her cheeks and she blotted them with a tissue.

"What do you know about vampires, Daria?"

"That they sleep in coffins and hate the sun . . . I know, but maybe it's only partly true. I do hate the sunlight. It hurts my eyes. And garlic, too. It makes me sick. Even the smell of it. Maybe the legends aren't quite right. Maybe I'm just a different kind of vampire. Why else would I do what I do?"

"Do you want to be a vampire, Daria?" Dr. Wells asked softly.

"No!" she shouted, the tears streaming down her face unimpeded, then again more softly, "No. Do you think I'm a vampire?" she asked.

"No, Daria. I don't believe in vampires. I think you're a young lady with a problem. And . . . I think if we work together, we can find out why you have this problem and what we can do about it."

There is the jingle of keys and the crisp sound of heavy feet. The dying

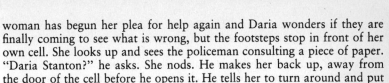

woman has begun her plea for help again and Daria wonders if they are finally coming to see what is wrong, but the footsteps stop in front of her own cell. She looks up and sees the policeman consulting a piece of paper. "Daria Stanton?" he asks. She nods. He makes her back up, away from the door of the cell before he opens it. He tells her to turn around and put her hands behind her back. He handcuffs her and makes her follow him.

She is surprised to see there is only one cell between hers and the main corridor, something that she hadn't noticed on the way in. The cop she saw earlier is still sitting there, still eating, or perhaps eating again. She wants to ask him why he doesn't at least check on the woman who is screaming, but he doesn't look up at her as she passes. She is taken down an endless maze of corridors, all covered with the same green tile, except where they branch out into hallways full of cells. Eventually, she is taken to a room where her cuffs are removed and she is told to wait. He is careless shutting the door behind him and she can see that it isn't locked, but she makes no move to go through it. What difference can it make. Her fate was decided long ago.

"Daria Stanton? Please sit down, I have some questions to ask you."

Even after six months it still felt strange, coming to this new building, walking down a new corridor. She still missed Dr. Wells and hated him for dying that way, without any warning, as though it had been an act against her, personally. This new doctor didn't feel like a doctor at all; letting her call him Mark. And there should be a law against anyone's shrink being so cute, with all those new-fangled ideas. She paused outside the door, pulled off her mirrored sunglasses, and adjusted her hair and makeup in the lenses.

"Morning, Mark," she said as she seated herself in his green padded chair by the window. She couldn't bring herself to lie down on the couch, because all she could think of was how much she wanted him lying there with her. Seated where she was, she could watch the street outside while they talked. Two boys were standing around the old slide-bolt gum machine that had stood outside Wexler's Drug Store for as long as she could remember. It was easy to tell by their attitude that they were up to something. The dark-haired boy looked around furtively several times, then started sliding the bolt back and forth.

"I have some news for you this morning," Dr. Bremner told her. "Good news, I hope." The blond child kicked the machine and tried the bolt again. "The reports of your blood workup are back and I've gone over them with Dr. Walinski. Your blood showed a marked anemia of a type known as iron-deficiency porphyria. Now, ordinarily, I wouldn't be telling a patient that it was good news that she was sick, but in your case, it could mean that your symptoms are purely physical." A woman walked down the street. The two boys stopped tampering with the machine, turned and stared into the drugstore window until she had passed ". . . a very rare disease. It is even more unusual for it to evince the symptoms that you have, but . . . it has been known to happen. Your body craves the iron porphyrins that it can't produce, and somehow, it knows what *you* don't . . . that whole blood is a source." The boys went back to the machine. One of them pulled a wire from his pocket and inserted it into the coin slot. "I've also talked with Dr. Ruth Tracey at the Eilman Clinic for Blood Disorders. She says your sensitivity to light and to garlic are all tied up in this too. For one thing, garlic breaks down old red blood cells. Just what a person with your condition can't afford to have happen." Once again the boys were interrupted and once again they removed themselves to the drugstore window. "Do you understand what all this means?"

Daria nodded morosely.

"How does it feel to know that there is a physiological cause for your problem?"

"I don't see what difference it makes," she said, brushing a wisp of straight black hair from her forehead in irritation. "Insanity, vampirism, porphyria? What difference does it make what name you put on it? Even my family barely speaks to me any more. Besides, it's getting worse. I can't even stand to go out during the day anymore, and look at this." She pulled the sunglasses from her face to show him the dark circles under her eyes.

"Yes, I know, but Dr. Tracey can help you. With the right medications your symptoms should disappear. Imagine a time when you can see someone cut themselves without being afraid of what you'll do. You'll be able to go to the beach and get a suntan for Chrissake."

Daria looked back out the window, but the boys were gone. She wasn't sure whether the half-empty globe had been full of gumballs a moment ago.

Hours—weeks—years later they bring her back to her cell. Though she has only been there since early evening, already it is like coming home. The chorus has changed. Two drunken, giggling voices have been added and someone is drumming on the bars with ringed fingers. The taunter still goads the gospel singer even though she has stopped singing and the dying woman is still dying, with a tough new voice telling her to do it already and shut up. Daria slumps back on her slab of metal, her back against the wall with her straight skirt hiked up so that her legs can be folded in front of her. She no longer cares what anybody sees. She has been questioned, photographed, and given one phone call. Mark will be there for the arraignment. He will see about getting her a lawyer. She has been told not to worry, that everything will be all right—but she is not worried . . . she knows that nothing will ever be all right for her again.

She stares at the dim and dirty green light that is always on and wonders if prison will be worse. From what she has read about penal institutions,

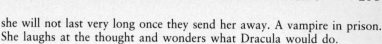

she will not last very long once they send her away. A vampire in prison. She laughs at the thought and wonders what Dracula would do.

The fire was warmth seeping into her body, making her feel alive for the first time in years. She inched herself a little closer to the hearth. Mark came into the room holding a pair of cocktail glasses. He placed one by her elbow and joined her on the rug.

"Daria, there are things I wanted to tell you. So many things that I just couldn't say while you were my patient. You do understand why I couldn't go on treating you? Not the way I felt."

She reached out and squeezed his hand, reluctant to turn her face away from the fire for even the time it would have taken to look at him. He stroked her hair. Why did it make her feel like purring? She wanted him to take her in his arms, but she was afraid. Unlike most twenty-year-old women, she had no idea what to do; how to react. The boys that she met had often told her that she was beautiful, flirted, made passes or asked her out, but the moment they found out anything about her, they always became frightened and backed off. Mark was different. He already knew everything, even though he didn't choose to believe it all.

He took her face in his hands and kissed her. At first she wanted to pull away, but soon a burning started inside of her that made the fireplace unnecessary.

Daria can no longer stand the boredom. She climbs on the bars of her cell just for something to do. It is morning. She can tell by the shuffling of feet and slamming of doors that come from the main corridor. She can tell by the food trays being brought down the hall, though none comes to her, and by the fact that the man in the chair has been replaced by a sloppy matron. She wonders if Mark is in the building yet. Probably. He has been in love with her since the first day she walked into his office, though she is convinced it is her condition and not herself that he loves. She would like to love him back, but though she needs him and wants him, truly enjoys his intimacy, she is sure that love is just another emotion that she cannot feel.

A different policeman stops outside her cell. He is carrying handcuffs, but he does not take them from his belt as he opens her cell door. "Time for your arraignment," he says cheerfully. Docile, she follows him down the same, and then a different, set of corridors. They take a long ride in a rickety elevator and when the doors open they are standing in a paneled hall. Spears of morning light stab through the windows making Daria cover her eyes. In the distance she can see a courtroom packed with people. Mark is there. He is standing by the double doors that lead inside. Someone is with him. Even on such short notice, he has found a lawyer—a friend of a friend. Mark takes her hand and they go through the double doors together. There are several cases to wait through before her name is called and he whispers reassurances to her while they sit there.

Finally, it is her turn, but the lawyer and Mark have taken that burden from her and she has no need to speak. Instead, she watches the judge. His face is puffy from sleep as he reads down the list of charges, aggravated assault, assault and battery . . . the list is long and Daria is surprised that they haven't thrown in witchcraft. The judge has probably slept through many such arraignments, but Daria knows that he will not sleep through this one. Indeed, she sees his eyes grow wide as the details of her crime are discussed. Interfering at the scene of an accident, obstructing the paramedics . . . there is no mercy in that face for her.

Then Mark begins to talk. Lovingly, he tells of her condition, of the work that Dr. Tracey is doing, of the hope for an imminent cure. He is so eloquent that for the very first time *she* is almost willing to believe that she is merely "sick." The judge's face softens. Illness is another matter. Daria has been so resigned to her fate that she is surprised to find that she has been freed. Released on her own recognizance until her trial. No bail. Mark throws his arms around her, but she is too stunned to hug him back.

"I love you," Mark tells her as he leads her out of the courtroom. He has brought glasses to shield her eyes from the sun.

A vein in his neck is throbbing.

"I love you too," she answers automatically. She tries not to stare at the throbbing vein. *This is a compulsion caused by illness,* she tells herself, *a chemical imbalance in the blood. It can be cured.*

"Daria, we're going to fight this. First we'll get you off on those ridiculous charges, and then Dr. Tracey is going to make you well. You'll see. Everything's going to be all right." He puts his arm around her shoulders, but something inside make her stiffen and pull away.

Once again she looks at the throbbing vein and wonders what it will be like not to feel this hunger. All it will take is just the right compound stabbed into her arm with a little glass needle. A second of pain.

No, she thinks to herself in the crowded aloneness of the jailhouse steps. She finds herself a well of resolve, of acceptance that she has never tapped before. She will no longer be put off by bottles of drugs, by diets that don't work, by hours of laborious talk. She will be what she is, the thing that makes her different, the thing that makes her herself. She is not just a young woman with a rare blood disease; she is a vampire, child of darkness, and she had been fighting it for way too long.

Allowing her expression to soften to a smile, she turns to Mark and places her hand gently on his neck, feeling the pulse of the vein under her thumb. "Yes, Mark, you're right," she says softly. "You *will* have to get me off on these charges." So many little blue veins in so many necks. She will have to stay free if she is to feed.

·······IV·······
THE
NON-HUMAN
VAMPIRE

Even if we limit our definition of the vampire to creatures who drink blood, there are numerous non-human vampires in the natural world—among them mosquitoes, fleas, bedbugs, ticks, gnats, and lice. Then there are leeches and spiders. And, finally, there are the vampire bats.

The vast majority of non-human vampires in fiction appear in children's humorous literature, where cute animal vampires have proliferated in recent years. There is "Bunnicula," a vampire rabbit who sucks the juices out of helpless fruits and vegetables. Created by James and Deborah Howe in 1980, Bunnicula has appeared in numerous pictures books, young adult novels, and even an animated television special. Bunnicula's competitors include the Vampire Cat series by Louise Munro Foley (1996 to present).

But the creatures explored in the following pages are *not* natural, in the usual understanding of the word. And that is what makes them especially interesting.

The vampire you will meet in Tanith Lee's "Bite-Me-Not or, Fleur de Feu," though not human, rouses great sympathy. Roger Zelazny's "The Stainless Steel Leech" has a strong comic dimension. All of the stories in this section, which include "The Spider" and "Negotium Perambulans," extend the fictional possibilities of vampires beyond those that simply mimic human form and behavior.

HANNS HEINZ EWERS
(1871–1943)

Hanns Heinz Ewers was a German writer (born in Düsseldorf); much of his fiction remains untranslated. He is noted mainly for a series of novels featuring anthropologist Frank Braun, a character who wields his influence over supposedly "inferior" people. Ewers is the author of Der Sanberlehrling *(1907, reprinted in the United States as* The Sorcerer's Apprentice *in 1927),* Vampir *(1921), and* Alraune *(also known as* The Mandrakes, *1911). His short fiction was collected in* Das Graven *(1908) and* Nachtmahr *(1922).*

Ewers led a complex and disturbing life; he was a spy in Mexico and the United States during World War I and an early member of the Nazi Party. He wrote the official biography of Horst Wessel, a Nazi officer killed by Communists in a street fight, as well as a biography of Edgar Allan Poe. Ewers's views about the link between German and Jewish destiny, as they are expressed in Vampir, *are macabre. There, the character Braun must drink the blood of his Jewish mistress—voluntarily offered by her—if he is to be an eloquent fund-raiser for the cause of Germany in World War I.*

The plot of Ewers's "The Spider" is not uncommon: There is a haunted house, castle, room, or cave. Someone is challenged to spend an hour, or a night in the dangerous place. He or she accepts the challenge and is found either dead or raving mad after the ordeal; or survives by being brave or clever.

What makes "The Spider" a superlative story, despite its well-worn plot, is the mimetic dialogue that Clairimonda, the vampire, and Richard Bracquemont, her victim, carry on together from windows on opposite sides of the street. Bracquemont calls it a game, but it seems more nearly a kind of simultaneous dance whose meaning becomes clear only at the story's end. The gesturing is surreal, unimaginable, and at the same time so apt for an encounter between a victim who yearns to be victimized and the creature who wants to victimize him. It is a fair, if disastrous, exchange.

THE SPIDER

When the student of medicine, Richard Bracquemont, decided to move into room #7 of the small Hotel Stevens, Rue Alfred Stevens (Paris 6), three persons had already hanged themselves from the cross-bar of the window in that room on three successive Fridays.

The first was a Swiss traveling salesman. They found his corpse on Saturday evening. The doctor determined that the death must have occurred between five and six o'clock on Friday afternoon. The corpse hung on a strong hook that had been driven into the window's cross-bar to serve as a hanger for articles of clothing. The window was closed, and the dead man had used the curtain cord as a noose. Since the window was very low, he hung with his knees practically touching the floor—a sign of the great discipline the suicide must have exercised in carrying out his design. Later, it was learned that he was a married man, a father. He had been a man of a continually happy disposition; a man who had achieved a secure place in life. There was not one written word to be found that would have shed light on his suicide . . . not even a will. Furthermore, none of his acquaintances could recall hearing anything at all from him that would have permitted anyone to predict his end.

The second case was not much different. The artist, Karl Krause, a high wire cyclist in the nearby Medrano Circus, moved into room #7 two days later. When he did not show up at Friday's performance, the director sent an employee to the hotel. There, he found Krause in the unlocked room hanging from the window cross-bar in circumstances exactly like those of the previous suicide. This death was as perplexing as the first. Krause was popular. He earned a very high salary, and had appeared to enjoy life at its fullest. Once again, there was no suicide note; no sinister hints. Krause's sole survivor was his mother to whom the son had regularly sent 300 marks on the first of the month.

For Madame Dubonnet, the owner of the small, cheap guesthouse whose clientele was composed almost completely of employees in a nearby Montmartre vaudeville theater, this second curious death in the same room had very unpleasant consequences. Already several of her guests had moved out, and other regular clients had not come back. She appealed for help to her personal friend, the inspector of police of the ninth precinct, who assured her that he would do everything in his power to help her. He pushed zealously ahead not only with the investigation into the grounds for the suicides of the two guests, but he also placed an officer in the mysterious room.

This man, Charles-Maria Chaumié, actually volunteered for the task.

Chaumié was an old "Marsouin," a marine sergeant with eleven years of service, who had lain so many nights at posts in Tonkin and Annam, and had greeted so many stealthily creeping river pirates with a shot from his rifle that he seemed ideally suited to encounter the "ghost" that everyone on Rue Alfred Stevens was talking about.

From then on, each morning and each evening, Chaumié paid a brief visit to the police station to make his report, which, for the first few days, consisted only of his statement that he had not noticed anything unusual. On Wednesday evening, however, he hinted that he had found a clue. Pressed to say more, he asked to be allowed more time before making any comment, since he was not sure that what he had discovered had any relationship to the two deaths, and he was afraid he might say something that would make him look foolish.

On Thursday, his behavior seemed a bit uncertain, but his mood was noticeably more serious. Still, he had nothing to report. On Friday morning, he came in very excited and spoke, half humorously, half seriously, of the strangely attractive power that his window had. He would not elaborate this notion and said that, in any case, it had nothing to do with the suicides; and that it would be ridiculous of him to say any more. When, on that same Friday, he failed to make his regular evening report, someone went to his room and found him hanging from the cross-bar of the window.

All the circumstances, down to the minutest detail, were the same here as in the previous cases. Chaumié's legs dragged along the ground. The curtain cord had been used for a noose. The window was closed, the door to the room had not been locked and death had occurred at six o'clock. The dead man's mouth was wide open, and his tongue protruded from it.

Chaumié's death, the third in as many weeks in room #7, had the following consequences: all the guests, with the exception of a German high-school teacher in room #16, moved out. The teacher took advantage of the occasion to have his rent reduced by a third. The next day, Mary Garden, the famous Opéra Comique singer, drove up to the Hotel Stevens and paid two hundred francs for the red curtain cord, saying it would bring her luck. The story, small consolation for Madame Dubonnet, got into the papers.

If these events had occurred in summer, in July or August, Madame Dubonnet would have secured three times that price for her cord, but as it was in the middle of a troubled year, with elections, disorders in the Balkans, bank crashes in New York, the visit of the King and Queen of England, the result was that the *affaire Rue Alfred Stevens* was talked of less than it deserved to be. As for the newspaper accounts, they were brief, being essentially the police reports word for word.

These reports were all that Richard Bracquemont, the medical student, knew of the matter. There was one detail about which he knew nothing because neither the police inspector nor any of the eyewitnesses had mentioned it to the press. It was only later, after what happened to the medical student, that anyone remembered that when the police removed Sergeant Charles-Maria Chaumié's body from the window cross-bar a large black spider crawled from the dead man's open mouth. A hotel porter flicked it away, exclaiming. "Ugh, another of those damned creatures." When in later investigations which concerned themselves mostly with Bracquemont the servant was interrogated, he said that he had seen a similar spider crawling on the Swiss traveling salesman's shoulder when his body was removed from the window cross-bar. But Richard Bracquemont knew nothing of all this.

It was more than two weeks after the last suicide that Bracquemont moved into the room. It was a Sunday. Bracquemont conscientiously recorded everything that happened to him in his journal. That journal now follows.

Monday, February 28

I moved in yesterday evening. I unpacked my two wicker suitcases and straightened the room a little. Then I went to bed. I slept so soundly that it was nine o'clock the next morning before a knock at my door woke me. It was my hostess, bringing me breakfast herself. One could read her concern for me in the eggs, the bacon and the superb *café au lait* she brought me. I washed and dressed, then smoked a pipe as I watched the servant make up the room.

So, here I am. I know well that the situation may prove dangerous, but I think I may just be the one to solve the problem. If, once upon a time, Paris was worth a mass (conquest comes at a dearer rate these days), it is well worth risking my life *pour un si bel enjeu*. I have at least one chance to win, and I mean to risk it.

As it is, I'm not the only one who has had this notion. Twenty-seven people have tried for access to the room. Some went to the police, some went directly to the hotel owner. There were even three women among the candidates. There was plenty of competition. No doubt the others are poor devils like me.

And yet, it was I who was chosen. Why? Because I was the only one who hinted that I had some plan—or the semblance of a plan. Naturally, I was bluffing.

These journal entries are intended for the police. I must say that it amuses me to tell those gentlemen how neatly I fooled them. If the Inspector has any sense, he'll say, "Hm. This Bracquemont is just the man we need." In any case, it doesn't matter what he'll say. The point is I'm here now, and I take it as a good sign that I've begun my task by bamboozling the police.

I had gone first to Madame Dubonnet, and it was she who sent me to the police. They put me off for a whole week—as they put off my rivals as well. Most of them gave up in disgust, having something better to do than hang around the musty squad room. The Inspector was beginning to get irritated at my tenacity. At last, he told me I was wasting my time. That the police had no use for bungling amateurs. "Ah, if only you had a plan. Then . . ."

On the spot, I announced that I had such a plan, though naturally I had no such thing. Still, I hinted that my plan was brilliant, but dangerous, that it might lead to the same end as that which had overtaken the police officer, Chaumié. Still, I promised to describe it to him if he would give me his word that he would personally put it into effect. He made excuses, claiming he was too busy but when he asked me to give him at least a hint of my plan, I saw that I had picqued his interest.

I rattled off some nonsense made up of whole cloth. God alone knows where it all came from. I told him that six o'clock of a Friday is an occult hour. It is the last hour of the Jewish week; the hour when Christ disappeared from his tomb and descended into hell. That he would do well to remember that the three suicides had taken place at approximately that hour. That was all I could tell him just then, I said, but I pointed him to *The Revelations of St. John.*

The Inspector assumed the look of a man who understood all that I had been saying, then he asked me to come back that evening.

I returned, precisely on time, and noted a copy of the *New Testament* on the Inspector's desk. I had, in the meantime, been at the *Revelations* myself, without however having understood a syllable. Perhaps the Inspector was cleverer than I. Very politely—nay—deferentially, he let me know that, despite my extremely vague intimations, he believed he grasped my line of thought and was ready to expedite my plan in every way.

And here, I must acknowledge that he has indeed been tremendously helpful. It was he who made the arrangement with the owner that I was to have anything I needed so long as I stayed in the room. The Inspector gave me a pistol and a police whistle, and he ordered the officers on the beat to pass through the Rue Alfred Stevens as often as possible, and to watch my window for any signal. Most important of all, he had a desk telephone installed which connects directly with the police station. Since the station is only four minutes away, I see no reason to be afraid.

Wednesday, March 1
Nothing has happened. Not yesterday. Not today.

Madame Dubonnet brought a new curtain cord from another room— the rooms are mostly empty, of course. Madame Dubonnet takes every opportunity to visit me, and each time she brings something with her. I have asked her to tell me again everything that happened here, but I have learned nothing new. She has her own opinion of the suicides. Her view is that the music hall artist, Krause, killed himself because of an unhappy love affair. During the last year that Krause lived in the hotel, a young woman had made frequent visits to him. These visits had stopped, just before his death. As for the Swiss gentleman, Madame Dubonnet confessed herself baffled. On the other hand, the death of the policeman was easy to explain. He had killed himself just to annoy her.

These are sad enough explanations, to be sure, but I let her babble on to take the edge off my boredom.

Thursday, March 3

Still nothing. The Inspector calls twice a day. Each time, I tell him that all is well. Apparently, these words do not reassure him.

I have taken out my medical books and I study, so that my self-imposed confinement will have some purpose.

Friday, March 4

I ate uncommonly well at noon. The landlady brought me half a bottle of champagne. It seemed a meal for a condemned man. Madame Dubonnet looked at me as if I were already three-quarters dead. As she was leaving, she begged me tearfully to come with her, fearing no doubt that I would hang myself "just to annoy her."

I studied the curtain cord once again. Would I hang myself with it? Certainly, I felt little desire to do so. The cord is stiff and rough—not the sort of cord one makes a noose of. One would need to be truly determined before one could imitate the others.

I am seated now at my table. At my left, the telephone. At my right, the revolver. I'm not frightened; but I am curious.

Six o'clock, the same evening

Nothing has happened. I was about to add, "Unfortunately." The fatal hour has come—and has gone, like any six o'clock on any evening. I won't hide the fact that I occasionally felt a certain impulse to go to the window, but for a quite different reason than one might imagine.

The Inspector called me at least ten times between five and six o'clock. He was as impatient as I was. Madame Dubonnet, on the other hand, is happy. A week has passed without someone in #7 hanging himself. Marvelous.

Monday, March 7

I have a growing conviction that I will learn nothing; that the previous suicides are related to the circumstances surrounding the lives of the three men. I have asked the Inspector to investigate the cases further, convinced that someone will find their motivations. As for me, I hope to stay here as long as possible. I may not conquer Paris here, but I live very well and I'm fattening up nicely. I'm also studying hard, and I am making real progress. There is another reason, too, that keeps me here.

Wednesday, March 9

So! I have taken one step more. Clarimonda.

I haven't yet said anything about Clarimonda. It is she who is my "third" reason for staying here. She is also the reason I was tempted to go to the window during the "fateful" hour last Friday. But of course, not to hang myself.

Clarimonda. Why do I call her that? I have no idea what her name is, but it ought to be Clarimonda. When finally I ask her name, I'm sure it will turn out to be Clarimonda.

I noticed her almost at once . . . in the very first days. She lives across the narrow street; and her window looks right into mine. She sits there, behind her curtains.

I ought to say that she noticed me before I saw her; and that she was obviously interested in me. And no wonder. The whole neighborhood knows I am here, and why. Madame Dubonnet has seen to that.

I am not of a particularly amorous disposition. In fact, my relations with women have been rather meager. When one comes from Verdun to Paris to study medicine, and has hardly money enough for three meals a day, one has something else to think about besides love. I am then not very experienced with women, and I may have begun my adventure with her stupidly. Never mind. It's exciting just the same.

At first, the idea of establishing some relationship with her simply did not occur to me. It was only that, since I was here to make observations, and, since there was nothing in the room to observe, I thought I might as well observe my neighbor—openly, professionally. Anyhow, one can't sit all day long just reading.

Clarimonda, I have concluded, lives alone in the small flat across the way. The flat has three windows, but she sits only before the window that looks into mine. She sits there, spinning on an old-fashioned spindle, such as my grandmother inherited from a great aunt. I had no idea anyone still used such spindles. Clarimonda's spindle is a lovely object. It appears to be made of ivory; and the thread she spins is of an exceptional fineness. She works all day behind her curtains, and stops spinning only as the sun goes down. Since darkness comes abruptly here in this narrow street and in this season of fogs, Clarimonda disappears from her place at five o'clock each evening.

I have never seen a light in her flat.

What does Clarimonda look like? I'm not quite sure. Her hair is black and wavy; her face pale. Her nose is short and finely shaped with delicate nostrils that seem to quiver. Her lips, too, are pale; and when she smiles, it seems that her small teeth are as keen as those of some beast of prey. Her eyelashes are long and dark; and her huge dark eyes have an intense glow. I guess all these details more than I know them. It is hard to see clearly through the curtains.

Something else: she always wears a black dress embroidered with a lilac motif; and black gloves, no doubt to protect her hands from the effects of her work. It is a curious sight: her delicate hands moving perpetually, swiftly grasping the thread, pulling it, releasing it, taking it up again; as if one were watching the indefatigable motions of an insect.

Our relationship? For the moment, still very superficial, though it *feels* deeper. It began with a sudden exchange of glances in which each of us noted the other. I must have pleased her, because one day she studied me a while longer, then smiled tentatively. Naturally, I smiled back. In this fashion, two days went by, each of us smiling more frequently with the passage of time. Yet something kept me from greeting her directly.

Until today. This afternoon, I did it. And Clarimonda returned my greeting. It was done subtly enough, to be sure, but I saw her nod.

Thursday, March 10

Yesterday, I sat for a long time over my books, though I can't truthfully say that I studied much. I built castles in the air and dreamed of Clarimonda.

I slept fitfully.

This morning, when I approached my window, Clarimonda was already in her place. I waved, and she nodded back. She laughed and studied me for a long time.

I tried to read, but I felt much too uneasy. Instead, I sat down at my window and gazed at Clarimonda. She too had laid her work aside. Her hands were folded in her lap. I drew my curtain wider with the window cord, so that I might see better. At the same moment, Clarimonda did the same with the curtains at her window. We exchanged smiles.

We must have spent a full hour gazing at each other.

Finally, she took up her spinning.

Saturday, March 12

The days pass, I eat and drink. I sit at the desk. I light my pipe; I look down at my book but I don't read a word, though I try again and again. Then I go to the window where I wave to Clarimonda. She nods. We smile. We stare at each other for hours.

Yesterday afternoon, at six o'clock, I grew anxious. The twilight came early, bringing with it something like anguish. I sat at my desk. I waited until I was invaded by an irresistible need to go to the window—not to hang myself; but just to see Clarimonda. I sprang up and stood beside the curtain where it seemed to me I had never been able to see so clearly, though it was already dark. Clarimonda was spinning, but her eyes looked into mine. I felt myself strangely contented even as I experienced a light sensation of fear.

The telephone rang. It was the Inspector tearing me out of my trance with his idiotic questions. I was furious.

This morning, the Inspector and Madame Dubonnet visited me. She is enchanted with how things are going. I have now lived for two weeks in room #7. The Inspector, however, does not feel he is getting results. I hinted mysteriously that I was on the trail of something most unusual. The jackass took me at my word and fulfilled my dearest wish. I've been allowed to stay in the room for another week. God knows it isn't Madame Dubonnet's cooking or wine-cellar that keeps me here. How quickly one can be sated with such things. No. I want to stay because of the window Madame Dubonnet fears and hates. That beloved window that shows me Clarimonda.

I have stared out of my window, trying to discover whether she ever leaves her room, but I've never seen her set foot on the street.

As for me, I have a large, comfortable armchair and a green shade over the lamp whose glow envelops me in warmth. The Inspector has left me with a huge packet of fine tobacco—and yet I cannot work. I read two or three pages only to discover that I haven't understood a word. My eyes see the letters, but my brain refuses to make any sense of them. Absurd. As if my brain were posted: "No Trespassing." It is as if there were no room in my head for any other thought than the one: Clarimonda. I push my book away; I lean back deeply into my chair. I dream.

Sunday, March 13

This morning I watched a tiny drama while the servant was tidying my room. I was strolling in the corridor when I paused before a small window in which a large garden spider had her web. Madame Dubonnet will not have it removed because she believes spiders bring luck, and she's had enough misfortunes in her house lately. Today, I saw a much smaller spider, a male, moving across the strong threads towards the middle of the web, but when his movements alerted the female, he drew back shyly to the edge of the web from which he made a second attempt to cross it. Finally, the female in the middle appeared attentive to his wooing, and stopped moving. The male tugged at a strand gently, then more strongly till the whole web shook. The female stayed motionless. The male moved quickly forward and the female received him quietly, calmly, giving herself over completely to his embraces. For a long minute, they hung together motionless at the center of the huge web.

Then I saw the male slowly extricating himself, one leg over the other. It was as if he wanted tactfully to leave his companion alone in the dream of love, but as he started away, the female, overwhelmed by a wild life, was after him, hunting him ruthlessly. The male let himself drop from a thread, the female followed, and for a while the lovers hung there, imitating a piece of art. Then they fell to the window-sill where the male, summoning all his strength, tried again to escape. Too late. The female already had him in her powerful grip, and was carrying him back to the center of the web. There, the place that had just served as the couch for their lascivious embraces took on quite another aspect. The lover wriggled, trying to escape from the female's wild embrace, but she was too much for him. It was not long before she had wrapped him completely in her thread, and he was helpless. Then she dug her sharp pincers into his body, and sucked full draughts of her young lover's blood. Finally, she detached herself from the pitiful and unrecognizable shell of his body and threw it out of her web.

So that is what love is like among these creatures. Well for me that I am not a spider.

Monday, March 14

I don't look at my books any longer. I spend my days at the window. When it is dark, Clarimonda is no longer there, but if I close my eyes, I continue to see her.

This journal has become something other than I intended. I've spoken about Madame Dubonnet, about the Inspector; about spiders and about Clarimonda. But I've said nothing about the discoveries I undertook to make. It can't be helped.

Tuesday, March 15

We have invented a strange game, Clarimonda and I. We play it all day long. I greet her; then she greets me. Then I tap my fingers on the windowpanes. The moment she sees me doing that, she too begins tapping. I wave to her; she waves back. I move my lips as if speaking to her; she does the same. I run my hand through my sleep-disheveled hair and instantly her hand is at her forehead. It is a child's game, and we both laugh over it. Actually, she doesn't laugh. She only smiles a gently contained smile. And I smile back in the same way.

The game is not as trivial as it seems. It's not as if we were grossly imitating each other—that would weary us both. Rather, we are communicating with each other. Sometimes, telepathically, it would seem, since Clarimonda follows my movements instantaneously almost before she has had time to see them. I find myself inventing new movements, or new combinations of movements, but each time she repeats them with disconcerting speed. Sometimes, I change the order of the movements to surprise her, making whole series of gestures as rapidly as possible; or I leave out some motions and weave in others, the way children play "Simon Says." What is amazing is that Clarimonda never once makes a mistake, no matter how quickly I change gestures.

That's how I spend my days . . . but never for a moment do I feel that I'm killing time. It seems, on the contrary, that never in my life have I been better occupied.

Wednesday, March 16

Isn't it strange that it hasn't occurred to me to put my relationship with Clarimonda on a more serious basis than these endless games. Last night, I thought about this . . . I can, of course, put on my hat and coat, walk down two flights of stairs, take five steps across the street and mount two flights to her door which is marked with a small sign that says "Clarimonda." Clarimonda what? I don't know. Something. Then I can knock and . . .

Up to this point I imagine everything very clearly, but I cannot see what should happen next. I know that the door opens. But then I stand before it, looking into a dark void. Clarimonda doesn't come. Nothing comes. Nothing is there, only the black, impenetrable dark.

Sometimes, it seems to me that there can be no other Clarimonda but the one I see in the window; the one who plays gesture-games with me. I cannot imagine a Clarimonda wearing a hat, or a dress other than her black dress with the lilac motif. Nor can I imagine a Clarimonda without black gloves. The very notion that I might encounter Clarimonda somewhere in the streets or in a restaurant eating, drinking or chatting is so improbable that it makes me laugh.

Sometimes I ask myself whether I love her. It's impossible to say, since I have never loved before. However, if the feeling that I have for Clarimonda is really—love, then love is something entirely different from anything I have seen among my friends or read about in novels.

It is hard for me to be sure of my feelings and harder still to think of anything that doesn't relate to Clarimonda or, what is more important, to our game. Undeniably, it is our game that concerns me. Nothing else— and this is what I understand least of all.

There is no doubt that I am drawn to Clarimonda, but with this attraction there is mingled another feeling, fear. No. That's not it either. Say rather a vague apprehension in the presence of the unknown. And this anxiety has a strangely voluptuous quality so that I am at the same time drawn to her even as I am repelled by her. It is as if I were moving in giant circles around her, sometimes coming close, sometimes retreating . . . back and forth, back and forth.

Once, I am sure of it, it will happen, and I will join her.

Clarimonda sits at her window and spins her slender, eternally fine thread, making a strange cloth whose purpose I do not understand. I am amazed that she is able to keep from tangling her delicate thread. Hers is surely a remarkable design, containing mythical beasts and strange masks.

Thursday, March 17

I am curiously excited. I don't talk to people any more. I barely say "hello" to Madame Dubonnet or to the servant. I hardly give myself time to eat. All I can do is sit at the window and play the game with Clarimonda. It is an enthralling game. Overwhelming.

I have the feeling something will happen tomorrow.

Friday, March 18

Yes. Yes. Something will happen today. I tell myself—as loudly as I can—that that's why I am here. And yet, horribly enough, I am afraid.

And in the fear that the same thing is going to happen to me as happened to my predecessors, there is strangely mingled another fear: a terror of Clarimonda. And I cannot separate the two fears.

I am frightened. I want to scream.

Six o'clock, evening

I have my hat and coat on. Just a couple of words.

At five o'clock, I was at the end of my strength. I'm perfectly aware now that there is a relationship between my despair and the "sixth hour" that was so significant in the previous weeks. I no longer laugh at the trick I played the Inspector.

I was sitting at the window, trying with all my might to stay in my chair but the window kept drawing me. I had to resume the game with Clarimonda. And yet, the window horrified me. I saw the others hanging there: the Swiss traveling salesman, fat, with a thick neck and a grey stubbly beard; the thin artist; and the powerful police sergeant. I saw them, one after the other, hanging from the same hook, their mouths open, their tongues sticking out. And then, I saw myself among them.

Oh, this unspeakable fear. It was clear to me that it was provoked as much by Clarimonda as by the cross-bar and the horrible hook. May she pardon me . . . but it is the truth. In my terror, I keep seeing the three men hanging there, their legs dragging on the floor.

And yet, the fact is I had not felt the slightest desire to hang myself; nor was I afraid that I would want to do so. No, it was the window I feared; and Clarimonda. I was sure that something horrid was going to happen. Then I was overwhelmed by the need to go to the window to stand before it. I had to . . .

The telephone rang. I picked up the receiver and before I could hear a word, I screamed. "Come. Come at once."

It was as if my shrill cry had in that instant dissipated the shadows from my soul. I grew calm. I wiped the sweat from my forehead. I drank a glass of water. Then I considered what I should say to the Inspector when he arrived. Finally, I went to the window. I waved and smiled. And Clarimonda too waved and smiled.

Five minutes later, the Inspector was here. I told him that I was getting to the bottom of the matter, but I begged him not to question me just then. That very soon I would be in a position to make important revelations. Strangely enough, though I was lying to him, I myself had the feeling that I was telling the truth. Even now, against my will. I have that same conviction.

The Inspector could not help noticing my agitated state of mind, especially since I apologized for my anguished cry over the telephone. Naturally, I tried to explain it to him, and yet I could not find a single reason to give for it. He said affectionately that there was no need ever to apologize to him; that he was always at my disposal; that that was his duty. It was better that he should come a dozen times to no effect rather than fail to be here when he was needed. He invited me to go out with him for the evening. It would be a distraction for me. It would do me good not to be alone for a while. I accepted the invitation though I was very reluctant to leave the room.

Saturday, March 19

We went to the *Gaieté Rochechouart*, *La Cigale*, and *La Lune Rousse*. The Inspector was right: It was good for me to get out and breathe the fresh air. At first, I had an uncomfortable feeling, as if I were doing something wrong; as if I were a deserter who had turned his back on the flag. But that soon went away. We drank a lot, laughed and chatted. This morning, when I went to my window, Clarimonda gave me what I thought was a look of reproach, though I may only have imagined it. How could she have known that I had gone out last night? In any case, the look lasted only for an instant, then she smiled again.

We played the game all day long.

Sunday, March 20

Only one thing to record: we played the game.

Monday, March 21

We played the game all day long.

Tuesday, March 22

Yes, the game. We played it again. And nothing else. Nothing at all.

Sometimes I wonder what is happening to me? What is it I want? Where is all this leading? I know the answer: there is nothing else I want except what is happening. *It* is what I want . . . what I long for. This only.

Clarimonda and I have spoken with each other in the course of the last few days, but very briefly; scarcely a word. Sometimes we moved our lips, but more often we just looked at each other with deep understanding.

I was right about Clarimonda's reproachful look because I went out with the Inspector last Friday. I asked her to forgive me. I said it was stupid of me, and spiteful to have gone. She forgave me, and I promised never to leave the window again. We kissed, pressing our lips against each of our windowpanes.

Wednesday, March 23

I know now that I love Clarimonda. That she has entered into the very fiber of my being. It may be that the loves of other men are different. But does there exist one head, one ear, one hand that is exactly like hundreds of millions of others? There are always differences, and it must be so with love. My love is strange, I know that, but is it any the less lovely because of that? Besides, my love makes me happy.

If only I were not so frightened. Sometimes my terror slumbers and I forget it for a few moments, then it wakes and does not leave me. The fear is like a poor mouse trying to escape the grip of a powerful serpent. Just wait a bit, poor sad terror. Very soon, the serpent love will devour you.

Thursday, March 24

I have made a discovery: I don't play with Clarimonda. She plays with me.

Last night, thinking as always about our game, I wrote down five new and intricate gesture patterns with which I intended to surprise Clarimonda today. I gave each gesture a number. Then I practiced the series, so I could do the motions as quickly as possible, forwards or backwards. Or sometimes only the even numbered ones, sometimes the odd. Or the first and the last of the five patterns. It was tiring work, but it made me happy and seemed to bring Clarimonda closer to me. I practiced for hours until I got all the motions down pat, like clockwork.

This morning, I went to the window. Clarimonda and I greeted each other, then our game began. Back and forth! It was incredible how quickly she understood what was to be done; how she kept pace with me.

There was a knock at the door. It was the servant bringing me my shoes. I took them. On my way back to the window, my eye chanced to fall on the slip of paper on which I had noted my gesture patterns. It was then that I understood: in the game just finished, *I had not made use of a single one of my patterns.*

I reeled back and had to hold on to the chair to keep from falling. It was unbelievable. I read the paper again—and again. It was still true: I had gone through a long series of gestures at the window, and not one of the patterns had been mine.

I had the feeling, once more, that I was standing before Clarimonda's wide open door, through which, though I stared, I could see nothing but a dark void. I knew, too, that if I chose to turn from the door now, I might be saved; and that I still had the power to leave. And yet, I did not leave—because I felt myself at the very edge of the mystery: as if I were holding the secret in my hands. "Paris! You will conquer Paris," I thought. And in that instant, Paris was more powerful than Clarimonda.

I don't think about that any more. Now, I feel only love. Love, and a delicious terror.

Still, the moment itself endowed me with strength. I read my notes again, engraving the gestures on my mind. Then I went back to the window only to become aware that *there was not one of my patterns that I wanted to use.* Standing there, it occurred to me to rub the side of my nose; instead I found myself pressing my lips to the windowpane. I tried to drum with my fingers on the window sill; instead, I brushed my fingers through my hair. And so I understood that it was not that Clarimonda did what I did. Rather, my gestures followed her lead and with such lightning rapidity that we seemed to be moving simultaneously. I, who had been so proud because I thought I had been influencing her, I was in fact being influenced by her. Her influence . . . so gentle . . . so delightful.

I have tried another experiment. I clenched my hands and put them in my pockets firmly intending not to move them one bit. Clarimonda raised her hand and, smiling at me, made a scolding gesture with her finger. I did not budge, and yet I could feel how my right hand *wished* to leave my pocket. I shoved my fingers against the lining, but against my will, my hand left the pocket; my arm rose into the air. In my turn, I made a scolding gesture with my finger and smiled. It seemed to me that it was not I who was doing all this. It was a stranger whom I was watching. But, of course, I was mistaken. It was I making the gesture, and the person watching me was the stranger; that very same stranger who, not long ago, was so sure that he was on the edge of a great discovery. In any case, it was not I.

Of what use to me is this discovery? I am here to do Clarimonda's will. Clarimonda, whom I love with an anguished heart.

Friday, March 25

I have cut the telephone cord. I have no wish to be continually disturbed by the idiotic inspector just as the mysterious hour arrives.

God. Why did I write that? Not a word of it is true. It is as if someone else were directing my pen.

But I want to . . . want to . . . to write the truth here . . . though it is costing me great effort. But I want to . . . once more . . . do what *I* want.

I have cut the telephone cord . . . ah . . .

Because I had to . . . there it is. Had to . . .

We stood at our windows this morning and played the game, which is now different from what it was yesterday. Clarimonda makes a movement and I resist it for as long as I can. Then I give in and do what she wants without further struggle. I can hardly express what a joy it is to be so conquered; to surrender entirely to her will.

We played. All at once, she stood up and walked back into her room, where I could not see her; she was so engulfed by the dark. Then she came back with a desk telephone, like mine, in her hands. She smiled and set the telephone on the window sill, after which she took a knife and cut the cord. Then I carried my telephone to the window where I cut the cord. After that, I returned my phone to its place.

That's how it happened . . .

I sit at my desk where I have been drinking tea the servant brought me. He has come for the empty teapot, and I ask him for the time, since my watch isn't running properly. He says it is five fifteen. Five fifteen . . .

I know that if I look out of my window, Clarimonda will be there making a gesture that I will have to imitate. I will look just the same. Clarimonda is there, smiling. If only I could turn my eyes away from hers.

Now she parts the curtain. She takes the cord. It is red, just like the cord in my window. She ties a noose and hangs the cord on the hook in the window cross-bar.

She sits down and smiles.

No. Fear is no longer what I feel. Rather, it is a sort of oppressive terror which I would not want to avoid for anything in the world. Its grip is irresistible, profoundly cruel, and voluptuous in its attraction.

I could go to the window, and do what she wants me to do, but I wait. I struggle. I resist though I feel a mounting fascination that becomes more intense each minute.

Here I am once more. Rashly, I went to the window where I did what Clarimonda wanted. I took the cord, tied a noose, and hung it on the hook . . .

Now, I want to see nothing else—except to stare at this paper. Because if I look, I know what she will do . . . now . . . at the sixth hour of the last day of the week. If I see her, I will have to do what she wants. Have to . . .

I won't see her . . .

I laugh. Loudly. No. I'm not laughing. Something is laughing in me, and I know why. It is because of my "I won't . . ."

I won't, and yet I know very well that I have to . . . have to look at her. I must . . . must . . . and then . . . all that follows.

If I still wait, it is only to prolong this exquisite torture. Yes, that's it. This breathless anguish is my supreme delight. I write quickly, quickly . . . just so I can continue to sit here; so I can attenuate these seconds of pain.

Again, terror. Again. I know that I will look toward her. That I will stand up. That I will hang myself.

That doesn't frighten me. That is beautiful . . . even precious.

There is something else. *What will happen afterwards?* I don't know, but since my torment is so delicious, I feel . . . feel that something horrible must follow.

Think . . . think . . . Write something. Anything at all . . . to keep from looking toward her . . .

My name . . . Richard Bracquemont. Richard Bracquemont . . . Richard Bracquemont . . . Richard . . .

I can't . . . go on. I must . . . no . . . no . . . must look at her . . . Richard Bracquemont . . . no . . . no more . . . Richard . . . Richard Bracque— . . .

The inspector of the ninth precinct, after repeated and vain efforts to telephone Richard, arrived at the Hotel Stevens at 6:05. He found the body of the student Richard Bracquemont hanging from the cross-bar of the window in room #7, in the same position as each of his three predecessors.

The expression on the student's face, however, was different, reflecting an appalling fear. Bracquemont's eyes were wide open and bulging from their sockets. His lips were drawn into a *rictus,* and his jaws were clamped together. A huge black spider whose body was dotted with purple spots lay crushed and nearly bitten in two between his teeth.

On the table, there lay the student's journal. The inspector read it and went immediately to investigate the house across the street. What he learned was that the second floor of that building had not been lived in for many months.

E. F. BENSON
(1867–1940)

Edward Frederic Benson was born and raised in England and was edu-cated at Cambridge. His brothers A. C. Benson and Robert Hugh Benson were also writers, but he was by far the most successful of the three. The brothers came from what we would now regard as a dysfunctional family; one reference book says that "their history reads like a TV soap opera."*

Benson published his first and most acclaimed novel, Dodo, *in 1893. The novel's popularity spawned two later sequels:* Dodo's Daughter *(1914; republished as* Dodo the Second*) and* Dodo Wonders *(1921). His second novel,* The Rubicon *(1894), fared less well with the critics. Then followed years of popularity with readers leavened by serious criticism from reviewers.*

Like many people of his generation Benson was fascinated by seances, psychic phenomena, and magic, and wrote about them in his fiction, in-cluding The Luck of the Vails *(1901) and* The Angel of Pain *(1906). His many other successful novels include* Mrs. Ames *(1912),* Queen Lucia *(1920),* Miss Mapp *(1922), and* Lucia in London *(1927). His writing expanded to other genres as well, including biographies of Queen Victoria, William Gladstone, and William II of Germany. His reminisces include* As We Were *(1930),* As We Are *(1932), and* Final Edition *(1940). Ben-son's short stories are well known, many displaying strong science fiction elements. Collections include* The Room in the Tower and Other Stories *(1912),* The Countess of Lowndes Square *(1912),* Visible and Invisible *(1923),* Spook Stories *(1928), and* More Spook Stories *(1934).*

"Negotium Perambulans" ("the plague that walks," in Latin) recalls M. R. James's "Count Magnus." But here, the victim of the vampiric creature clearly, even dearly, deserves his end. As for the Thing itself, the subject of the story, there is hardly a monster in fiction that is quite as wet and loathsome.

**The Penguin Encyclopedia of Horror and the Supernatural* (Viking, 1986).

NEGOTIUM PERAMBULANS

The casual tourist in West Cornwall may just possibly have noticed, as he bowled along over the bare high plateau between Penzance and the Land's End, a dilapidated signpost pointing down a steep lane and bearing on its battered finger the faded inscription "Polearn 2 miles," but probably very few have had the curiosity to traverse those two miles in order to see a place to which their guide-books award so cursory a notice. It is described there, in a couple of unattractive lines, as a small fishing village with a church of no particular interest except for certain carved and painted wooden panels (originally belonging to an earlier edifice) which form an altar-rail. But the church at St. Creed (the tourist is reminded) has a similar decoration far superior in point of preservation and interest, and thus even the ecclesiastically disposed are not lured to Polearn. So meager a bait is scarce worth swallowing, and a glance at the very steep lane which in dry weather presents a carpet of sharp-pointed stones, and after rain a muddy watercourse, will almost certainly decide him not to expose his motor or his bicycle to risks like these in so sparsely populated a district. Hardly a house has met his eye since he left Penzance, and the possible trundling of a punctured bicycle for half a dozen weary miles seems a high price to pay for the sight of a few painted panels.

Polearn, therefore, even in the high noon of the tourist season, is little liable to invasion, and for the rest of the year I do not suppose that a couple of folk a day traverse those two miles (long ones at that) of steep and stony gradient. I am not forgetting the postman in this exiguous estimate, for the days are few when, leaving his pony and cart at the top of the hill, he goes as far as the village, since but a few hundred yards down the lane there stands a large white box, like a sea-trunk, by the side of the road, with a slit for letters and a locked door. Should he have in his wallet a registered letter or be the bearer of a parcel too large for insertion in the square lips of the sea-trunk, he must needs trudge down the hill and deliver the troublesome missive, leaving it in person on the owner, and receiving some small reward of coin or refreshment for his kindness. But such occasions are rare, and his general routine is to take out of the box such letters as may have been deposited there, and insert in their place such letters as he has brought. These will be called for, perhaps that day or perhaps the next, by an emissary from the Polearn post-office. As for the fishermen of the place, who, in their export trade, constitute the chief link of movement between Polearn and the outside world, they would not dream of taking their catch up the steep lane and so, with six miles farther of travel, to the market at Penzance. The sea route is shorter and easier, and they deliver their wares to the pier-head. Thus, though the sole industry of Polearn is sea-fishing, you will get no fish there unless you have bespoken your requirements to one of the fishermen. Back come the trawlers as empty as a haunted house, while their spoils are in the fish-train that is speeding to London.

Such isolation of a little community, continued, as it has been, for centuries, produces isolation in the individual as well, and nowhere will you find greater independence of character than among the people of Polearn. But they are linked together, so it has always seemed to me, by some mysterious comprehension: it is as if they had all been initiated into some ancient rite, inspired and framed by forces visible and invisible. The winter storms that batter the coast, the vernal spell of the spring, the hot, still summers, the season of rains and autumnal decay, have made a spell which, line by line, has been communicated to them, concerning the powers, evil and good, that rule the world, and manifest themselves in ways benignant or terrible . . .

I came to Polearn first at the age of ten, a small boy, weak and sickly, and threatened with pulmonary trouble. My father's business kept him in London, while for me abundance of fresh air and a mild climate were considered essential conditions if I was to grow to manhood. His sister had married the vicar of Polearn, Richard Bolitho, himself native to the place, and so it came about that I spent three years, as a paying guest, with my relations. Richard Bolitho owned a fine house in the place, which he inhabited in preference to the vicarage, which he let to a young artist, John Evans, on whom the spell of Polearn had fallen for from year's beginning to year's end he never let it. There was a solid roofed shelter, open on one side to the air, built for me in the garden, and here I lived and slept, passing scarcely one hour out of the twenty-four behind walls and windows. I was out on the bay with the fisher-folk, or wandering along the gorse-clad cliffs that climbed steeply to right and left of the deep combe where the village lay, or pottering about on the pier-head, or bird's-nesting in the bushes with the boys of the village. Except on Sunday and for the few daily hours of my lessons, I might do what I pleased so long as I remained in the open air. About the lessons there was nothing formidable; my uncle conducted me through flowering bypaths among the thickets of arithmetic, and made pleasant excursions into the elements of Latin grammar, and above all, he made me daily give him an account, in clear and grammatical sentences, of what had been occupying my mind or my movements. Should I select to tell him about a walk along the cliffs, my speech must be orderly, not vague, slip-shod notes of what I had observed. In this way, too, he trained my observation, for he would bid me tell him what flowers were in bloom, and what birds hovered fishing over the sea or were building in the bushes. For that I owe him a perennial gratitude, for to observe and to express my thoughts in the clear spoken word became my life's profession.

But far more formidable than my weekday tasks was the prescribed routine for Sunday. Some dark embers compounded of Calvinism and mysticism smoldered in my uncle's soul, and made it a day of terror. His sermon in the morning scorched us with a foretaste of the eternal fires reserved for unrepentant sinners, and he was hardly less terrifying at the children's service in the afternoon. Well do I remember his exposition of the doctrine of guardian angels. A child, he said, might think himself secure in such angelic care, but let him beware of committing any of those numerous offenses which would cause his guardian to turn his face from him, for as sure as there were angels to protect us, there were also evil and awful presences which were ready to pounce; and on them he dwelt with peculiar gusto. Well, too, do I remember in the morning sermon his commentary on the carved panels of the altar-rails to which I have already alluded. There was the angel of the Annunciation there, and the angel of the Resurrection, but not less was there the witch of Endor, and, on the fourth panel, a scene that concerned me most of all. This fourth panel (he came down from his pulpit to trace its time-worn features) represented the lych-gate of the church-yard at Polearn itself, and indeed the resemblance when thus pointed out was remarkable. In the entry stood the figure of a robed priest holding up a Cross, with which he faced a terrible creature like a gigantic slug, that reared itself up in front of him. That, so ran my uncle's interpretation, was some evil agency, such as he had spoken about to us children, of almost infinite malignity and power, which could alone be combated by firm faith and a pure heart. Below ran the legend "Negotium perambulans in tenebris" from the ninety-first Psalm. We should find it translated there, "the pestilence that walketh in darkness," which but feebly rendered the Latin. It was more deadly to the soul than any pestilence that can only kill the body: it was the Thing, the Creature, the Business that trafficked in the outer Darkness, a minister of God's wrath on the unrighteous . . .

I could see, as he spoke, the looks which the congregation exchanged with each other, and knew that his words were evoking a surmise, a remembrance. Nods and whispers passed between them, they understood to what he alluded, and with the inquisitiveness of boyhood I could not rest till I had wormed the story out of my friends among the fisher-boys, as, next morning, we sat basking and naked in the sun after our bathe. One knew one bit of it, one another, but it pieced together into a truly alarming legend. In bald outline it was as follows:

A church far more ancient than that in which my uncle terrified us every Sunday had once stood not three hundred yards away, on the shelf of level ground below the quarry from which its stones were hewn. The owner of the land had pulled this down, and erected for himself a house on the same site out of these materials, keeping, in a very ecstasy of wickedness, the altar, and on this he dined and played dice afterwards. But as he grew old some black melancholy seized him, and he would have lights burning there all night, for he had deadly fear of the darkness. On one winter evening there sprang up such a gale as was never before known, which broke in the windows of the room where he had supped, and extinguished the lamps. Yells of terror brought in his servants, who found him lying on the floor with the blood streaming from his throat. As they entered some huge black shadow seemed to move away from him, crawled across the floor and up the wall and out of the broken window.

"There he lay a-dying," said the last of my informants, "and him that had been a great burly man was withered to a bag o' skin, for the critter had drained all the blood from him. His last breath was a scream, and he hollered out the same words as passon read off the screen."

"*Negotium perambulans in tenebris*," I suggested eagerly.

"Thereabouts. Latin anyhow."

"And after that?" I asked.

"Nobody would go near the place, and the old house rotted and fell in ruins till three years ago, when along comes Mr. Dooliss from Penzance, and built the half of it up again. But he don't care much about such critters, nor about Latin neither. He takes his bottle of whisky a day and gets drunk's a lord in the evening. Eh, I'm gwine home to my dinner."

Whatever the authenticity of the legend, I had certainly heard the truth about Mr. Dooliss from Penzance, who from that day became an object of keen curiosity on my part, the more so because the quarry-house adjoined my uncle's garden. The Thing that walked in the dark failed to stir my imagination, and already I was so used to sleeping alone in my shelter that the night had no terrors for me. But it would be intensely exciting to wake at some timeless hour and hear Mr. Dooliss yelling, and conjecture that the Thing had got him.

But by degrees the whole story faded from my mind, overscored by the more vivid interests of the day, and, for the last two years of my outdoor life in the vicarage garden, I seldom thought about Mr. Dooliss and the possible fate that might await him for his temerity in living in the place where that Thing of darkness had done business. Occasionally I saw him over the garden fence, a great yellow lump of a man, with slow and staggering gait, but never did I set eyes on him outside his gate, either in the village street or down on the beach. He interfered with none, and no one interfered with him. If he wanted to run the risk of being the prey of the legendary nocturnal monster, or quietly drink himself to death, it was his affair. My uncle, so I gathered, had made several attempts to see him when first he came to live at Polearn, but Mr. Dooliss appeared to have no use for parsons, but said he was not at home and never returned the call.

After three years of sun, wind, and rain, I had completely outgrown my early symptoms and had become a tough, strapping youngster of thirteen. I was sent to Eton and Cambridge, and in due course ate my dinners and became a barrister. In twenty years from that time I was earning a yearly income of five figures, and had already laid by in sound securities a sum that brought me dividends which would, for one of my simple tastes and frugal habits, supply me with all the material comforts I needed on this side of the grave. The great prizes of my profession were already within my reach, but I had no ambition beckoning me on, nor did I want a wife and children, being, I must suppose, a natural celibate. In fact there was only one ambition which through these busy years had held the lure of blue and far-off hills to me, and that was to get back to Polearn, and live once more isolated from the world with the sea and the gorse-clad hills for play-fellows, and the secrets that lurked there for exploration. The spell of it had been woven about my heart, and I can truly say that there had hardly passed a day in all those years in which the thought of it and the desire for it had been wholly absent from my mind. Though I had been in frequent communication with my uncle there during his lifetime, and, after his death, with his widow who still lived there, I had never been back to it since I embarked on my profession, for I knew that if I went there, it would be a wrench beyond my power to tear myself away again. But I had made up my mind that when once I had provided for my own independence, I would go back there not to leave it again. And yet I did leave it again, and now nothing in the world would induce me to turn down the lane from the road that leads from Penzance to the Land's End, and see the sides of the combe rise steep above the roofs of the village and hear the gulls chiding as they fish in the bay. One of the things invisible, of the dark powers, leaped into light, and I saw it with my eyes.

The house where I had spent those three years of boyhood had been left for life to my aunt, and when I made known to her my intention of coming back to Polearn, she suggested that, till I found a suitable house or found her proposal unsuitable, I should come to live with her.

"The house is too big for a lone old woman," she wrote, "and I have often thought of quitting and taking a little cottage sufficient for me and my requirements. But come and share it, my dear, and if you find me troublesome, you or I can go. You may want solitude—most people in Polearn do—and will leave me. Or else I will leave you: one of the main reasons of my stopping here all these years was a feeling that I must not let the old house starve. Houses starve, you know, if they are not lived in. They die a lingering death; the spirit in them grows weaker and weaker, and at last fades out of them. Isn't this nonsense to your London notions? . . ."

Naturally I accepted with warmth this tentative arrangement, and on an evening in June found myself at the head of the lane leading down to Polearn, and once more I descended into the steep valley between the hills. Time had stood still apparently for the combe, the dilapidated signpost (or its successor) pointed a rickety finger down the lane, and a few hundred yards farther on was the white box for the exchange of letters. Point after remembered point met my eye, and what I saw was not shrunk, as is often the case with the revisited scenes of childhood, into a smaller scale. There stood the post-office, and there the church and close beside it the vicarage, and beyond, the tall shrubberies which separated the house for which I was bound from the road, and beyond that again the gray roofs of the quarry-house damp and shining with the moist evening wind from the sea. All was exactly as I remembered it, and, above all, that sense of seclusion and isolation. Somewhere above the tree-tops climbed the lane which joined the main road to Penzance, but all that had become immeasurably distant. The years that had passed since last I turned in at the well-known gate faded like a frosty breath, and vanished in this warm, soft air. There were law-courts somewhere in memory's dull book which, if I cared to turn the pages, would tell me that I had made a name and a great income there. But the dull book was closed now, for I was back in Polearn, and the spell was woven around me again.

And if Polearn was unchanged, so too was Aunt Hester, who met me at the door. Dainty and china-white she had always been, and the years had not aged but only refined her. As we sat and talked after dinner she spoke of all that had happened in Polearn in that score of years, and yet somehow the changes of which she spoke seemed but to confirm the immutability of it all. As the recollection of names came back to me, I asked her about the quarry-house and Mr. Dooliss, and her face gloomed a little as with the shadow of a cloud on a spring day.

"Yes, Mr. Dooliss," she said, "poor Mr. Dooliss, how well I remember him, though it must be ten years and more since he died. I never wrote to you about it, for it was all very dreadful, my dear, and I did not want to darken your memories of Polearn. Your uncle always thought that something of the sort might happen if he went on in his wicked, drunken ways, and worse than that, and though nobody knew exactly what took place, it was the sort of thing that might have been anticipated."

"But what more or less happened, Aunt Hester?" I asked.

"Well, of course I can't tell you everything, for no one knew it. But he was a very sinful man, and the scandal about him at Newlyn was shocking. And then he lived, too, in the quarry-house . . . I wonder if by any chance you remember a sermon of your uncle's when he got out of the pulpit and explained that panel in the altar-rails, the one, I mean, with the horrible creature rearing itself up outside the lych-gate?"

"Yes, I remember perfectly," said I.

"Ah. It made an impression on you, I suppose, and so it did on all who heard him, and that impression got stamped and branded on us all when the catastrophe occurred. Somehow Mr. Dooliss got to hear about your uncle's sermon, and in some drunken fit he broke into the church and smashed the panel to atoms. He seems to have thought that there was some magic in it, and that if he destroyed that he would get rid of the terrible fate that was threatening him. For I must tell you that before he committed that dreadful sacrilege he had been a haunted man: he hated and feared darkness, for he thought that the creature on the panel was on his track, but that as long as he kept lights burning it could not touch him. But the panel, to his disordered mind, was the root of his terror, and so, as I said, he broke into the church and attempted—you will see why I said 'attempted'—to destroy it. It certainly was found in splinters next morning, when your uncle went into church for matins, and knowing Mr. Dooliss's fear of the panel, he went across to the quarry-house afterwards and taxed him with its destruction. The man never denied it; he boasted of what he had done. There he sat, though it was early morning, drinking his whisky.

" 'I've settled your Thing for you,' he said, 'and your sermon too. A fig for such superstitions.'

"Your uncle left him without answering his blasphemy, meaning to go straight into Penzance and give information to the police about this outrage to the church, but on his way back from the quarry-house he went into the church again, in order to be able to give details about the damage, and there in the screen was the panel, untouched and uninjured. And yet he had himself seen it smashed, and Mr. Dooliss had confessed that the destruction of it was his work. But there it was, and whether the power of God had mended it or some other power, who knows?"

This was Polearn indeed, and it was the spirit of Polearn that made me accept all Aunt Hester was telling me as attested fact. It had happened like that. She went on in her quiet voice.

"Your uncle recognized that some power beyond police was at work, and he did not go to Penzance or give informations about the outrage, for the evidence of it had vanished."

A sudden spate of skepticism swept over me.

"There must have been some mistake," I said. "It hadn't been broken . . ."

She smiled.

"Yes, my dear, but you have been in London so long," she said. "Let me, anyhow, tell you the rest of my story. That night, for some reason, I could not sleep. It was very hot and airless; I dare say you will think that the sultry conditions accounted for my wakefulness. Once and again, as I went to the window to see if I could not admit more air, I could see from it the quarry-house, and I noticed the first time that I left my bed that it was blazing with lights. But the second time that I saw that it was all in darkness, and as I wondered at that, I heard a terrible scream, and the moment afterwards the steps of someone coming at full speed down the road outside the gate. He yelled as he ran; 'Light, light!' he called out. 'Give me light, or it will catch me!' It was very terrible to hear that, and I went to rouse my husband, who was sleeping in the dressing-room across the passage. He wasted no time, but by now the whole village was aroused by the screams, and when he got down to the pier he found that all was over. The tide was low, and on the rocks at its foot was lying the body of Mr. Dooliss. He must have cut some artery when he fell on those sharp edges of stone, for he had bled to death, they thought, and though he was a big burly man, his corpse was but skin and bones. Yet there was no pool of blood round him, such as you would have expected. Just skin and bones as if every drop of blood in his body had been sucked out of him!"

She leaned forward.

"You and I, my dear, know what happened," she said, "or at least can guess. God has His instruments of vengeance on those who bring wickedness into places that have been holy. Dark and mysterious are His ways."

Now what I should have thought of such a story if it had been told me in London I can easily imagine. There was such an obvious explanation: the man in question had been a drunkard, what wonder if the demons of delirium pursued him? But here in Polearn it was different.

"And who is in the quarry-house now?" I asked. "Years ago the fisherboys told me the story of the man who first built it and of his horrible end. And now again it has happened. Surely no one has ventured to inhabit it once more?"

I saw in her face, even before I asked that question, that somebody had done so.

"Yes, it is lived in again," said she, "for there is no end to the blindness . . . I don't know if you remember him. He was tenant of the vicarage many years ago."

"John Evans," said I.

"Yes. Such a nice fellow he was too. Your uncle was pleased to get so good a tenant. And now—"

She rose.

"Aunt Hester, you shouldn't leave your sentences unfinished," I said.

She shook her head.

"My dear, that sentence will finish itself," she said. "But what a time of night! I must go to bed, and you too, or they will think we have to keep lights burning here through the dark hours."

Before getting into bed I drew my curtains wide and opened all the windows to the warm tide of the sea air that flowed softly in. Looking out into the garden I could see in the moonlight the roof of the shelter, in which for three years I had lived, gleaming with dew. That, as much as anything, brought back the old days to which I had now returned, and they seemed of one piece with the present, as if no gap of more than twenty years sundered them. The two flowed into one like globules of mercury uniting into a softly shining globe, of mysterious lights and reflections. Then, raising my eyes a little, I saw against the black hill-side the windows of the quarry-house still alight.

Morning, as is so often the case, brought no shattering of my illusion. As I began to regain consciousness, I fancied that I was a boy again waking up in the shelter in the garden, and though, as I grew more widely awake, I smiled at the impression, that on which it was based I found to be indeed true. It was sufficient now as then to be here, to wander again on the cliffs, and hear the popping of the ripened seed-pods on the gorse-bushes; to stray along the shore to the bathing-cove, to float and drift and swim in the warm tide, and bask on the sand, and watch the gulls fishing, to lounge on the pier-head with the fisher-folk, to see in their eyes and hear in their quiet speech the evidence of secret things not so much known to them as part of their instincts and their very being. There were powers and presences about me; the white poplars that stood by the stream that babbled down the valley knew of them, and showed a glimpse of their knowledge sometimes, like the gleam of their white underleaves; the very cobbles that paved the street were soaked in it . . . All that I wanted was to lie there and grow soaked in it too; unconsciously, as a boy, I had done that, but now the process must be conscious. I must know what stir of forces, fruitful and mysterious, seethed along the hill-side at noon, and sparkled at night on the sea. They could be known, they could even be controlled by those who were masters of the spell, but never could they be spoken of, for they were dwellers in the innermost, grafted into the eternal life of the world. There were dark secrets as well as these clear, kindly powers, and to these no doubt belonged the *negotium perambulans in tenebris* which, though of deadly malignity, might be regarded not only as evil, but as the avenger of sacrilegious and impious deeds . . . All this was part of the spell of Polearn, of which the seeds had long lain dormant in me. But now they were sprouting, and who knew what strange flower would unfold on their stems?

It was not long before I came across John Evans. One morning, as I lay on the beach, there came shambling across the sand a man stout and middle-aged with the face of Silenus. He paused as he drew near and regarded me from narrow eyes.

"Why, you're the little chap that used to live in the parson's garden," he said. "Don't you recognize me?"

I saw who it was when he spoke: his voice, I think, instructed me, and recognizing it, I could see the features of the strong, alert young man in this gross caricature.

"Yes, you're John Evans," I said. "You used to be very kind to me: you used to draw pictures for me."

"So I did, and I'll draw you some more. Been bathing? That's a risky performance. You never know what lives in the sea, nor what lives on the land for that matter. Not that I heed them. I stick to work and whisky. God! I've learned to paint since I saw you, and drink too for that matter. I live in the quarry-house, you know, and it's a powerful thirsty place. Come and have a look at my things if you're passing. Staying with your aunt, are you? I could do a wonderful portrait of her. Interesting face; she knows a lot. People who live at Polearn get to know a lot, though I don't take much stock in that sort of knowledge myself."

I do not know when I have been at once so repelled and interested. Behind the mere grossness of the face there lurked something which, while it appalled, yet fascinated me. His thick lisping speech had the same quality. And his paintings, what would they be like? . . .

"I was just going home," I said. "I'll gladly come in, if you'll allow me."

He took me through the untended and overgrown garden into the house which I had never yet entered. A great gray cat was sunning itself in the window, and an old woman was laying lunch in a corner of the cool hall into which the door opened. It was built of stone, and the carved moldings let into the walls, the fragments of gargoyles and sculptured images, bore testimony to the truth of its having been built out of the demolished church. In one corner was an oblong and carved wooden table littered with a painter's apparatus and stacks of canvases leaned against the walls.

He jerked his thumb towards a head of an angel that was built into the mantelpiece and giggled.

"Quite a sanctified air," he said, "so we tone it down for the purposes of ordinary life by a different sort of art. Have a drink? No? Well, turn over some of my pictures while I put myself to rights."

He was justified in his own estimate of his skill: he could paint (and apparently he could paint anything), but never have I seen pictures so inexplicably hellish. There were exquisite studies of trees, and you knew that something lurked in the flickering shadows. There was a drawing of his cat sunning itself in the window, even as I had just now seen it, and yet it was no cat but some beast of awful malignity. There was a boy stretched naked on the sands, not human, but some evil thing which had come out of the sea. Above all there were pictures of his garden overgrown and jungle-like, and you knew that in the bushes were presences ready to spring out on you . . .

"Well, do you like my style?" he said as he came up, glass in hand. (The tumbler of spirits that he held had not been diluted.) "I try to paint the essence of what I see, not the mere husk and skin of it, but its nature, where it comes from and what gave it birth. There's much in common between a cat and a fuchsia-bush if you look at them closely enough. Everything came out of the slime of the pit, and it's all going back there. I should like to do a picture of you some day. I'd hold the mirror up to Nature, as that old lunatic said."

After the first meeting I saw him occasionally throughout the months of that wonderful summer. Often he kept to his house and to his painting for days together, and then perhaps some evening I would find him lounging on the pier, always alone, and every time we met thus the repulsion and interest grew, for every time he seemed to have gone farther along a path of secret knowledge towards some evil shrine where complete initiation awaited him . . . And then suddenly the end came.

I had met him thus one evening on the cliffs while the October sunset still burned in the sky, but over it with amazing rapidity there spread from the west a great blackness of cloud such as I have never seen for denseness. The light was sucked from the sky, the dusk fell in ever thicker layers. He suddenly became conscious of this.

"I must get back as quick as I can," he said. "It will be dark in a few minutes, and my servant is out. The lamps will not be lit."

He stepped out with extraordinary briskness for one who shambled and could scarcely lift his feet, and soon broke out into a stumbling run. In the gathering darkness I could see that his face was moist with the dew of some unspoken terror.

"You must come with me," he panted, "for so we shall get the lights burning the sooner. I cannot do without light."

I had to exert myself to the full to keep up with him, for terror winged him, and even so I fell behind, so that when I came to the garden gate, he was already half-way up the path to the house. I saw him enter, leaving the door wide, and found him fumbling with matches. But his hand so trembled that he could not transfer the light to the wick of the lamp.

"But what's the hurry about?" I asked.

Suddenly his eyes focused themselves on the open door behind me, and he jumped from his seat beside the table which had once been the altar of God, with a gasp and a scream.

"No, no!" he cried. "Keep it off! . . ."

I turned and saw what he had seen. The Thing had entered and now was swiftly sliding across the floor towards him, like some gigantic caterpillar. A stale phosphorescent light came from it, for though the dusk had grown to blackness outside, I could see it quite distinctly in the awful light of its own presence. From it too there came an odor of corruption and decay, as from slime that has long lain below water. It seemed to have no head, but on the front of it was an orifice of puckered skin which opened and shut and slavered at the edges. It was hairless, and slug-like in shape and in texture. As it advanced its fore-part reared itself from the ground, like a snake about to strike, and it fastened on him . . .

At that sight, and with the yells of his agony in my ears, the panic which had struck me relaxed into a hopeless courage, and with palsied, impotent hands I tried to lay hold of the Thing. But I could not: though something material was there, it was impossible to grasp it; my hands sunk in it as in thick mud. It was like wrestling with a nightmare.

I think that but a few seconds elapsed before all was over. The screams of the wretched man sank to moans and mutterings as the Thing fell on him: he panted once or twice and was still. For a moment longer there came gurglings and sucking noises, and then it slid out even as it had entered. I lit the lamp which he had fumbled with, and there on the floor he lay, no more than a rind of skin in loose folds over projecting bones.

ROGER ZELAZNY
(1937–1995)

Roger Zelazny, a Hugo and Nebula award-winning writer, grew up in Euclid, Ohio. He earned an undergraduate degree from Case Western Reserve University and a masters degree from Columbia University. He was employed by the Social Security Administration from 1962 to 1969 in Cleveland and Baltimore, after which he wrote full time. He published his first story, "Passion Play," in Amazing Stories magazine in 1962. He eventually took on the pseudonym Harrison Denmark.

In the 1960s, Zelazny became a leading figure of the "new wave" of science fiction writing, together with Samuel R. Delany, Thomas M. Disch, and Ursula K. Le Guin. These authors shifted emphasis from the external world of the sciences to a more internal, sociological, and psychological perspective.

Zelazny's best early work is assembled in Four for Tomorrow (1967) and The Doors of His Face, the Lamps of His Mouth, and Other Stories (1971). Novels include the award-winning Lord of Light (1967), Isle of the Dead (1969), and the immensely popular and critically acclaimed Amber series, starting with Nine Princes in Amber (1970). His later works include Deus Irae (with Phillip K. Dick; 1976), Doorways in the Sand (1976), Roadmarks (1979), The Last Defender of Camelot (1980), Uncommon Variations (1983), and Eye of Cat (1982). Zelazny's last novel, Donnerjack (1997), was co-written with Jane Lindskold, while in one of his last published works, he completed a novel started by the late Alfred Bester, entitled Psychoshop (1998).

"The Stainless Steel Leech" is an ingeniously imagined tragicomedy of a were-robot (as in were-wolf, were-tiger) whose best friend is a sadly dwindling vampire, and how the two play out their destiny together. The story's genial, even comic, tone is a delicate counterpoint to what is essentially a sad account of obsolescence.

THE STAINLESS STEEL LEECH

They're really afraid of this place.

During the day they'll clank around the headstones, if they're ordered to, but even Central can't make them search at night, despite the ultras and the infras—and they'll never enter a mausoleum.

Which makes things nice for me.

They're superstitious; it's a part of the circuitry. They were designed to serve man, and during his brief time on earth, awe and devotion, as well as dread, were automatic things. Even the last man, dead Kennington, commanded every robot in existence while he lived. His person was a thing of veneration, and all his orders were obeyed.

And a man is a man, alive or dead—which is why the graveyards are a combination of hell, heaven, and strange feedback, and will remain apart from the cities so long as the earth endures.

But even as I mock them they are looking behind the stones and peering into the gullies. They are searching for—and afraid they might find—me.

I, the unjunked, am legend. Once out of a million assemblies a defective such as I might appear and go undetected, until too late.

At will, I could cut the circuit that connected me with Central Control, and be a free 'bot, and master of my own movements. I liked to visit the cemeteries, because they were quiet and different from the maddening stamp-stamp of the presses and the clanking of the crowds; I liked to look at the green and red and yellow and blue things that grew about the graves. And I did not fear these places, for that circuit, too, was defective. So when I was discovered they removed my vite-box and threw me on the junk heap.

But the next day I was gone, and their fear was great.

I no longer posses a self-contained power unit, but the freak coils within my chest act as storage batteries. They require frequent recharging, however, and there is only one way to do that.

The werebot is the most frightful legend whispered among the gleaming steel towers, when the night wind sighs with its burden of fears out of the past, from days when non-metal beings walked the earth. The half-lifes; the preyers upon order, still cry darkness within the vite-box of every 'bot.

I, the discontent, the unjunked, live here in Rosewood Park, among the dogwood and myrtle, the headstones and broken angels, with Fritz—another legend—in our deep and peaceful mausoleum

Fritz is a vampire, which is a terrible and tragic thing. He is so under-nourished that he can no longer move about, but he cannot die either, so he lies in his casket and dreams of times gone by. One day, he will ask me to carry him outside into the sunlight, and I will watch him shrivel and dim into peace and nothingness and dust. I hope he does not ask me soon.

We talk. At night, when the moon is full and he feel strong enough, he tells me of his better days, in places called Austria and Hungary, where he, too, was feared and hunted.

". . . But only a stainless steel leech can get blood out of a stone—or a robot," he said last night. "It is a proud and lovely thing to be a stainless steel leech—you are possibly the only one of your kind in existence. Live up to your reputation! Hound them! Drain them! Leave your mark on a thousand steel throats!"

And he was right. He is always right. And he knows more about these things than I.

"Kennington!" his thin, bloodless lips smiled. "Oh, what a duel we fought! He was the last man on earth, and I the last vampire. For ten years I tried to drain him. I got at him twice, but he was from the Old Country and knew what precautions to take. Once he learned of my existence, he issued a wooden stake to every robot—but I had forty-two graves in those days and they never found me. They did come close, though. . . .

"But at night, ah, at night!" he chuckled. "Then things were reversed! I was the hunter and he the prey!

"I remember his frantic questing after the last few sprays of garlic and wolfsbane on earth, the crucifix assembly lines he kept in operation around the clock—irreligious soul that he was! I was genuinely sorry when he died, in peace. Not so much because I hadn't gotten to drain him properly, but because he was a worthy opponent and a suitable antagonist. What a game we played!"

His husky voiced weakened.

"He sleeps a scant three hundred paces from here, bleaching and dry. His is the great marble tomb by the gate. . . . Please gather roses tomorrow and place them upon it."

I agreed that I would, for there is a closer kinship between the two of us than between myself and any 'bot, despite the dictates of resemblance. And I must keep my word, before this day passes into evening and although there are searchers above, for such is the law of my nature.

"Damn them! (He taught me that word.) Damn them!" I say. "I'm coming up! Beware, gentle 'bots! I shall walk among you and you shall not know me. I shall join in the search, and you will think I am one of you. I shall gather the red flowers for dead Kennington, rubbing shoulders with you, and Fritz will smile at the joke."

I climb the cracked and hollow steps, the east already spilling twilight, and the sun half-lidded in the west.

I emerge.

The roses live on the wall across the road. From great twisting tubes of vine, with heads brighter than any rust, they burn like danger lights on a control panel, but moistly.

One, two, three roses for Kennington. Four, five . . .

"What are you doing, 'bot?"

"Gathering roses."

"You are supposed to be searching for the werebot. Has something damaged you?"

"No, I'm all right," I say, and I fix him where he stands, by bumping against his shoulder. The circuit completed, I drain his vite-box until I am filled.

"You are the werebot!" he intones weakly.

He falls with a crash.

. . . Six, seven, eight roses for Kennington, dead Kennington, dead as the 'bot at my feet—more dead—for he once lived a full, organic life, nearer to Fritz's or my own than to theirs.

"What happened here, 'bot?"

"He is stopped, and I am picking roses," I tell them.

There are four 'bots and an Over.

"It is time you left this place," I say. "Shortly it will be night and the werebot will walk. Leave, or he will end you."

"You stopped him!" says the Over. "You are the werebot!"

I bunch all the flowers against my chest with one arm and turn to face them. The Over, a large special-order 'bot, moves toward me. Others are approaching from all directions. He had sent out a call.

"You are a strange and terrible thing," he is saying, "and you must be junked, for the sake of the community."

He seizes me and I drop Kennington's flowers.

I cannot drain him. My coils are already loaded near their capacity, and he is specially insulated.

There are dozens around me now, fearing and hating. They will junk me and I will lie beside Kennington.

"Rust in peace," they will say. . . . I am sorry that I cannot keep my promise to Fritz.

"Release him!"

No!

It is shrouded and moldering Fritz in the doorway of the mausoleum, swaying, clutching at the stone. He always knows. . . .

"Release him! I, a human, order it."

He is ashen and gasping, and the sunlight is doing awful things to him.

—The ancient circuits click and suddenly I am free.

"Yes, master," says the Over. "We did not know. . . ."

"Seize that robot!"

He points a shaking emaciated finger at him.

"He is the werebot," he gasps. "Destroy him! The one gathering flowers was obeying my orders. Leave him here with me."

He falls to his knees and the final darts of day pierce his flesh.

"And go! All the rest of you! Quickly! It is my order that no robot ever enter another graveyard again!"

He collapses within and I know that now there are only bones and bits of rotted shroud on the doorstep of our home.

Fritz has had his final joke—a human masquerade.

I take the roses to Kennington, as the silent 'bots file out through the gate forever, bearing the unprotesting Overbot with them. I place the roses at the foot of the monument—Kennington's and Fritz's—the monument of the last, strange, truly living ones.

Now only I remain unjunked.

In the final light of the sun I see them drive a stake through the Over's vite-box and bury him at the crossroads.

Then they hurry back toward their towers of steel, of plastic.

I gather up what remains of Fritz and carry him down to his box. The bones are brittle and silent.

. . . It is a very proud and very lonely thing to be a stainless steel leech.

TANITH LEE
(b. 1947)

Tanith Lee, who has written children's books and sword-and-sorcery novels for adults, is the master of a truly distinguished and sensuous prose style. Her first fantasy novel, The Birthgrave, *was published in 1975; since then she has published more than fifty books and 130 short stories. Her novels include the Scarabae Blood Opera series, which began with* Dark Dance *(1992); her Unicorn seriess for young adults including* Black Unicorn *(1991),* Gold Unicorn *(1993), and* Red Unicorn *(1997); as well as* Lycanthia *(1981),* Anackire *(1983), and* The Gods Are Thirsty *(1996). Lee has also written dozens of short stories collected into many volumes, among them* Dreams of Dark and Light *(1986),* Forests of the Night *(1989), and* Women as Demons: The Male Perception of Women Through Space and Time *(1989).*

The originality and poetic power of "Bite-Me-Not or, Fleur de Feu" is truly astonishing. This is a simple Cinderella tale transformed into an epic romance. Rohise, the little slave in the duke's kitchen, is our Cinderella, living within a castle sealed against the intrusion of a race of vampires. The magnificent black-winged vampire prince, Feroluce, finds a way to break into the castle. There he is set upon by a chained lion that wounds him, allowing him to be captured and caged by the inhabitants of the castle. Though Rohise falls in love with him, he is doomed to be killed at dawn and to have his blood poured over the plant known as fleur de fleu or flower of fire. This plant grows in a secret garden of the castle, and its flower, if it ever blooms, repels vampires.

The rest of the story explores the slow progress toward love of these two, Rohise and Feroluce, who are different species. With such vast differences between them, it takes Lee's truly epic imagination to bring these two together in a believable way.

Lee's prose is baroque, richly metaphoric. At its best, as in this story, her imagery is perfect for the sort of medieval allegorical tapestry she is weaving. The language is grandiose indeed, but so is the conception she has of her story. That her prose should slip perceptibly into near poetry is not surprising.

One last word: the reader should not have qualms about the quasi-French verses that Lee uses from time to time. Invariably, their meaning is made clear within the text itself.

BITE-ME-NOT OR, FLEUR DE FEU

In the tradition of young girls and windows, the young girl looks out of this one. It is difficult to see anything. The panes of the window are heavily leaded, and secured by a lattice of iron. The stained glass of lizard-green and storm-purple is several inches thick. There is no red glass in the window. The color red is forbidden in the castle. Even the sun, behind the glass, is a storm sun, a green-lizard sun.

The young girl wishes she had a gown of palest pastel rose—the nearest affinity to red which is never allowed. Already she has long dark beautiful eyes, a long white neck. Her long hair is however hidden in a dusty scarf and she wears rags. She is a scullery maid. As she scours dishes and mops stone floors, she imagines she is a princess floating through the upper corridors, gliding to the dais in the Duke's hall. The Cursed Duke. She is sorry for him. If he had been her father, she would have sympathized and consoled him. His own daughter is dead, as his wife is dead, but these things, being to do with the cursing, are never spoken of. Except, sometimes, obliquely.

"*Rohise!*" dim voices cry now, full of dim scolding soon to be actualized.

The scullery maid turns from the window and runs to have her ears boxed and a broom thrust into her hands.

Meanwhile, the Cursed Duke is prowling his chamber, high in the East Turret carved with swans and gargoyles. The room is lined with books, swords, lutes, scrolls, and has two eerie portraits, the larger of which represents his wife, and the smaller his daughter. Both ladies look much the same with their pale, egg-shaped faces, polished eyes, clasped hands. They do not really look like his wife or daughter, nor really remind him of them.

There are no windows at all in the turret, they were long ago bricked up and covered with hangings. Candles burn steadily. It is always night in the turret. Save, of course, by night there are particular *sounds* all about it, to which the Duke is accustomed, but which he does not care for. By night, like most of his court, the Cursed Duke closes his ears with softened tallow. However, if he sleeps, he dreams, and hears in the dream the beating of wings. . . . Often, the court holds loud revel all night long.

The Duke does not know Rohise the scullery maid has been thinking of him. Perhaps he does not even know that a scullery maid is capable of thinking at all.

Soon the Duke descends from the turret and goes down, by various stairs and curving passages, into a large, walled garden on the east side of the castle.

It is a very pretty garden, mannered and manicured, which the gardeners keep in perfect order. Over the tops of the high, high walls, where delicate blooms bell the vines, it is just possible to glimpse the tips of sun-baked mountains. But by day the mountains are blue and spiritual to look at, and seem scarcely real. They might only be inked on the sky.

A portion of the Duke's court is wandering about in the garden, playing games or musical instruments, or admiring painted sculptures, or the flora, none of which is red. But the Cursed Duke's court seems vitiated this noon. Nights of revel take their toll.

As the Duke passes down the garden, his courtiers acknowledge him deferentially. He sees them, old and young alike, all doomed as he is, and the weight of his burden increases.

At the furthest, most eastern end of the garden, there is another garden, sunken and rather curious, beyond a wall with an iron door. Only the Duke possesses the key to this door. Now he unlocks it and goes through. His courtiers laugh and play and pretend not to see. He shuts the door behind him.

The sunken garden, which no gardener ever tends, is maintained by other, spontaneous, means. It is small and square, lacking the hedges and the paths of the other, the sundials and statues and little pools. All the sunken garden contains is a broad paved border, and at its center a small plot of humid earth. Growing in the earth is a slender bush with slender velvet leaves.

The Duke stands and looks at the bush only a short while.

He visits it every day. He has visited it every day for years. He is waiting for the bush to flower. Everyone is waiting for this. Even Rohise, the scullery maid, is waiting, though she does not, being only sixteen, born in the castle and uneducated, properly understand why.

The light in the little garden is dull and strange, for the whole of it is roofed over by a dome of thick smoky glass. It makes the atmosphere somewhat depressing, although the bush itself gives off a pleasant smell, rather resembling vanilla.

Something is cut into the stone rim of the earth-plot where the bush grows. The Duke reads it for perhaps the thousandth time. O, *fleur de feu*—

When the Duke returns from the little garden into the large garden, locking the door behind him, no one seems truly to notice. But their obeisances now are circumspect.

One day, he will perhaps emerge from the sunken garden leaving the door wide, crying out in a great voice. But not yet. Not today.

The ladies bend to the bright fish in the pools, the knights pluck for them blossoms, challenge each other to combat at chess, or wrestling, discuss the menagerie lions; the minstrels sing of unrequited love. The pleasure garden is full of one long and weary sigh.

"Oh flurda fur

"Pourma souffrance—"

Sings Rohise as she scrubs the flags of the pantry floor.

"Ned ormey par,

"May say day mwar—"

"What are you singing, you slut?" someone shouts, and kicks over her bucket.

Rohise does not weep. She tidies her bucket and soaks up the spilled water with her cloths. She does not know what the song, because of which she seems, apparently, to have been chastised, means. She does not understand the words that somehow, somewhere—perhaps from her own dead mother—she learned by rote.

In the hour before sunset, the Duke's hall is lit by flambeaux. In the high windows, the casements of oil-blue and lavender glass and glass like storms and lizards, are fastened tight. The huge window by the dais was long ago obliterated, shut up, and a tapestry hung of gold and silver tissue with all the rubies pulled out and emeralds substituted. It describes the subjugation of a fearsome unicorn by a maiden, and huntsmen.

The court drifts in with its clothes of rainbow from which only the color red is missing.

Music for dancing plays. The lean pale dogs pace about, alert for tidbits as dish on dish comes in. Roast birds in all their plumage glitter and die a second time under the eager knives. Pastry castles fall. Pink and amber fruits, and green fruits and black, glow beside the goblets of fine yellow wine.

The Cursed Duke eats with care and attention, not with enjoyment. Only the very young of the castle still eat in that way, and there are not so many of those.

The murky sun slides through the stained glass. The musicians strike up more wildly. The dances become boisterous. Once the day goes out, the hall will ring to *chanson,* to drum and viol and pipe. The dogs will bark, no language will be uttered except in a bellow. The lions will roar from the menagerie. On some nights the cannons are set off from the battlements, which are now all of them roofed in, fired out through narrow mouths just wide enough to accommodate them, the charge crashing away in thunder down the darkness.

By the time the moon comes up and the castle rocks to its own cacophony, exhausted Rohise has fallen fast asleep in her cupboard bed in the attic. For years, from sunset to rise, nothing has woken her. Once, as a child, when she had been especially badly beaten, the pain woke her and she heard a strange silken scratching, somewhere over her bed. But she thought it a rat, or a bird. Yes, a bird, for later it seemed to her there were also wings. . . . But she forgot all this half a decade ago. Now she sleeps deeply and dreams of being a princess, forgetting, too, how the Duke's daughter died. Such a terrible death, it is better to forget.

"The sun shall not smite thee by day, neither the moon by night," intones the priest, eyes rolling, his voice like a bell behind the Duke's shoulder.

"Ne moi mords pas," whispers Rohise in her deep sleep. "Ne mwar mor par, ne par mor mwar. . . ."

And under its impenetrable dome, the slender bush has closed its fur leaves also to sleep. O flower of fire, oh fleur de fur. Its blooms, though it has not bloomed yet, bear the ancient name *Nona Mordica*. In light parlance they call it Bite-Me-Not. There is a reason for that.

He is the Prince of a proud and savage people. The pride they acknowledge, perhaps they do not consider themselves to be savages, or at least believe that savagery is the proper order of things.

Feroluce, that is his name. It is one of the customary names his kind give their lords. It has connotations with diabolic royalty and, too, with a royal flower of long petals curved like scimitars. Also the name might be the partial anagram of another name. The bearer of that name was also winged.

For Feroluce and his people are winged beings. They are more like a nest of dark eagles than anything, mounted high among the rocky pilasters and pinnacles of the mountain. Cruel and magnificent, like eagles, the somber sentries motionless as statuary on the ledge-edges, their sable wings folded about them.

They are very alike in appearance (less a race or tribe, more a flock, an unkindness of ravens). Feroluce also, black-winged, black-haired, aquiline of feature, standing on the brink of star-dashed space, his eyes burning through the night like all the eyes along the rocks, depthless red as claret.

They have their own traditions of art and science. They do not make or read books, fashion garments, discuss God or metaphysics or men. Their cries are mostly wordless and always mysterious, flung out like ribbons over the air as they wheel and swoop and hang in wicked cruciform, between the peaks. But they sing, long hours, for whole nights at a time, music that has a language only they know. All their wisdom and theosophy, and all their grasp of beauty, truth or love, is in the singing.

They look unloving enough, and so they are. Pitiless fallen angels. A traveling people, they roam after sustenance. Their sustenance is blood. Finding a castle, they accepted it, every bastion and wall, as their prey. They have preyed on it and tried to prey on it for years.

In the beginning, their calls, their songs, could lure victims to the feast. In this way, the tribe or unkindness of Feroluce took the Duke's wife, somnambulist, from a midnight balcony. But the Duke's daughter, the first victim, they found seventeen years ago, benighted on the mountain side. Her escort and herself they left to the sunrise, marble figures, the life drunk away.

Now the castle is shut, bolted and barred. They are even more attracted by its recalcitrance (a woman who says "No"). They do not intend to go away until the castle falls to them.

· By night, they fly like huge black moths round and round the carved turrets, the dull-lit leaded windows, their wings invoking a cloudy tindery wind, pushing thunder against thundery glass.

They sense they are attributed to some sin, reckoned a punishing curse, a penance, and this amuses them at the level whereon they understand it.

They also sense something of the flower, the *Nona Mordica*. Vampires have their own legends.

But tonight Feroluce launches himself into the air, speeds down the sky on the black sails of his wings, calling, a call like laughter or derision. This morning, in the tween-time before the light began and the sun-to-be drove him away to his shadowed eyrie in the mountain-guts, he saw a chink in the armor of the beloved refusing-woman-prey. A window, high in an old neglected tower, a window with a small eyelet which was cracked.

Feroluce soon reaches the eyelet and breathes on it, as if he would melt it. (His breath is sweet. Vampires do not eat raw flesh, only blood, which is a perfect food and digests perfectly, while their teeth are sound of necessity.) The way the glass mists at breath intrigues Feroluce. But presently he taps at the cranky pane, taps, then claws. A piece breaks away, and now he sees how it should be done.

Over the rims and upthrusts of the castle, which is only really another mountain with caves to Feroluce, the rumble of the Duke's revel drones on.

Feroluce pays no heed. He does not need to reason, he merely knows, *that* noise masks *this*—as he smashes in the window. Its panes were all faulted and the lattice rusty. It is, of course, more than that. The magic of Purpose has protected the castle, and, as in all balances, there must be, or come to be, some balancing contradiction, some flaw. . . .

The people of Feroluce do not notice what he is at. In a way, the dance with their prey has debased to a ritual. They have lived almost two decades on the blood of local mountain beasts, and bird-creatures like themselves brought down on the wing. Patience is not, with them, a virtue. It is a sort of foreplay, and can go on, in pleasure, a long, long while.

Feroluce intrudes himself through the slender window. Muscularly slender himself, and agile, it is no feat. But the wings catch, are a trouble. They follow him because they must, like two separate entities. They have been cut a little on the glass, and bleed.

He stands in a stony small room, shaking bloody feathers from him, snarling, but without sound.

Then he finds the stairway and goes down.

There are dusty landings and neglected chambers. They have no smell of life. But then there comes to be a smell. It is the scent of a nest, a colony of things, wild creatures, in constant proximity. He recognizes it. The light of his crimson eyes precedes him, deciphering blackness. And then other eyes, amber, green and gold, spring out like stars all across his path.

Somewhere an old torch is burning out. To the human eye, only mounds and glows would be visible, but to Feroluce, the Prince of the vampires, all is suddenly revealed. There is a great stone area, barred with bronze and iron, and things stride and growl behind the bars, or chatter and flee, or only stare. And there, without bars, though bound by ropes of brass to rings of brass, three brazen beasts.

Feroluce, on the steps of the menagerie, looks into the gaze of the Duke's lions. Feroluce smiles, and the lions roar. One is the king, its mane like war-plumes. Feroluce recognizes the king and the king's right to challenge, for this is the lions' domain, their territory.

Feroluce comes down the stair and meets the lion as it leaps the length of its chain. To Feroluce, the chain means nothing, and since he has come close enough, very little either to the lion.

To the vampire Prince the fight is wonderful, exhilarating and meaningful, intellectual even, for it is colored by nuance, yet powerful as sex.

He holds fast with his talons, his strong limbs wrapping the beast which is almost stronger than he, just as its limbs wrap him in turn. He sinks his teeth in the lion's shoulder, and in fierce rage and bliss begins to draw out the nourishment. The lion kicks and claws at him in turn. Feroluce feels the gouges like fire along his shoulders, thighs, and hugs the lion more nearly as he throttles and drinks from it, loving it, jealous of it, killing it. Gradually the mighty feline body relaxes, still clinging to him, its cat teeth embedded in one beautiful swanlike wing, forgotten by both.

In a welter of feathers, stripped skin, spilled blood, the lion and the angel lie in embrace on the menagerie floor. The lion lifts its head, kisses the assassin, shudders, lets go.

Feroluce glides out from under the magnificent deadweight of the cat. He stands. And pain assaults him. His lover has severely wounded him.

Across the menagerie floor, the two lionesses are crouched. Beyond them, a man stands gaping in simple terror, behind the guttering torch. He had come to feed the beasts, and seen another feeding, and now is paralyzed. He is deaf, the menagerie-keeper, previously an advantage saving him the horror of nocturnal vampire noises.

Feroluce starts toward the human animal swifter than a serpent, and checks. Agony envelops Feroluce and the stone room spins. Involuntarily, confused, he spreads his wings for flight, there in the confined chamber. But only one wing will open. The other, damaged and partly broken, hangs like a snapped fan. Feroluce cries out, a beautiful singing note of despair and anger. He drops fainting at the menagerie keeper's feet.

The man does not wait for more. He runs away through the castle, screaming invective and prayer, and reaches the Duke's hall and makes the whole hall listen.

All this while, Feroluce lies in the ocean of almost-death that is sleep or swoon, while the smaller beasts in the cages discuss him, or seem to.

And when he is raised, Feroluce does not wake. Only the great drooping bloody wings quiver and are still. Those who carry him are more than ever revolted and frightened, for they have seldom seen blood. Even the food for the menagerie is cooked almost black. Two years ago, a gardener slashed his palm on a thorn. He was banished from the court for a week.

But Feroluce, the center of so much attention, does not rouse. Not until the dregs of the night are stealing out through the walls. Then some nervous instinct invests him. The sun is coming and this is an open place, he struggles through unconsciousness and hurt, through the deepest most bladed waters, to awareness.

And finds himself in a huge bronze cage, the cage of some animal appropriated for the occasion. Bars, bars all about him, and not to be got rid of, for he reaches to tear them away and cannot. Beyond the bars, the Duke's hall, which is only a pointless cold glitter to him in the maze of pain and dying lights. Not an open place, in fact, but too open for his kind. Through the window-spaces of thick glass, muddy sunglare must come in. To Feroluce it will be like swords, acids, and burning fire—

Far off he hears wings beat and voices soaring. His people search for him, call and wheel and find nothing.

Feroluce cries out, a gravel shriek now, and the persons in the hall rush back from him, calling on God. But Feroluce does not see. He has tried to answer his own. Now he sinks down again under the coverlet of his broken wings, and the wine-red stars of his eyes go out.

"And the Angel of Death," the priest intones, "shall surely pass over, but yet like the shadow, not substance—"

The smashed window in the old turret above the menagerie tower has been sealed with mortar and brick. It is a terrible thing that it was for so long overlooked. A miracle that only one of the creatures found and entered by it. God, the Protector, guarded the Cursed Duke and his court. And the magic that surrounds the castle, that too held fast. For from the possibility of a disaster was born a bloom of great value: Now one of the monsters is in their possession. A prize beyond price.

Caged and helpless, the fiend is at their mercy. It is also weak from its battle with the noble lion, which gave its life for the castle's safety (and will be buried with honor in an ornamented grave at the foot of the Ducal family tomb). Just before the dawn came, the Duke's advisers advised him, and the bronze cage was wheeled away into the darkest area of the hall, close by the dais where once the huge window was but is no more. A barricade of great screens was brought, and set around the cage, and the top of it covered. No sunlight now can drip into the prison to harm the specimen. Only the Duke's ladies and gentlemen steal in around the screens and see, by the light of a candlebranch, the demon still lying in its trance of pain and bloodloss. The Duke's alchemist sits on a stool nearby, dictating many notes to a nervous apprentice. The alchemist, and the apothecary for that matter, are convinced the vampire, having drunk the lion almost dry, will recover from its wounds. Even the wings will mend.

The Duke's court painter also came. He was ashamed presently, and went away. The beauty of the demon affected him, making him wish to paint it, not as something wonderfully disgusting, but as a kind of superlative man, vital and innocent, or as Lucifer himself, stricken in the sorrow of his colossal Fall. And all that has caused the painter to pity the fallen one, mere artisan that the painter is, so he slunk away. He knows, since the alchemist and the apothecary told him, what is to be done.

Of course much of the castle knows. Though scarcely anyone has slept or sought sleep, the whole place rings with excitement and vivacity. The Duke has decreed, too, that everyone who wishes shall be a witness. So he is having a progress through the castle, seeking every nook and cranny, while, let it be said, his architect takes the opportunity to check no other windowpane has cracked.

From room to room the Duke and his entourage pass, through corridors, along stairs, through dusty attics and musty storerooms he has never seen, or if seen has forgotten. Here and there some retainer is come on. Some elderly women are discovered spinning like spiders up under the eaves, half-blind and complacent. They curtsy to the Duke from a vague recollection of old habit. The Duke tells them the good news, or rather, his messenger, walking before, announces it. The ancient women sigh and whisper, are left, probably forget. Then again, in a narrow courtyard, a simple boy, who looks after a dovecote, is magnificently told. He has a fit from alarm, grasping nothing; and the doves who love and understand him (by not trying to) fly down and cover him with their soft wings as the Duke goes away. The boy comes to under the doves as if in a heap of warm snow, comforted.

It is on one of the dark staircases above the kitchen that the gleaming entourage sweeps round a bend and comes on Rohise the scullery maid, scrubbing. In these days, when there are so few children and young servants, labor is scarce, and the scullerers are not confined to the scullery.

Rohise stands up, pale with shock, and for a wild instant thinks that, for some heinous crime she has committed in ignorance, the Duke has come in person to behead her.

"Hear then, by the Duke's will," cries the messenger. "One of Satan's night-demons, which do torment us, has been captured and lies penned in the Duke's hall. At sunrise tomorrow, this thing will be taken to that sacred spot where grows the bush of the Flower of the Fire, and here its foul blood shall be shed. Who then can doubt the bush will blossom, and save us all, by the Grace of God."

"And the Angel of Death," intones the priest, on no account to be omitted, "shall surely—"

"Wait," says the Duke. He is as white as Rohise. "Who is this?" he asks. "Is it a ghost?"

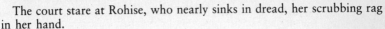

The court stare at Rohise, who nearly sinks in dread, her scrubbing rag in her hand.

Gradually, despite the rag, the rags, the rough hands, the court too begins to see.

"Why, it is a marvel."

The Duke moves forward. He looks down at Rohise and starts to cry. Rohise thinks he weeps in compassion at the awful sentence he is here to visit on her, and drops back on her knees.

"No, no," says the Duke tenderly. "Get up. Rise. You are so like my child, my daughter—"

Then Rohise, who knows few prayers, begins in panic to sing her little song as an orison:

"Oh fleur de feu
"Pour ma souffrance—"

"Ah!" says the Duke. "Where did you learn that song?"

"From my mother," says Rohise. And, all instinct now, she sings again:

"O flurda fur,
"Pourma souffrance
"Ned orney par
"May say day mwar—"

It is the song of the fire-flower bush, the *Nona Mordica,* called Bite-Me-Not. It begins, and continues: *Oh flower of fire, For my misery's sake, Do not sleep but aid me; wake!* The Duke's daughter sang it very often. In those days the shrub was not needed, being just a rarity of the castle. Invoked as an amulet, on a mountain road, the rhyme itself had besides proved useless.

The Duke takes the dirty scarf from Rohise's hair. She is very, very like his lost daughter, the same pale smooth oval face, the long white neck and long dark polished eyes, and the long dark hair. (Or is it that she is very, very like the painting?)

The Duke gives instructions and Rohise is borne away.

In a beautiful chamber, the door of which has for seventeen years been locked, Rohise is bathed and her hair is washed. Oils and scents are rubbed into her skin. She is dressed in a gown of palest most pastel rose, with a girdle sewn with pearls. Her hair is combed, and on it is set a chaplet of stars and little golden leaves. "Oh, your poor hands," say the maids, as they trim her nails. Rohise has realized she is not to be executed. She has realized the Duke has seen her and wants to love her like his dead daughter. Slowly, an uneasy stir of something, not quite happiness, moves through Rohise. Now she will wear her pink gown, now she will sympathize with and console the Duke. Her daze lifts suddenly.

The dream has come true. She dreamed of it so often it seems quite normal. The scullery was the thing which never seemed real.

She glides down through the castle and the ladies are astonished by her grace. The carriage of her head under the starry coronet is exquisite. Her voice is quiet and clear and musical, and the foreign tone of her mother, long unremembered, is quite gone from it. Only the roughened hands give her away, but smoothed by unguents, soon they will be soft and white.

"Can it be she is truly the princess returned to flesh?"

"Her life was taken so early—yes, as they believe in the Spice-Lands, by some holy dispensation, she might return."

"She would be about the age to have been conceived the very night the Duke's daughter d— That is, the very night the bane began—"

Theosophical discussion ensues. Songs are composed.

Rohise sits for a while with her adoptive father in the East Turret, and he tells her about the books and swords and lutes and scrolls, but not about the two portraits. Then they walk out together, in the lovely garden in the sunlight. They sit under a peach tree, and discuss many things, or the Duke discusses them. That Rohise is ignorant and uneducated does not matter at this point. She can always be trained. She has the basic requirements: docility, sweetness. There are many royal maidens in many places who know as little as she.

The Duke falls asleep under the peach tree. Rohise listens to the love-songs her own (her very own) courtiers bring her.

When the monster in the cage is mentioned, she nods as if she knows what they mean. She supposes it is something hideous, a scaring treat to be shown at dinner time, when the sun has gone down.

When the sun moves towards the western line of mountains just visible over the high walls, the court streams into the castle and all the doors are bolted and barred. There is an eagerness tonight in the concourse.

As the light dies out behind the colored windows that have no red in them, covers and screens are dragged away from a bronze cage. It is wheeled out into the center of the great hall.

Cannons begin almost at once to blast and bang from the roof holes. The cannoneers have had strict instructions to keep up the barrage all night without a second's pause.

Drums pound in the hall. The dogs start to bark. Rohise is not surprised by the noise, for she has often heard it from far up, in her attic, like a sea-wave breaking over and over through the lower house.

She looks at the cage cautiously, wondering what she will see. But she sees only a heap of blackness like ravens, and then a tawny dazzle, torch-light on something like human skin. "You must not go down to look," says the Duke protectively, as his court pours about the cage. Someone pokes between the bars with a gemmed cane, trying to rouse the nightmare which lies quiescent there. But Rohise must be spared this.

So the Duke calls his actors, and a slight, pretty play is put on through-out dinner, before the dais, shutting off from the sight of Rohise the

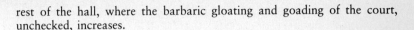

rest of the hall, where the barbaric gloating and goading of the court, unchecked, increases.

The Prince Feroluce becomes aware between one second and the next. It is the sound—heard beyond all others—of the wings of his people beating at the stones of the castle. It is the wings which speak to him, more than their wild orchestral voices. Besides these sensations, the anguish of healing and the sadism of humankind are not much.

Feroluce opens his eyes. His human audience, pleased, but afraid and squeamish, backs away, and asks each other for the two thousandth time if the cage is quite secure. In the torchlight the eyes of Feroluce are more black than red. He stares about. He is, though captive, imperious. If he were a lion or a bull, they would admire this 'nobility.' But the fact is, he is too much like a man, which serves to point up his supernatural differences unbearably.

Obviously, Feroluce understands the gist of his plight. Enemies have him penned. He is a show for now, but ultimately to be killed, for with the intuition of the raptor he divines everything. He had thought the sunlight would kill him, but that is a distant matter, now. And beyond all, the voices and the voices of the wings of his kindred beat the air outside this room-caved mountain of stone.

And so, Feroluce commences to sing, or at least, this is how it seems to the rabid court and all the people gathered in the hall. It seems he sings. It is the great communing call of his kind, the art and science and religion of the winged vampires, his means of telling them, or attempting to tell them, what they must be told before he dies. So the sire of Feroluce sang, and the grandsire, and each of his ancestors. Generally they died in flight, falling angels spun down the gulches and enormous stairs of distant peaks, singing. Feroluce, immured, believes that his cry is somehow audible.

To the crowd in the Duke's hall the song is merely that, a song, but how glorious. The dark silver voice, turning to bronze or gold, whitening in the higher registers. There seem to be words, but in some other tongue. This is how the planets sing, surely, or mysterious creatures of the sea.

Everyone is bemused. They listen, astonished.

No one now remonstrates with Rohise when she rises and steals down from the dais. There is an enchantment which prevents movement and coherent thought. Of all the roomful, only she is drawn forward. So she comes close, unhindered, and between the bars of the cage, she sees the vampire for the first time.

She has no notion what he can be. She imagined it was a monster or a monstrous beast. But it is neither. Rohise, starved for so long of beauty and always dreaming of it, recognizes Feroluce inevitably as part of the dream-come-true. She loves him instantly. Because she loves him, she is not afraid of him.

She attends while he goes on and on with his glorious song. He does not see her at all, or any of them. They are only things, like mist, or pain. They have no character or personality or worth; abstracts.

Finally, Feroluce stops singing. Beyond the stone and the thick glass of the siege, the wing-beats, too, eddy into silence.

Finding itself mesmerized, silent by night, the court comes to with a terrible joint start, shrilling and shouting, bursting, exploding into a compensation of sound. Music flares again. And the cannons in the roof, which have also fallen quiet, resume with a tremendous roar.

Feroluce shuts his eyes and seems to sleep. It is his preparation for death.

Hands grasp Rohise. "Lady—step back, come away. So close! It may harm you—"

The Duke clasps her in a father's embrace. Rohise, unused to this sort of physical expression, is unmoved. She pats him absently.

"My lord, what will be done?"

"Hush, child. Best you do not know."

Rohise persists.

The Duke persists in not saying.

But she remembers the words of the herald on the stair, and knows they mean to butcher the winged man. She attends thereafter more carefully to snatches of the bizarre talk about the hall, and learns all she needs. At earliest sunrise, as soon as the enemy retreat from the walls, their captive will be taken to the lovely garden with the peach trees. And so to the sunken garden of the magic bush, the fire-flower. And there they will hang him up in the sun through the dome of smoky glass, which will be slow murder to him, but they will cut him, too, so his blood, the stolen blood of the vampire, runs down to water the roots of the fleur de feu. And who can doubt that, from such nourishment, the bush will bloom? The blooms are salvation. Wherever they grow it is a safe place. Whoever wears them is safe from the draining bite of demons. Bite-Me-Not, they call it; vampire-repellent.

Rohise sits the rest of the night on her cushions, with folded hands, resembling the portrait of the princess, which is not like her.

Eventually the sky outside alters. Silence comes down beyond the wall, and so within the wall, and the court lifts its head, a corporate animal scenting day.

At the intimation of sunrise the black plague has lifted and gone away, and might never have been. The Duke, and almost all his castle full of men, women, children, emerge from the doors. The sky is measureless and bluely grey, with one cherry rift in the east that the court refers to as "mauve," since dawns and sunsets are never any sort of red here.

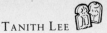

They move through the dimly lightening garden as the last stars melt. The cage is dragged in their midst.

They are too tired, too concentrated now, the Duke's people, to continue baiting their captive. They have had all the long night to do that, and to drink and opine, and now their stamina is sharpened for the final act.

Reaching the sunken garden, the Duke unlocks the iron door. There is no room for everyone within, so mostly they must stand outside, crammed in the gate, or teetering on erections of benches that have been placed around, and peering in over the walls through the glass of the dome. The places in the doorway are the best, of course; no one else will get so good a view. The servants and lower persons must stand back under the trees and only imagine what goes on. But they are used to that.

Into the sunken garden itself there are allowed to go the alchemist and the apothecary, and the priest, and certain sturdy soldiers attendant on the Duke, and the Duke. And Feroluce in the cage.

The east is all 'mauve' now. The alchemist has prepared sorcerous safe-guards which are being put into operation, and the priest, never to be left out, intones prayers. The bulge-thewed soldiers open the cage and seize the monster before it can stir. But drugged smoke has already been wafted into the prison, and besides, the monster has prepared itself for hopeless death and makes no demur.

Feroluce hangs in the arms of his loathing guards, dimly aware the sun is near. But death is nearer, and already one may hear the alchemist's apprentice sharpening the knife an ultimate time.

The leaves of the *Nona Mordica* are trembling, too, at the commencement of the light, and beginning to unfurl. Although this happens every dawn, the court points to it with optimistic cries. Rohise, who has claimed a position in the doorway, watches it too, but only for an instant. Though she has sung of the flue de fur since childhood, she had never known what the song was all about. And in just this way, though she has dreamed of being the Duke's daughter most of her life, such an event was never really comprehended either, and so means very little.

As the guards haul the demon forward to the plot of humid earth where the bush is growing, Rohise darts into the sunken garden, and lightning leaps in her hands. Women scream and well they might. Rohise has stolen one of the swords from the East Turret, and now she flourishes it, and now she has swung it and a soldier falls, bleeding red, red, *red,* before them all.

Chaos enters, as in yesterday's play, shaking its tattered sleeves. The men who hold the demon rear back in horror at the dashing blade and the blasphemous gore, and the mad girl in her princess's gown. The Duke makes a pitiful bleating noise, but no one pays him any attention.

The east glows in and like the liquid on the ground.

Meanwhile, the ironically combined sense of impending day and spilled hot blood have penetrated the stunned brain of the vampire. His eyes open and he sees the girl wielding her sword in a spray of crimson as the last guard lets go. Then the girl has run to Feroluce. Though, or because, her face is insane, it communicates her purpose, as she thrusts the sword's hilt into his hands.

No one has dared approach either the demon or the girl. Now they look on in horror and in horror grasp what Feroluce has grasped.

In that moment the vampire springs, and the great swanlike wings are reborn at his back, healed and whole. As the doctors predicted, he has mended perfectly, and prodigiously fast. He takes to the air like an arrow, unhindered, as if gravity does not any more exist. As he does so, the girl grips him about the waist, and slender and light, she is drawn upward too. He does not glance at her. He veers towards the gateway, and tears through it, the sword, his talons, his wings, his very shadow beating men and bricks from his path.

And now he is in the sky above them, a black star which has not been put out. They see the wings flare and beat, and the swirling of a girl's dress and unbound hair, and then the image dives and is gone into the shade under the mountains, as the sun rises.

It is fortunate, the mountain shade in the sunrise. Lion's blood and enforced quiescence have worked wonders, but the sun could undo it all. Luckily the shadow, deep and cold as a pool, envelops the vampire, and in it there is a cave, deeper and colder. Here he alights and sinks down, sloughing the girl, whom he has almost forgotten. Certainly he fears no harm from her. She is like a pet animal, maybe, like the hunting dogs or wolves or lammergeyers that occasionally the unkindness of vampires have kept by them for a while. That she helped him is all he needs to know. She will help again. So when, stumbling in the blackness, she brings him in her cupped hands water from a cascade at the poolcave's back, he is not surprised. He drinks the water, which is the only other substance his kind imbibe. Then he smooths her hair, absently, as he would pat or stroke the pet she seems to have become. He is not grateful, as he is not suspicious. The complexities of his intellect are reserved for other things. Since he is exhausted he falls asleep, and since Rohise is exhausted she falls asleep beside him, pressed to his warmth in the freezing dark. Like those of Feroluce, as it turns out, her thoughts are simple. She is sorry for distressing the Cursed Duke. But she has no regrets, for she could no more have left Feroluce to die than she could have refused to leave the scullery for the court.

The day, which had only just begun, passes swiftly in sleep.

Feroluce wakes as the sun sets, without seeing anything of it. He unfolds himself and goes to the cave's entrance, which now looks out on a whole sky of stars above a landscape of mountains. The castle is far below, and to the eyes of Rohise as she follows him, invisible. She does not even look for it, for there is something else to be seen.

The great dark shapes of angels are wheeling against the peaks, the stars. And their song begins, up in the starlit spaces. It is a lament, their mourning, pitiless and strong, for Feroluce, who has died in the stone heart of the thing they prey upon.

The tribe of Feroluce do not laugh, but, like a bird or wild beast, they have a kind of equivalent to laughter. This Feroluce now utters, and like a flung lance he launches himself into the air.

Rohise at the cave mouth, abandoned, forgotten, unnoted even by the mass of vampires, watches the winged man as he flies towards his people. She supposes for a moment that she may be able to climb down the tortuous ways of the mountain, undetected. Where then should she go? She does not spend much time on these ideas. They do not interest or involve her. She watches Feroluce and, because she learned long ago the uselessness of weeping, she does not shed tears, though her heart begins to break.

As Feroluce glides, body held motionless, wings outspread on a downdraft, into the midst of the storm of black wings, the red stars of eyes ignite all about him. The great lament dies. The air is very still.

Feroluce waits then. He waits, for the aura of his people is not as he has always known it. It is as if he had come among emptiness. From the silence, therefore, and from nothing else, he learns it all. In the stone he lay and he sang of his death, as the Prince must, dying. And the ritual was completed, and now there is the threnody, the grief, and thereafter the choosing of a new Prince. And none of this is alterable. He is dead. Dead. It cannot and will not be changed.

There is a moment of protest, then, from Feroluce. Perhaps his brief sojourn among men has taught him some of their futility. But as the cry leaves him, all about the huge wings are raised like swords. Talons and teeth and eyes burn against the stars. To protest is to be torn in shreds. He is not of their people now. They can attack and slaughter him as they would any other intruding thing. *Go,* the talons and the teeth and the eyes say to him. *Go far off.*

He is, dead. There is nothing left him but to die.

Feroluce retreats. He soars. Bewildered, he feels the power and energy of his strength and the joy of flight, and cannot understand how this is, if he is dead. Yet he *is* dead. He knows it now.

So he closes his eyelids, and his wings. Spear swift he falls. And something shrieks, interrupting the reverie of nihilism. Disturbed, he opens his wings, shudders, turns like a swimmer, finds a ledge against his side and two hands outstretched, holding him by one shoulder, and by his hair.

"No," says Rohise. (The vampire cloud, wheeling away, have not heard her; she does not think of them.) His eyes stay shut. Holding him, she kisses these eyelids, his forehead, his lips, gently, as she drives her nails into his skin to hold him. The black wings beat, tearing to be free and fall and die. "No," say Rohise. "I love you," she says. "My life is your life." These are the words of the court and of courtly love songs. No matter, she means them. And though he cannot understand her language or her sentiments, yet her passion, purely that, communicates itself, strong and burning as the passions of his kind, who generally love only one thing, which is scarlet. For a second her intensity fills the void which now contains him. But then he dashes himself away from the ledge, to fall again, to seek death again.

Like a ribbon, clinging to him still, Rohise is drawn from the rock and falls with him.

Afraid, she buries her head against his breast, in the shadow of wings and hair. She no longer asks him to reconsider. This is how it must be. *Love* she thinks again, in the instant before they strike the earth. Then that instant comes, and is gone.

Astonished, she finds herself still alive, still in the air. Touching so close feathers have been left on the rocks, Feroluce has swerved away, and upward. Now, conversely, they are whirling towards the very stars. The world seems miles below. Perhaps they will fly into space itself. Perhaps he means to break their bones instead on the cold face of the moon.

He does not attempt to dislodge her, he does not attempt any more to fall and die. But as he flies, he suddenly cries out, terrible lost lunatic cries.

They do not hit the moon. They do not pass through the stars like static rain.

But when the air grows thin and pure there is a peak like a dagger standing in their path. Here, he alights. As Rohise lets go of him, he turns away. He stations himself, sentry-fashion, in the manner of his tribe, at the edge of the pinnacle. But watching for nothing. He has not been able to choose death. His strength and the strong will of another, these have hampered him. His brain has become formless darkness. His eyes glare, seeing nothing.

Rohise, gasping a little in the thin atmosphere, sits at his back, watching for him, in case any harm may come near him.

At last, harm does come. There is a lightening in the east. The frozen, choppy sea of the mountains below and all about, grows visible. It is a marvelous sight, but holds no marvel for Rohise. She averts her eyes from the exquisitely penciled shapes, looking thin and translucent as paper, the rivers of mist between, the glimmer of nacreous ice. She searches for a blind hole to hide in.

There is a pale yellow wound in the sky when she returns. She grasps Feroluce by the wrist and tugs at him. "Come," she says. He looks at her vaguely, as if seeing her from the shore of another country. "The sun," she says. "Quickly."

The edge of the light runs along his body like a razor. He moves by instinct now, following her down the slippery dagger of the peak, and so eventually into a shallow cave. It is so small it holds him like a coffin. Rohise closes the entrance with her own body. It is the best she can do. She sits facing the sun as it rises, as if prepared to fight. She hates the sun for his sake. Even as the light warms her chilled body, she curses it. Till light and cold and breathlessness fade together.

When she wakes, she looks up into twilight and endless stars, two of which are red. She is lying on the rock by the cave. Feroluce leans over her, and behind Feroluce his quiescent wings fill the sky.

She has never properly understood his nature: Vampire. Yet her own nature, which tells her so much, tells her some vital part of herself is needful to him, and that he is danger, and death. But she loves him, and is not afraid. She would have fallen to die with him. To help him by her death does not seem wrong to her. Thus, she lies still, and smiles at him to reassure him he will not struggle. From lassitude, not fear, she closes her eyes. Presently she feels the soft weight of hair brush by her cheek, and then his cool mouth rests against her throat. But nothing more happens. For some while, they continue in this fashion, she yielding, he kneeling over her, his lips on her skin. Then he moves a little away. He sits, regarding her. She, knowing the unknown act has not been completed, sits up in turn. She beckons to him mutely, telling him with her gestures and her expression *I consent. Whatever is necessary.* But he does not stir. His eyes blaze, but even of these she has no fear. In the end he looks away from her, out across the spaces of the darkness.

He himself does not understand. It is permissible to drink from the body of a pet, the wolf, the eagle. Even to kill the pet, if need demands. Can it be, outlawed from his people, he has lost their composite soul? Therefore, is he soulless now? It does not seem to him he is. Weakened and famished though he is, the vampire is aware of a wild tingling of life. When he stares at the creature which is his food, he finds he sees her differently. He has borne her through the sky, he has avoided death, by some intuitive process, for her sake, and she has led him to safety, guarded him from the blade of the sun. In the beginning it was she who rescued him from the human things which had taken him. She cannot be human, then. Not pet, and not prey. For no, he could not drain her of blood, as he would not seize upon his own kind, even in combat, to drink and feed. He starts to see her as beautiful, not in the way a man beholds a woman, certainly, but as his kind revere the sheen of water in dusk, or flight, or song. There are no words for this. But the life goes on tingling through him. Though he is dead, life.

In the end, the moon does rise, and across the open face of it something wheels by. Feroluce is less swift than was his wont, yet he starts in pursuit, and catches and brings down, killing on the wing, a great night bird. Turning in the air, Feroluce absorbs its liquors. The heat of life now, as well as its assertion, courses through him. He returns to the rock perch, the glorious flaccid bird dangling from his hand. Carefully, he tears the glory of the bird in pieces, plucks the feathers, splits the bones. He wakes the companion (asleep again from weakness) who is not pet or prey, and feeds her morsels of flesh. At first she is unwilling. But her hunger is so enormous and her nature so untamed that quite soon she accepts the slivers of raw fowl.

Strengthened by blood, Feroluce lifts Rohise and bears her gliding down the moon-slit quill-backed land of the mountains, until there is a rocky cistern full of cold, old rains. Here they drink together. Pale white primroses grow in the fissures where the black moss drips. Rohise makes a garland and throws it about the head of her beloved when he does not expect it. Bewildered but disdainful, he touches at the wreath of primroses to see if it is likely to threaten or hamper him. When it does not, he leaves it in place.

Long before dawn this time, they have found a crevice. Because it is so cold, he folds his wings about her. She speaks of her love to him, but he does not hear, only the murmur of her voice, which is musical and does not displease him. And later, she sings him sleepily the little song of the fleur de fur.

There comes a time then, brief, undated, chartless time, when they are together, these two creatures. Not together in any accepted sense, of course, but together in the strange feeling or emotion, instinct or ritual, that can burst to life in an instant or flow to life gradually across half a century, and which men call *Love.*

They are not alike. No, not at all. Their differences are legion and should be unpalatable. He is a supernatural thing and she a human thing, he was a lord and she a scullery sloven. He can fly, she cannot fly. And he is male, she female. What other items are required to make them enemies? Yet they are bound, not merely by love, they are bound by all they are, the very stumbling blocks. Bound, too, because they are doomed. Because the stumbling blocks have doomed them; everything has. Each has been exiled out of their own kind. Together, they cannot even communicate with each other, save by looks, touches, sometimes by sounds, and by songs neither understands, but which each comes to value since the other appears to value them, and since they give expression to that other. Nevertheless, the binding of the doom, the greatest binding, grows, as it holds them fast to each other, mightier and stronger.

Although they do not know it, or not fully, it is the awareness of doom that keeps them there, among the platforms and steps up and down, and the inner cups, of the mountains.

Here it is possible to pursue the airborne hunt, and Feroluce may now and then bring down a bird to sustain them both. But birds are scarce. The richer lower slopes, pastured with goats, wild sheep and men—they lie far off and far down from this place as a deep of the sea. And Feroluce does not conduct her there, nor does Rohise ask that he should, or try to lead the way, or even dream of such a plan.

But yes, birds are scarce, and the pastures far away, and winter is coming. There are only two seasons in these mountains. High summer, which dies, and the high cold which already treads over the tips of the air and the rock, numbing the sky, making all brittle, as though the whole landscape might snap in pieces, shatter.

How beautiful it is to wake with the dusk, when the silver webs of night begin to form, frost and ice, on everything. Even the ragged dress—once that of a princess—is tinseled and shining with this magic substance, even the mighty wings—once those of a prince—each feather is drawn glittering with thin rime. And oh, the sky, thick as a daisy-field with the white stars. Up there, when they have fed and have strength, they fly, or, Feroluce flies and Rohise flies in his arms, carried by his wings. Up there in the biting chill like a pane of ghostly vitreous, they have become lovers, true blind lovers, embraced and linked, their bodies a bow, coupling on the wing. By the hour that this first happened the girl had forgotten all she had been, and he had forgotten too that she was anything but the essential mate. Sometimes, borne in this way, by wings and by fire, she cries out as she hangs in the ether. These sounds, transmitted through the flawless silence and amplification of the peaks, scatter over tiny half-buried villages countless miles away, where they are heard in fright and taken for the shrieks of malign invisible devils, tiny as bats, and armed with the barbed stings of scorpions. There are always misunderstandings.

After a while, the icy prologues and the stunning starry fields of winter nights give way to the main argument of winter.

The liquid of the pool, where the flowers made garlands, has clouded and closed to stone. Even the volatile waterfalls are stilled, broken cascades of glass. The wind tears through the skin and hair to gnaw the bones. To weep with cold earns no compassion of the cold.

There is no means to make fire. Besides, the one who was Rohise is an animal now, or a bird, and beasts and birds do not make fire, save for the phoenix in the Duke's bestiary. Also, the sun is fire, and the sun is a foe. Eschew fire.

There begin the calendar months of hibernation. The demon lovers too must prepare for just such a measureless winter sleep, that gives no hunger, asks no action. There is a deep cave they have lined with feathers and withered grass. But there are no more flying things to feed them. Long, long ago, the last warm frugal feast, long, long ago the last flight, joining, ecstasy and song. So, they turn to their cave, to stasis, to sleep. Which each understands, wordlessly, thoughtlessly, is death.

What else? He might drain her of blood, he could persist some while on that, might even escape the mountains, the doom. Or she herself might leave him, attempt to make her way to the places below, and perhaps she could reach them, even now. Others, lost here, have done so. But neither considers these alternatives. The moment for all that is past. Even the death-lament does not need to be voiced again.

Installed, they curl together in their bloodless, icy nest, murmuring a little to each other, but finally still.

Outside, the snow begins to come down. It falls like a curtain. Then the winds take it. Then the night is full of the lashing of whips, and when the sun rises it is white as the snow itself, its flames very distant, giving nothing. The cave mouth is blocked up with snow. In the winter, it seems possible that never again will there be a summer in the world.

Behind the modest door of snow, hidden and secret, sleep is quiet as stars, dense as hardening resin. Feroluce and Rohise turn pure and pale in the amber, in the frigid nest, and the great wings lie like a curious articulated machinery that will not move. And the withered grass and the flowers are crystallized, until the snows shall melt.

At length, the sun deigns to come closer to the earth, and the miracle occurs. The snow shifts, crumbles, crashes off the mountains in rage. The waters hurry after the snow, the air is wrung and racked by splittings and splinterings, by rushes and booms. It is half a year, or it might be a hundred years, later.

Open now, the entry to the cave. Nothing emerges. Then, a flutter, a whisper. Something does emerge. One black feather, and caught in it, the petal of a flower, crumbling like dark charcoal and white, drifting away into the voids below. Gone. Vanished. It might never have been.

But there comes another time (half a year, a hundred years), when an adventurous traveler comes down from the mountains to the pocketed villages the other side of them. He is a swarthy cheerful fellow, you would not take him for herbalist or mystic, but he has in a pot a plant he found high up in the staring crags, which might after all contain anything or nothing. And he shows the plant, which is an unusual one, having slender, dark and velvety leaves, and giving off a pleasant smell like vanilla. "See, the *Nona Mordica,*" he says. "The Bite-Me-Not. The flower that repels vampires."

Then the villagers tell him an odd story, about a castle in another country, besieged by a huge flock, a menace of winged vampires, and how the Duke waited in vain for the magic bush that was in his garden, the Bite-Me-Not, to flower and save them all. But it seems there was a curse on this Duke, who on the very night his daughter was lost, had raped a serving woman, as he had raped others before. But this woman conceived. And bearing the fruit, or flower, of this rape, damaged her, so she lived only a year or two after it. The child grew up unknowing, and in the end betrayed her own father by running away to the vampires, leaving the Duke demoralized. And soon after he went mad, and himself stole out one night, and let the winged fiends into his castle, so all there perished.

"Now if only the bush had flowered in time, as your bush flowers, all would have been well," the villagers cry.

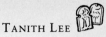

The traveler smiles. He in turn does not tell them of the heap of peculiar bones, like parts of eagles mingled with those of a woman and a man. Out of the bones, from the heart of them, the bush was rising, but the traveler untangled the roots of it with care; it looks sound enough now in its sturdy pot, all of it twining together. It seems as if two separate plants are growing from a single stem, one with blooms almost black, and one pink-flowered, like a young sunset.

"Flur de fur," says the traveler, beaming at the marvel, and his luck.

Fleur de feu. Oh flower of fire. That fire is not hate or fear, which makes flowers come, not terror or anger or lust, it is love that is the fire of the Bite-Me-Not, love which cannot abandon, love which cannot harm. Love which never dies.

THE COMIC VAMPIRE

D espite the link between horror and humor (they both depend upon distortion and excess), comparatively little vampire comedy has been written. While satirists and stand-up comedians are perfectly comfortable poking fun at every aspect of human existence, blood may be a problem. Blood, as has been pointed out, is a substance singularly laden with meaning—most of it of a very serious sort. And there are only a certain number of clever remarks that can be made about it.

The film industry, though, has had quite a bit of fun with vampires. Abbott and Costello have met Dracula to good effect in *Abbott and Costello Meet Frankenstein* (1948). John Carradine in *Billy the Kid versus Dracula* (1966) enhances the film's campiness so that it becomes sheer comedy. Then there is *Love at First Bite* (1979), in which Susan St. James and George Hamilton play with the big 1970s questions of commitment and recreational sex. And in *The Fearless Vampire Killer* (1967), a chaste chambermaid finds her crucifix powerless against the Jewish vampire that has come to ravish her.

In print, humorous vampires mostly lend themselves to short pieces with funny punch lines and trick endings, as in the stories collected here. Nonetheless, some brave authors have attempted to explore the lighter side of undeath at novel length. *Tabitha fffoulkes* by John Linssen (1978) is a genuine romantic comedy about the rocky relationship between a modern young woman and her vampiric suitor. *The Goldcamp Vampire, or The Sanguinary Sourdough* by Elizabeth Ann Scarborough (1987), is a light-hearted romp set in Jack London's Yukon. *Suckers,* by Anne Billson (1993), is something considerably nastier, a biting black comedy set in Thatcherite London. *Suckers* contains one of the most audacious and perversely amusing end-of-chapter cliffhangers ever conceived: when the heroine goes undercover at a vampires-only pub, her menstrual period suddenly begins.

The definitive vampire comedy has probably yet to be written, but the stories selected here, including the Dracula story by filmmaker Woody Allen, do reveal untapped veins of humor in the conventions of traditional vampire fiction.

FREDERIC BROWN
(1906–1972)

Born in Cincinnati, Ohio, Frederic Brown attended the University of Cincinnati and Hanover College in Indiana. He was a detective story and science fiction writer, and a working journalist for the Milwaukee Journal for many years.

Brown is perhaps most famous for his detective novels, especially The Fabulous Clipjoint (1947), but his science fiction stories are well loved for their humor and elegance. His most well-known science fiction novel, What Mad Universe (1949), is a complex alternate-worlds story. Brown was also attracted to humor writing, making many of his shorter works essentially extended jokes. His collection entitled Nightmares and Geezenstacks (1961) merged with another, Honeymoon in Hell (1958), into an omnibus edition, entitled And the Gods Laughed (1987). Brown's other science fiction works include The Lights in the Sky are Stars (1953) and Martians Go Home (1955).

Many of his previously uncollected stories have recently been published, including "Homicide Sanitarium" (1984), "Before She Kills" (1984), "The Freak Show Murders" (1985), "Thirty Corpses Every Thursday" (1986), "Who Was that Blonde I Saw You Kill Last Night?" (1988), "The Water-Walker" (1990), and "The Pickled Punks" (1991).

The story that follows is typical of Brown's specialty, which is the tiny, explosive joke. So as not to risk spoiling the joke, no annotation or commentary is offered here. Still, readers may want to keep in mind what it is that you can't get from a turnip.

BLOOD

In their time machine, Vron and Dreena, last two survivors of the race of vampires, fled into the future to escape annihilation. They held hands and consoled one another in their terror and their hunger.

In the twenty-second century mankind had found them out, had discovered that the legend of vampires living secretly among humans was not a legend at all, but fact. There had been a pogrom that had found and killed every vampire but these two, who had already been working on a time machine and who had finished in time to escape in it. Into the future, far enough into the future that the very word *vampire* would be forgotten so they could again live unsuspected—and from their loins regenerate their race.

"I'm hungry, Vron. Awfully hungry."

"I too, Dreena dear. We'll stop again soon."

They had stopped four times already and had narrowly escaped dying each time. They had *not* been forgotten. The last stop, half a million years back, had shown them a world gone to the dogs—quite literally: human beings were extinct and dogs had become civilized and man-like. Still they had been recognized for what they were. They'd managed to feed once, on the blood of a tender young bitch, but then they'd been hounded back to their time machine and into flight again.

"Thanks for stopping," Dreena said. She sighed.

"Don't thank me," said Vron grimly. "This is the end of the line. We're out of fuel and we'll find none here—by now all radioactives will have turned to lead. We live here . . . or else."

They went out to scout. "Look," said Dreena excitedly, pointing to something walking toward them. "A new creature! The dogs are gone and something else has taken over. And surely we're forgotten."

The approaching creature was telepathic. "I have heard your thoughts," said a voice inside their brains. "You wonder whether we know 'vampires,' whatever they are. We do not."

Dreena clutched Vron's arm in ecstasy. "Freedom!" she murmured hungrily. "And *food!*"

"You also wonder," said the voice, "about my origin and evolution. All life today is vegetable. I—" He bowed low to them. "I, a member of the dominant race, was once what you called a turnip."

CHARLES BEAUMONT
(1929–1967)

Chicago-born Charles Nutt was self-educated after his second year of high school. He wrote under several pseudonyms, including Charles Beaumont, Keith Grantland, C. B. Lovehill, and S. M. Tenneshaw. It was as Beaumont, under which he wrote "Blood Brother" and most of his science fiction, that he was best known.

Nutt began publishing his brand of horror mixed with science fiction with "The Devil, You Say?" for Amazing Stories in 1951. He published many short story collections, including The Hunger (1957), Yonder (1958), Night Ride and Other Journeys (1960), The Magic Man (1965), and The Edge (1966). His work combines humor with horror in a very effective style that downplays the grimness of the subject matter. He also worked as a writer for genre movies, among them Queen of Outer Space (1958), The Premature Burial (1962), The Wonderful World of the Brothers Grimm (1962), The Haunted Palace (1963), The Seven Faces of Dr. Lao (1964), and The Masque of the Red Death (1964). Several of these films were directed by the famous director Roger Corman, well known for his horror and science fiction genre movies. Nutt also wrote numerous scripts for television, including some work for The Twilight Zone.

"Blood Brother," like satire generally, succeeds because it takes its target seriously. Nutt examines vampire lore with a pragmatic eye, showing us that a twentieth-century urban vampire has almost unsolvable problems. The joke, as the story's ending reveals, is that there are people out there who can solve these problems rather simply.

BLOOD BROTHER

"Now then," said the psychiatrist, looking up from his note pad, "when did you first discover that you were dead?"

"Not dead," said the pale man in the dark suit. "Undead."

"I'm sorry."

"Just try to keep it straight. If I were dead, I'd be in great shape. That's the trouble, though. I can't die."

"Why not?"

"Because I'm not alive."

"I see." The psychiatrist made a rapid notation. "Now, Mr. Smith, I'd like you to start at the beginning, and tell me the whole story."

The pale man shook his head. "At twenty-five dollars an hour," he said, "are you kidding? I can barely afford to have my cape cleaned once a month."

"I've been meaning to ask you about that. Why do you wear it?"

"You ever hear of a vampire without a cape? It's part of the whole schmear, that's all. *I* don't know why!"

"Calm yourself."

"Calm yourself! I wish I could. I tell you, Doctor, I'm going right straight out of my skull. Look at this!" The man who called himself Smith put out his hands. They were a tremblous blur of white. "And look at this!" He pulled down the flaps beneath his eyes, revealing an intricate red lacework of veins. "Believe me," he said, flinging himself upon the couch, "another few days of this and I'll be ready for the funny farm!"

The psychiatrist picked a mahogany letter opener off his desk and tapped his palm. "I would appreciate it," he said, "if you would make an effort to avoid those particular terms."

"All right," said the pale man. "But you try living on blood for a year, and see how polite you are. I mean—"

"The beginning, Mr. Smith."

"Well, I met this girl, Dorcas, and she bit me."

"Yes?"

"That's all. It doesn't take much, you know."

The psychiatrist removed his glasses and rubbed his eyes. "As I understand it," he said, "you think you're a vampire."

"No," said Smith. "I *think* I'm a human being, but I *am* a vampire. That's the hell of it. I can't seem to adjust."

"How do you mean?"

"Well, the hours for instance. I used to have very regular habits. Work from nine to five, home, a little TV, maybe, into bed by ten, up at six-thirty. Now—" He shook his head violently from side to side. "You know how it is with vampires."

"Let's pretend I don't," said the psychiatrist, soothingly. "Tell me. How is it?"

"Like I say, the hours. Everything's upside-down. That's why I made this appointment with you so late. See, you're supposed to sleep during the *day* and work at *night*."

"Why?"

"Boy, you've got me. I asked Dorcas, that's the girl bit me, and she said she'd try and find out, but nobody seems to be real sure about it."

"Dorcas," said the psychiatrist, pursing his lips. "That's an unusual name."

"Dorcas Schultz is an unusual girl, I'll tell you. A real nut. She's on that late-late TV show, you know? The one that runs all those crummy old horror movies?" Smith scraped a stain from his cloak with his finger-nail. "Maybe you know her. She recommended you."

"It's possible. But let's get back to you. You were speaking of the hours."

Smith wrung his hands. "They're murdering me," he said. "Eight fly-by-night jobs I've had—eight!—and lost every one!"

"Would you care to explain that?"

"Nothing to explain. I just can't stay awake, that's all. I mean, every night—I mean every *day*—I toss and turn for hours and then when I finally *do* doze off, boom, it's nightfall and I've got to get out of the coffin."

"The coffin?"

"Yeah. That's another sweet wrinkle. The minute you go bat, you're supposed to give up beds and take a casket. Which is not only sick, but expensive as *hell*." Smith shook his head angrily. "First you got to buy the damn thing. Do you know the cost of the average casket?"

"Well—" began the psychiatrist.

"Astronomical! Completely out of proportion. I'm telling you, it's a racket! For anything even halfway decent you're going to drop five bills, easy. But that's just the initial outlay. Then there's the cartage and the cleaning bills."

"I don't—"

"Seventy-five to a hundred every month, month in, month out."

"I'm afraid I—"

"The grave dirt, man. Sacking out in a coffin isn't bad enough, no, you've got to line it with *soil from the family plot*. I ask you, who's got a family plot these days? Have you?"

"No, but—"

"Right. So what do you do? You go out and buy one. Then you bring home a couple pounds of dirt and spread it around in the coffin. Wake up at night and you're *covered* with it." Smith clicked his tongue exasperatedly. "If you could just wear pajamas—but no, the rules say the full bit. Ever *hear* of anything so crazy? You can't even take off your *shoes*, for cry eye!" He began to pace. "Then there's the bloodstains."

The psychiatrist lowered his pad, replaced his glasses, and regarded his patient with a not incurious eye.

"I must go through twenty white shirts a month," continued Smith. "Even at two-fifty a shirt, that's a lot of dough. You're probably thinking, Why isn't he more careful? Well, listen, I try to be. But it isn't like eating a bowl of tomato soup, you know." A shudder, or something like a shudder, passed over the pale man. "That's another thing. The diet. I mean, I always used to like my steaks rare, but this is ridiculous! Blood for breakfast, blood for lunch, blood for dinner. Uch—just the thought of it makes me queasy to the stomach!" Smith flung himself back onto the couch and closed his eyes. "It's the monotony that gets you," he said, "although there's plenty else to complain about. You know what I mean?"

"Well," said the psychiatrist, clearing his throat, "I—"

"Filthy stuff! And the routines I have to go through to get it! What if you had to rob somebody every time you wanted a hamburger—I mean, just supposing. That's the way it is with me. I tried stocking up on plasma, but that's death warmed over. A few nights of it and you've got to go after the real thing, it doesn't matter *how* many promises you've made to yourself."

"The real thing?"

"I don't like to talk about it," said Smith, turning his head to the wall. "I'm actually a very sensitive person, know what I mean? Gentle. Kind. Never could stand violence, not even as a kid. Now . . ." He sobbed wrackingly, leaped to his feet, and resumed pacing. "Do you think I *enjoy* biting people? Do you think I don't *know* how disgusting it is? But, I tell you, *I can't help it!* Every few nights I get this terrible urge . . ."

"Yes?"

"You'll hate me."

"No, Mr. Smith."

"Yes you will. Everybody does. Everybody hates a vampire." The pale man withdrew a large silk handkerchief from his pocket and daubed at sudden tears. "It isn't fair," he choked. "After all, we didn't *ask* to become what we are, did we? Nobody ever thinks of that."

"You feel, then, that you are being persecuted?"

"Damn right," said Smith. "And you know why? I'll tell you why. Because I *am* being persecuted. That's why. Have you ever heard a nice thing said about a vampire? Ever in your whole life? No. Why? Because people hate us. But I'll tell you something even sillier. They *fear* us, too!" The pale man laughed a wild, mirthless laugh. "*Us*," he said. "The most helpless creatures on the face of the Earth! Why, it doesn't take *anything* to knock us over. If we don't cut our throats trying to shave—you know the mirror bit: no reflection—we stand a chance to land flat on our back because the neighbor downstairs is cooking garlic. Or bring us a little running water, see what happens. We flip our lids. Or silver bullets. *Daylight,* for crying out loud. If I'm not back in that stupid coffin by dawn, zow, I'm out like a light. So I'm out late, and time sort of gets away from me, and I look at my watch and I've got ten minutes. What do I do? Any other vampire in his right mind, he changes into a bat and flies. Not me. You know why?"

The psychiatrist shook his head.

"Because I can't stand the ugly things. They make me sick just to look at, let alone be. And then there's all the hassle of taking off your clothes and all. So I grab a cab and just pray there isn't any traffic. Boy. Or take these." He smiled for the first time, revealing two large pointed incisors. "What do you imagine happens to us when our choppers start to go? I've had this one on the left filled it must be half a dozen times. The dentist says if I was smart I'd have 'em all yanked out and a nice denture put in. Sure. Can't you just see me trying to rip out somebody's throat with a pair of false teeth? Or take the routine with the wooden stake. It used to be that was kind of a secret. Now with all these lousy movies, the whole *world* is in on the gag. I ask you, Doctor, how are you supposed to be able to sleep when you know that everybody in the block is just itching to find you so they can drive a piece of wood into your heart? Huh? Man, you talk about *sick!* Those people are in *really* bad shape!" He shuddered again. "I'll tell you about the jazz with crosses, but frankly, even thinking about it makes me jumpy. You know what? I have to walk three blocks out of my way to avoid the church I used to go to every Sunday. But don't get the idea it's just churches. No, it's *anything.* Cross your fingers and I'll start sweating. Lay a fork over a knife and I'll probably jump right out the window. So then what happens? I splatter myself all over the sidewalk, right? But do I die? Oh, hell, no. Doc, listen! You've got to help me! If you don't, I'm going to go off my gourd, I know it!"

The psychiatrist folded his note pad and smiled. "Mr. Smith," he said, "you may be surprised to learn that yours is a relatively simple problem . . . with a relatively simple cure."

"Really?" asked the pale man.

"To be sure," said the psychiatrist. "Just lie down on the couch there. That's it. Close your eyes. Relax. Good." The psychiatrist rose from his chair and walked to his desk. "While it is true that this syndrome is something of a rarity," he said, "I do not foresee any great difficulty." He picked something off the top of the desk and returned. "It is primarily a matter of adjustment and of right thinking. Are you quite relaxed?"

Smith said that he was.

"Good," said the psychiatrist. "Now we begin the cure." With which comment he raised his arm high in the air, held it there for a moment, then plunged it down, burying the mahogany letter opener to its hilt in Mr. Smith's heart.

Seconds later, he was dialing a telephone number.

"Is Dorcas there?" he asked, idly scratching the two circular marks on his neck. "Tell her it's her fiancé."

WOODY ALLEN
(b. 1935)

America's most creative, and often funniest, filmmaker, Woody Allen, was born Allen Stewart Konigsberg in Brooklyn, New York. He was educated at New York University and at the City College of New York.

Allen began his career as a comedy writer and a stand-up comedian, drawing most of his material from events or fantasies in his own life and finding humor in his own insecurities. In his comedy routines and films, Allen often depicts himself as the prototypical modern man, one living in a perpetual state of anxiety, hexed by women, the certainty of death, and the guilt-ridden vestiges of inherited religion. There is a direct line leading from Y. L. Peretz's Yiddish sufferer, "Silent Bontsche," through Charlie Chaplin's Little Tramp to Woody Allen's endlessly beset schlimazel (klutz), an endlessly baffled New York City Jew around whom the contemporary world whirls.

Allen's film triumphs, almost too numerous to list, include such favorites as Annie Hall (1977), Manhattan (1979), Broadway Danny Rose (1984), The Purple Rose of Cairo (1985), and Mighty Aphrodite (1995). His written works include Getting Even (1971), Without Feathers (1975), and The Complete Prose of Woody Allen (1991).

That Allen turned his attention to Count Dracula should not surprise us. Nor should it surprise us that Allen's Count Dracula has an uncanny resemblance to the schlimazel Allen has made famous. In any case, here we have the fruit of that excursion: The answer to the question of what happens to a vampire whose sense of sunrise and sunset is discombobulated by a total eclipse of the sun.

COUNT DRACULA

Somewhere in Transylvania, Dracula the monster lies sleeping in his coffin, waiting for night to fall. As exposure to the sun's rays would surely cause him to perish, he stays protected in the satin-lined chamber bearing his family name in silver. Then the moment of darkness comes, and through some miraculous instinct the fiend emerges from the safety of his hiding place and, assuming the hideous forms of the bat or the wolf, he prowls the countryside, drinking the blood of his victims. Finally, before the first rays of his archenemy, the sun, announce a new day, he hurries back to the safety of his hidden coffin and sleeps, as the cycle begins anew.

Now he starts to stir. The fluttering of his eyelids are a response to some age-old, unexplainable instinct that the sun is nearly down and his time is near. Tonight, he is particularly hungry and as he lies there, fully awake now, in red-lined Inverness cape and tails, waiting to feel with uncanny perception the precise moment of darkness before opening the lid and emerging, he decides who this evening's victims will be. The baker and his wife, he thinks to himself. Succulent, available, and unsuspecting. The thought of the unwary couple whose trust he has carefully cultivated excites his blood lust to a fever pitch, and he can barely hold back these last seconds before climbing out of the coffin to seek his prey.

Suddenly he knows the sun is down. Like an angel of hell, he rises swiftly, and changing into a bat, flies pell-mell to the cottage of his tantalizing victims.

"Why, Count Dracula, what a nice surprise," the baker's wife says, opening the door to admit him. (He has once again assumed human form, as he enters their home, charmingly concealing his rapacious goal.)

"What brings you here so early?" the baker asks.

"Our dinner date," the Count answers. "I hope I haven't made an error. You did invite me for tonight, didn't you?"

"Yes, tonight, but that's not for seven hours."

"Pardon me?" Dracula queries, looking around the room puzzled.

"Or did you come by to watch the eclipse with us?"

"Eclipse?"

"Yes. Today's the total eclipse."

"What?"

"A few moments of darkness from noon until two minutes after. Look out the window."

"Uh-oh—I'm in big trouble."

"Eh?"

"And now if you'll excuse me . . ."

"What, Count Dracula?"

"Must be going—aha—oh, god . . ." Frantically he fumbles for the door knob.

"Going? You just came."

"Yes—but—I think I blew it very badly . . ."

"Count Dracula, you're pale."

"Am I? I need a little fresh air. It was nice seeing you . . ."

"Come. Sit down. We'll have a drink."

"Drink? No, I must run. Er—you're stepping on my cape."

"Sure. Relax. Some wine."

"Wine? Oh no, gave it up—liver and all that, you know. And now I really must buzz off. I just remembered, I left the lights on at my castle—bills'll be enormous . . ."

"Please," the baker says, his arm around the Count in firm friendship. "You're not intruding. Don't be so polite. So you're early."

"Really, I'd like to stay but there's a meeting of old Roumanian Counts across town and I'm responsible for the cold cuts."

"Rush, rush, rush. It's a wonder you don't get a heart attack."

"Yes, right—and now—"

"I'm making Chicken Pilaf tonight," the baker's wife chimes in. "I hope you like it."

"Wonderful, wonderful," the Count says, with a smile, as he pushes her aside into some laundry. Then, opening a closet door by mistake, he walks in. "Christ, where's the goddamn front door?"

"Ach," laughs the baker's wife, "such a funny man, the Count."

"I knew you'd like that," Dracula says, forcing a chuckle, "now get out of my way." At last he opens the front door but time has run out on him.

"Oh, look, Mama," says the baker, "the eclipse must be over. The sun is coming out again."

"Right," says Dracula, slamming the front door. "I've decided to stay. Pull down the window shades quickly—*quickly!* Let's move it!"

"What window shades?" asks the baker.

"There are none, right? Figures. You got a basement in this joint?"

"No," says the wife affably, "I'm always telling Jarslov to build one but he never listens. That's some Jarslov, my husband."

"I'm all choked up. Where's the closet?"

"You did that one already, Count Dracula. Unt Mama and I laughed at it."

"Ach—such a funny man, the Count."

"Look, I'll be in the closet. Knock at seven-thirty." And with that, the Count steps inside the closet and slams the door.

"Hee-hee—he is so funny, Jarslov."

"Oh, Count. Come out of the closet. Stop being a big silly." From inside the closet comes the muffled voice of Dracula.

"Can't—please—take my word for it. Just let me stay here. I'm fine. Really."

"Count Dracula, stop the fooling. We're already helpless with laughter."

"Can I tell you, I love this closet."

"Yes, but . . ."

"I know, I know . . . it seems strange, and yet here I am, having a ball. I was just saying to Mrs. Hess the other day, give me a good closet and I can stand in it for hours. Sweet woman, Mrs. Hess. Fat but sweet . . . Now, why don't you run along and check back with me at sunset. Oh, Ramona, la da da de da da de, Ramona . . ."

Now the Mayor and his wife, Katia, arrive. They are passing by and have decided to pay a call on their good friends, the baker and his wife.

"Hello, Jarslov. I hope Katia and I are not intruding?"

"Of course not, Mr. Mayor. Come out, Count Dracula! We have company!"

"Is the Count here?" asks the Mayor surprised.

"Yes, and you'll never guess where," says the baker's wife.

"It's so rare to see him around this early. In fact I can't ever remember seeing him around in the daytime."

"Well, he's here. Come out, Count Dracula!"

"Where is he?" Katia asks, not knowing whether to laugh or not.

"Come on out now! Let's go!" The baker's wife is getting impatient.

"He's in the closet," says the baker, apologetically.

"Really?" asks the Mayor.

"Let's go," says the baker with mock good humor as he knocks on the closet door. "Enough is enough. The Mayor's here."

"Come on out, Dracula," His Honor shouts, "let's have a drink."

"No, go ahead. I've got some business in here."

"In the closet?"

"Yes, don't let me spoil your day. I can hear what you're saying. I'll join in if I have anything to add."

Everyone looks at one another and shrugs. Wine is poured and they all drink.

"Some eclipse today," the Mayor says, sipping from his glass.

"Yes," the baker agrees. "Incredible."

"Yeah. Thrilling," says a voice from the closet.

"What, Dracula?"

"Nothing, nothing. Let it go."

And so the time passes, until the Mayor can stand it no longer and forcing open the door to the closet, he shouts, "Come on, Dracula. I always thought you were a mature man. Stop this craziness."

The daylight streams in, causing the evil monster to shriek and slowly dissolve to a skeleton and then to dust before the eyes of the four people present. Leaning down to the pile of white ash on the closet floor, the baker's wife shouts, "Does this mean dinner's off tonight?"

·······VI·······
THE HEROIC VAMPIRE

Is vampirism an unnatural plague or merely another alternative lifestyle? One hundred years after *Dracula,* readers are finding it easier to identify with vampiric protagonists and even admire them. In a more secular and hostile age, where undeath is not automatically synonymous with damnation, even Dracula can be a hero if seen from the right point of view. Over the last few decades fictional vampires have been transformed from remorseless seducers and killers, to tormented souls wrestling with an affliction beyond their control, to, increasingly, genuinely heroic figures who are morally superior to the petty, short-lived humans who surround them. It is not surprising that more and more young readers identify with the vampire who is exiled from normal experience, a sexual experimenter, a sensualist, and, above all, someone who has found a way to stay young.

There has been a steady drifting of audience or reader sympathy in favor of the vampire, perhaps beginning with the film *Dracula* (1931), in which Bela Lugosi as the title character is fascinating, though perhaps not congenial. Film Draculas following Lugosi have been increasingly attractive figures.

This trend achieved greater visibility in the 1960s, with the creation of Barnabas Collins on television's *Dark Shadows* and the popular comic book heroine Vampirella, and accelerated rapidly from there. Even more admirable and altruistic is Chelsea Quinn Yarbro's popular creation, the Count Saint-Germain. Introduced in *Hôtel Transylvania* in 1977, Saint-Germain is perhaps the purest example of the heroic vampire in modern fiction; he has defended the innocent and battled the corrupt in nearly a dozen books and has a passionate fan following. Although few other vampires can live up to his sterling example, several other sympathetic vampire protagonists do grace, with their sometimes uneasy consciences, the annals of modern vampire fiction.

One person's vampire hero, though, can be another person's worst nightmare, and sometimes it can be difficult to tell the good vampires from the bad, especially when they all leave large body counts behind. But one characteristic of vampires, we recall, is their ability to change shape. So perhaps we should not be too surprised when they transform from monsters to heroes . . . and back again.

CHELSEA QUINN YARBRO
(b. 1942)

Born and raised in Berkeley, California, Chelsea Quinn Yarbro has published more than fifty books, sixty short stories, and a handful of essays and reviews in almost three decades as a professional writer. Her work covers many genres: horror, science fiction, fantasy, thriller, mystery, historical, romantic suspense, young adult, and westerns.

Yarbro is perhaps best known for her immensely popular vampire novels featuring the Count Saint-Germain, the first of which, Hôtel Transylvania (1977), is excerpted here. The others include The Palace (1978), Blood Games (1979), Path of the Eclipse (1981), Tempting Fate (1982), Out of the House of Life (1990), Darker Jewels (1993), Better in the Dark (1993), Mansions of Darkness (1996), and Writ in Blood (1997). She is writing a trilogy of novels about Count Dracula's wives, the first of which is The Angry Angel (1998).

The trick that both Yarbro and Anne Rice have accomplished—inventing heroic, admirable vampires—seems beyond comprehension. In the presence of such protagonists, readers must reconcile their elegance with the fact that they sustain themselves by taking the blood of other humans. Still, Yarbro's Saint-Germain is charming and attractive, and the author reassures us that he never takes more blood than he needs—and then only from willing victims. Among his other skills, he has learned how to temporarily outwit the requirement that vampires sleep in their native soil: he has had that soil built into the soles of his shoes!

Excerpt from
HÔTEL TRANSYLVANIA

Excerpt from one of a series of letters written by le Baron
Clotaire de Saint Sebastien to the absent members of his Circle; undated:

. . . The chapel may be reached by a secret tunnel that leads from
the Seine to the abandoned vaults of the monastery that stood near the
river over five hundred years ago. You will find the entrance to the
tunnel on the river side of Quai Malaquais between la rue des Saints
Péres and la rue de Seine. The tunnel is reinforced with heavy stones,
and you should bring a club with you, for there are many rats.

. . . On the other side of the burial vaults is the chapel. It is rumored
that practices of our sort were in effect there as long ago as the reign
of the Spider King, which is auspicious. Certainly it has seen more
recent use, for La Voison mentioned it and several others like it in and
around Paris, to many of that Circle, to which my grandfather
belonged.

The chapel itself is almost directly under Hôtel Transylvania. I find
myself amused by this contrast. Above us, our splendid equals will be
playing at dice, and risking several generations' fortune on the turn of
a card, thinking that they have found the answer to power and fame,
while we, far under their feet, will perform the rituals that will bring
us power as they do not know exists, and the control of France more
potent than the throne.

Let me warn you: apparently there is some means of access to the
chapel from Hôtel Transylvania, although I have not discovered it, and
it is doubtful that the owners of the Hôtel or the staff are aware of it.
But you will admit that it would be most unfortunate if any of our
number should use it, and even more important if any unlucky member
of the Hôtel's staff should happen to discover our presence. For that,
and other reasons, I will insist that each of you take turns standing
guard. You will not be deprived of the delights of our sacrifice, or the
use of our offering, who I find will be excellent. Even the slight taste
I have had of her tells me that it will be a splendid thing to destroy
her. But we must be secret. Reflection on the scandal that accompanied
the last discovery of a Circle should make the need for these precautions
obvious to you. One Affair of the Poisons is enough for France. I will
not tolerate any of you being so clumsy as was Montespan.

As I write this last message the hour of one has struck. I charge you to be at the chapel by the third hour of the morning, as we have planned. It may be a good thing that we have moved to the chapel ahead of the planned time for it reduces our chance of discovery and allows more leisure to make the offerings acceptable.

If you fail me in this, I will know you for my enemy, and will deal with you accordingly at my first opportunity. If you will not bow before Satan, you may still be of use to him, and to me. Think of the dismal fate of others who have stood against me, and let your decision reflect the benefit of your contemplations.

Until the third hour of the morning, then, and the first ritual, when we will offer on the altar the body of one who has betrayed me, be certain that you are in my thoughts—for advantage and luxury beyond your fondest hopes, or destruction, as you choose. It is my honor to be

> Your most devoted
> Baron Clotaire de Saint Sebastien

Water darkened the stones of the tunnel, and on the uneven flags that served as flooring, there was a thin film of slime, making it difficult to walk. A pervasive fetid odor filled the close air, making even the torches seem dimmed by the stench.

"Do not drop him!" Saint Sebastien ordered to the men who followed him through the tunnel.

Achille Cressie, who bore the shoulders of Robert de Montalia, complained, "Why did you have to drug him? We should have bound him."

"So that you could be entertained by his dear words, Achille?" Saint Sebastien's tone was poisonously sweet.

This did not have the expected effect on Achille, who chuckled unpleasantly. "You should have heard him in the tack room. How he despised himself when his flesh warmed to me."

De les Radeux, who held de Montalia's legs, gave a deprecating sigh. "It is all very well for you to boast of your prowess, Achille, but you will not let anyone watch, or share." He slid on the watery ooze, cursing.

"Pay attention!" Saint Sebastien barked out the order.

"He is heavy," de les Radeux insisted, sulking.

"All the more reason for you to keep your mind on what you are doing and away from your vain rivalry with Achille. If you cannot do as you are told, you are of no use to me."

De les Radeux muttered an imprecation under his breath, but steadied his grip on the drugged Robert de Montalia, going the rest of the way into the vault in silence.

The air was somewhat better there, not so close, and since the ancient stones were farther away from the river, the vault did not have that clammy cold that had made the tunnel so unbearable. Yet, it was a gloomy place. In the niches around the walls were the partially mummified remains of monks who had died three hundred years before. A closer look showed that most of the bodies had been profaned and that the crucifixes that had lain in their skeletal fingers had been replaced by phalluses, and that where consecrated oil had marked their foreheads as those belonging to God, there were now dried reddish stains in the symbol of Satan.

Saint Sebastien held his torch higher, and went quickly through the vault, arriving at last at a thick door set in the wall. The door was somewhat out of place in the Romanesque setting, for its design was recent, the strong iron hinges and other fittings still showing traces of oil to prevent rust, and the carving on the door indicated to what perverse use the chapel beyond had been put.

The door yawned open on nearly silent fittings, revealing the first area of the chapel beyond. Saint Sebastien sighed as he held the door for Cressie and de les Radeux. It would be an easy matter now. They had escaped detection, and there was no evidence that the chapel had been found and cleansed of the demonic presence.

Saint Sebastien walked farther into the chapel, his torch bringing light to the crude murals that adorned the walls, showing all the excesses of Satanic worship. Saint Sebastien smiled at one particularly horrendous representation, then went to the altar, saying to the panting men behind him, "Here, I think. Strip him and tie him down. I do not want to have to subdue him again."

De les Radeux said at his surliest, "I am honored to do this." He glared at the altar, at Saint Sebastien, at the man he carried. This was not at all what he had anticipated. He had been told that the ceremonies of the Circle were grand occasions. His uncle Beauvrai had dwelt lovingly on the complex gratifications that were offered for every desire as well as the opportunity to advance in power through these practices. But here he was in a cold stone room, under the ground, carrying le Marquis de Montalia and bowing and scraping to Saint Sebastien as if Saint Sebastien were king or archangel and he was the lowest peasant in France. To make matters worse, the damp had quite ruined his satin coat and fine white-silk hose. He wished now that he had had the foresight to keep his riding boots on.

With a last grunt, de les Radeux and Achille Cressie hoisted Robert de Montalia onto the altar, and set about pulling his clothes off, a task that proved to be surprisingly difficult.

It took Saint Sebastien about ten minutes to recite the required incantations as he lit the fifteen torches that lined the walls. The brightness grew, but the flickering of the torches made that brightness unsteady, a leaping, irregular illumination that gave weird life to the grotesque paintings on the walls.

A noise beyond the door brought Saint Sebastien's attention to the task at hand. He called out the password and waited for a response. The proper words came back, and he went to open the door.

Jueneport stood there, Madelaine in his arms. "Where do you want her?"

Saint Sebastien studied the limp figure. "I think we must put her where she can watch what we do to her father. Perhaps there." He motioned to the inverted crucifix that hung over the altar.

"It doesn't look safe to me," Jueneport said slowly. "She's strong enough to pull it out of the wall."

"I see your point." Saint Sebastien considered for a moment longer. "We could tie her there. She would then see what is done to her father, and we would see what is her reaction. An excellent combination." He had pointed to the screen that had once guarded part of the sanctuary, when the chapel had been used by the monks and not the Circles who had come to own it.

"It is strong," Jueneport agreed. "Very well. I imagine there are ropes available?"

"Behind the altar. Take what you need."

Jueneport nodded, then went to where de les Radeux and Achille Cressie worked to secure Robert de Montalia to the altar. Achille worked more slowly, pausing every now and then to run his hands over the nude body, an unpleasant light in his face as he said, "We could bind his organ as well. That way, his pain would be doubled, as would our sport."

De les Radeux shot him a look of tolerant disgust. "Is your lust all that goads you to this, Achille? Have you no other desires?"

The laughter that greeted these questions made Saint Sebastien turn, angered. "None of that, Achille, or I will forbid you to take part in the celebration."

Achille pouted, then shrugged and negligently returned to his task.

Now there was another knock at the door, and the passwords were once again exchanged. De la Sept-Nuit came in, his eyes searching for and finding the pathetic figure of Madelaine. He gestured to the bag he held. "These are the robes, mon Baron. They are all prepared, and need only your curse before we don them."

Saint Sebastien traced the pentagram in the air and said a few syllables of backward Latin. "You may dress whenever you like. Make sure your own garments are out of the way."

"I will." De la Sept-Nuit went away to a side alcove and returned several minutes later in the pleated silk robe of the Circle. It resembled a soutane, but the pleated silk clung to the body in a way no priestly garb did, and the neck opening ran the length of the robe to the hem, so that the material opened to reveal the body as de la Sept-Nuit walked across the chapel.

"I have put your robe aside," de la Sept-Nuit said. "Yours is the red with the embroidery, is that not so?"

"Yes. If you will take this torch and put it in place by the altar. I will invest myself. Are the bracelets there as well?"

"Two of silver, one of black glass. They're with the robe. You will find them. They are still wrapped as you want them to be."

"I am pleased to hear it. That is to your advantage."

De la Sept-Nuit shook his head. "You know what reward I would most enjoy." He waved a languid hand toward Madelaine, whom Jueneport had finished binding to the heavy screen. She was naked, and bruises were beginning to show on her flesh.

"Perhaps. With Tite dead, perhaps." He strolled away to put on his robes.

When he returned, the rest of the Circle had arrived and were concluding the preparations for the first ceremony. Châteaurose was now a little the worse for drink, but he knew the motions well enough that he would complete them without hazard.

"Have the sacrifices wakened yet?" Saint Sebastien asked as he came down the aisle toward the altar. He was gorgeous now in the heavy red silk which hung open showing his lean, hard body that had been only lightly touched by age. Gone was the polish that marked his public dealings, and in its place was a terrible mastery, made even stronger by the signs of office he wore around his neck, the sign of the pentagram and the obscene crucifix.

"Not yet, though the woman is stirring."

"They must be awake in twenty minutes. See to it that they are." He turned away and ignored the efforts of his Circle to force Madelaine and her father to be roused.

Beauvrai strode over to Saint Sebastien. "Well, Clotaire, how is your revenge?" Out of his ridiculous court finery, he was no longer the foppish fool he often appeared to be. In the black-silk robe none of his absurdity remained, and only the malice in him shone at full force, no longer hampered by his outward trappings.

"I have not tasted it yet. But soon. Soon."

"What for Robert? Have you thought of it?"

"Of course." He fingered the two medallions that hung halfway down his chest. "It will please you, mon Baron."

"I hope so." He turned aside, saying under his breath, "That nephew of mine is rather an ass, Clotaire."

"He seemed so to me as well," Saint Sebastien agreed at his most silky. "One would think he was too foolish to live."

"My point precisely." He bowed to Saint Sebastien and walked off to take his place in the first rank of worshipers.

At last Achille Cressie thought to bring two pails of water, and these he threw over Madelaine and Robert de Montalia. He was satisfied as he heard the woman stutter and her father gag. "I think we are ready," he said, very satisfied.

"That is good. We are very near the hour." Saint Sebastien came forward and plucked painfully at Madelaine's breasts and her cheeks. This brought a quick cry in response, and Saint Sebastien was reassured. "Yes, my dear," he said softly, caressingly, "it is I. You have not fled me."

Madelaine half-opened her violet eyes, and felt herself turn an icy cold that had little to do with the water that had drenched her. "Saint-Germain," she whispered in her desperation.

Saint Sebastien achieved a magnificent sneer. "So you long for that hoaxing fop, do you?" He reached out and slapped her face. "It is not that impostor who has you now." He turned away from the fury in her face and walked to the altar.

"He is awake," Achille told Saint Sebastien. "You have only to touch him to see the disgust in his face." He demonstrated this in superb imitation of Saint Sebastien's grand and evil manner.

"You have done well, Achille. I may let you enjoy yourself again before we dispatch Robert." He put one insolent hand on Robert's cold flesh. "How sad, my friend, that I cannot offer you a blanket. But you have my promise that I will see that you are warmed in other ways. You know that I always keep my promises."

Robert, whose jaw had tightened steadily through this new indignity, spat once, most accurately, at Saint Sebastien, then forced himself once again to stoic silence.

"You will make it worse for yourself, Robert." Saint Sebastien stood back, then lifted his arms and called out to the members of the Circle, who waited, robed and silent, before him. "We are met in the name of Satan, that we may grow in his power and his great strength, which is the strength of the great lie. We meet that we may join him in power, be with him in potency and in savagery, and to that end we bring him sacrifices."

"We bring him sacrifices," the Circle chanted.

"Lives, paid in blood, in degradation."

"In blood and degradation."

Madelaine, her arms aching from the bonds that held her to the screen, her body already hurt from the cruelty of the men gathered in the debauched chapel, felt herself sway in her bonds, almost overcome with fear and wretchedness. And she knew that for her the heinous men had not even begun to do what they were capable of doing. She remembered that there would be forty days for her destruction. She told herself in the back of her thoughts that they could not succeed, that she would be missed, and her father, that someone would find her, save her. Again she felt her soul reach out for Saint-Germain, filled with her yearning for him as much as with her panic-stricken desire for escape. But she did not know if she could dare to hope, not with the chanting growing louder.

"This forsworn one, your betrayer, Satan!"

"Your betrayer!"

"Brought back again to make expiation for his duplicity." Saint Sebastien held aloft a curiously curved dagger, letting the blade flash in the quivering torchlight.

"Your betrayer!"

Saint Sebastien put the point of the dagger against Robert de Montalia's chest, and with concentrated precision he cut the pentagram into his skin. "He is marked as yours, Satan!"

"Marked!" This triumphant shout covered the groans that Robert could not hold back.

"For your strength is not to be spurned, and your power is not mocked!"

"Power and strength are yours alone!"

Madelaine shook her head, as if the very motion would shut out the sounds that assaulted her. She could not look at her father as he steeled himself against further outrage, and she would not look at Saint Sebastien. The chanting got louder.

"Let him taste of your wrath!"

"Let him taste of your wrath!" came the shout from the Circle as Saint Sebastien brought the blade swiftly down and held up Robert's ear as a gory trophy. A great cry from the Circle combined with Robert de Montalia's scream, and the noise continued rising like a wave as Saint Sebastien put the ear to his mouth and licked it. The Circle surged forward, hysteria pulling them toward the ghastly spectacle. Saint Sebastien motioned for silence, the dagger held high as he waited.

His dramatic effect was quite destroyed when a voice spoke from the rear of the chapel, a voice that was beautifully modulated, and tinged with a slight Piedmontese accent. "I am glad I am in time, gentlemen," said le Comte de Saint-Germain.

Relief, more weakening than her terror had been, filled Madelaine, turning her very bones to water. The tears she had held back welled in her eyes, and a pang sharp as Saint Sebastien's knife lodged itself in her breast.

The members of the Circle turned, each member's face showing that dazed stupidity that often comes with being wakened from a sound sleep. Their movements were jerky, and the momentum of their ferocity faltered.

Saint-Germain came down the aisle toward the terrible altar. All of the elegant frippery of manner had vanished with his splendid clothes. Now his movements suited the tight riding coat of black leather worn over tight woolen breeches that were also black. His high boots were wide-cuffed, and the simple shirt under the coat was adorned with Russian embroidery showing a pattern of steppe wildflowers known as tulips. He carried no sword or other weapon, and was alone.

Saint Sebastien watched him, wrath showing in his narrowed eyes and malicious smile. He nodded, motioning his Circle to keep back. "*Ragoczy*," he said. "I did not believe. I did not recognize . . ."

Saint-Germain inclined his head. "I have told you before that appearances are deceiving."

"But that was thirty years ago." He moved closer, the dagger held tightly in his hand.

"Was it? I will take your word for it." If he knew that he was in danger, nothing but the hot stare of his eyes suggested it.

"Your father, then?" Saint Sebastien closed in on Saint-Germain, almost near enough to strike.

"I was not aware that I had changed so much in that time." He had taken in the chapel and its uses when he entered it, and now he was prepared to deal with Saint Sebastien on his own ground. He touched the small locketlike receptacle that hung on a chain around his neck.

Saint Sebastien had already raised his dagger, and was about to make a sudden rush, when Saint-Germain's arm shot out, seized Saint Sebastien's shoulder, not to hold him back, but to pull him forward, sending him hurtling past Saint-Germain to crash into the stack of ruined pews at the back of the chapel.

Saint-Germain glanced toward Saint Sebastien, then directed his penetrating eyes to the members of the Circle who stood around the altar. "How absurd you are," he said lightly. "You should see yourselves standing there in your fine robes, with your manhood, if you can call it that, peeking out at the world like so many birds." He waited for the hostile words to stop. "You are foolish. Do you think that you will enhance your place in the world, obtain power and position, by following Saint Sebastien's orders? It is *his* position and power that your profane offices enhance. It is *his* desires that are met. And you, thinking that you get these things for yourselves, give yourself to him without question. If I were the one you worship, I would think poorly of your practices."

Beauvrai was the first to object. "You think we're stupid, you, who came here with nothing to protect you. . . ."

Saint-Germain held up the locket on the chain. "I beg your pardon, Baron. I have this. You are not so far removed from the faith you were born to that you cannot recognize a pyx."

The Circle, which had been growing restless, now became hushed again.

"You are asking yourselves if this is genuine." He held the pyx higher. "You may try to touch it if you like. I understand the burns are instantaneous." He waited, while the silk-robed men held back. "I see."

A sudden noise behind him made him turn, and in that moment he cursed himself for not being sure that Saint Sebastien was unconscious, for now the leader of the Circle was rushing toward Madelaine, and although he no longer carried a dagger, there was a wickedly broken piece of planking in his hands, and this he held ready to strike.

At that moment, the hush, the almost somnambulistic trance that had held the Circle members to their clumsiness and to Saint-Germain's control, ruptured with the explosiveness of a Dutch dyke bursting to let in the sea. With an awful shout, the men in the silken robes flung themselves at Saint-Germain.

Excerpt from a note written by l'Abbé Ponteneuf to his cousin, le Comtesse d'Argenlac, dated November 5, 1743:

. . . From my heart of hearts I pray God that He will comfort you and open your eyes to the glory that awaits all good Christians beyond the grave and the shadow of death. It is my duty to write this letter to you, my poor cousin, but even now my pen falters and I cannot find it in me to tell you what has befallen. I beseech you to marshal your heart to greet this terrible news with true fortitude, for all of us who know and love you cannot but wish that you would never have to endure the ordeal that is now before you.

It was rather less than an hour ago when a coach called for me, to take me to a church on the outskirts of the city. You may imagine my surprise at this unlikely request, for it is not usual to have such a request forthcoming at so late an hour. But I have not been a priest for twenty years without learning to accept what God sends me without complaint. So it was that I went in the coach to the church to which I have already alluded. We arrived in good time, and I was immediately ushered into the sanctuary, where an awesome sight met my eyes. There, laid out before me, were the bodies of three men. One was a mountebank, from the look of him, and I did not know anything of him. Another was one of Saint Sebastien's servants, whom I recognized by the livery. Saint Sebastien is such an unrepentant sinner of all the Deadly Sins that I did not know the man himself, but his master is not likely to have set his feet on a path toward Our Lord and His Sweet Mother.

It is the third man I must speak of, and it stops my heart to say this. The third man was le Comte d'Argenlac, your own beloved husband, whom you have loved so tenderly, and who has always been your staunch protector. It is further my most unpleasant duty to inform you that he did not die by accident or an act of God. He was, my unfortunate cousin, cold-bloodedly slain by a person or persons unknown.

The curé at this church has given me the use of his study that I might send you news immediately. His understanding is not great, but he is a good man, and I have told him that le Comte is known to me, and that it is only appropriate that you, as my cousin, should hear of this tragedy from one who has the knowledge of your particular circumstances.

Do not let yourself be overwhelmed. Pray to Mary for the saving of your husband's soul. You will find that such religious exercise does much to alleviate your grief, which must surely consume you otherwise. I have often remarked that when God made Woman as helpmeet to Man, He made her prey to whims and weaknesses that her mate does not know. The excellent solace of Scripture will help you to control those emotions which must fill your breast as you read this. . . .

I will take it upon myself to see that le Comte's body is removed to his parish church immediately, and that such notice as must be given of his death be delivered to the proper authorities. If you are not too incapacitated by this terrible event, perhaps, you will allow me to visit you and read with you the Great Words that will assuage your sorrow.

In the name of God, Who even now welcomes your beloved husband to the Glories of Paradise, I am always

Your obedient cousin,
L'Abbé Ponteneuf, S.J.

ANNE RICE
(b. 1941)

Born Howard Allen O'Brien, Anne Rice was raised in New Orleans and later attended San Francisco State University. A prolific writer, she works in more than one genre and under more than one name; she writes as Anne Rampling for her mainstream fiction, and as A. N. Rocquelaire for her works of sadomasochistic pornography. However, she is best known for the Vampire Chronicles, written under her own name. The first volume in this series, Interview with the Vampire *(1976), was heralded as bringing a new direction in vampire fiction, and established her as the foremost, and the most ambitious, writer on vampire themes in the world. In this series, which also includes* The Vampire Lestat *(1985),* The Queen of the Damned *(1988),* The Tale of the Body Thief *(1992), and* Memnoch the Devil *(1995), she has created an epic genealogy of the vampire gods and shown them living among us as a superbly beautiful, mostly immortal, endlessly youthful and good-looking race. Their lovemaking has proved titillating to readers, perhaps speaking to the psychological hungers of people sidelined from contemporary culture.*

Another fascinating element in Rice's work, and one exploited by Bram Stoker in Dracula, *is the way in which the deadly amorous adventures of her characters are occasionally framed by religious discourse, imparting a glow of high seriousness to her novels.*

As with Stoker's Dracula, *the vampire of this short story—who is the master referred to in the title—remains a mysterious figure, visible only to Julie, the story's protagonist. The alluring power of a house also plays a role, as Julie becomes entranced with the Rampling estate, defying her father's dying wish that the place be torn down.*

THE MASTER OF RAMPLING GATE

Rampling Gate: It was so real to us in those old pictures, rising like a fairytale castle out of its own dark wood. A wilderness of gables and chimneys between those two immense towers, grey stone walls mantled in ivy, mullioned windows reflecting the drifting clouds.

But why had Father never gone there? Why had he never taken us? And why on his deathbed, in those grim months after Mother's passing, did he tell my brother, Richard, that Rampling Gate must be torn down stone by stone? Rampling Gate that had always belonged to Ramplings, Rampling Gate which had stood for over four hundred years.

We were in awe of the task that lay before us, and painfully confused. Richard had just finished four years at Oxford. Two whirlwind social seasons in London had proven me something of a shy success. I still preferred scribbling poems and stories in the quiet of my room to dancing the night away, but I'd kept that a good secret, and though we were not spoilt children, we had enjoyed the best of everything our parents could give. But now the carefree years were ended. We had to be careful and wise.

And our hearts ached as, sitting together in Father's booklined study, we looked at the old pictures of Rampling Gate before the small coal fire. "Destroy it, Richard, as soon as I am gone," Father had said.

"I just don't understand it, Julie," Richard confessed, as he filled the little crystal glass in my hand with sherry. "It's the genuine article, that old place, a real fourteenth-century manor house in excellent repair. A Mrs. Blessington, born and reared in the village of Rampling, has apparently managed it all these years. She was there when Uncle Baxter died, and he was last Rampling to live under that roof."

"Do you remember," I asked, "the year that Father took all these pictures down and put them away?"

"I shall never forget that!" Richard said. "How could I? It was so peculiar, and so unlike Father, too." He sat back, drawing slowly on his pipe. "There had been that bizarre incident in Victoria Station, when he had seen that young man."

"Yes, exactly," I said, snuggling back into the velvet chair and looking into the tiny dancing flames in the grate. "You remember how upset Father was?"

Yet it was simple incident. In fact nothing really happened at all. We couldn't have been more than six and eight at the time and we had gone to the station with Father to say farewell to friends. Through the window of a train Father saw a young man who startled and upset him. I could remember the face clearly to this day. Remarkably handsome, with a narrow nose and well drawn eyebrows, and a mop of lustrous brown hair. The large black eyes had regarded Father with the saddest expression as Father had drawn us back and hurried us away.

"And the argument that night, between Father and Mother," Richard said thoughtfully. "I remember that we listened on the landing and we were so afraid."

"And Father said *he* wasn't content to be master of Rampling Gate anymore; *he* had come to London and revealed himself. An unspeakable horror, that is what he called it, that *he* should be so bold."

"Yes, exactly, and when Mother tried to quiet him, when she suggested that he was imagining things, he went into a perfect rage."

"But who could it have been, the master of Rampling Gate, if Father wasn't the master? Uncle Baxter was long dead by then."

"I just don't know what to make of it," Richard murmured. "And there's nothing in Father's papers to explain any of it at all." He examined the most recent of the pictures, a lovely tinted engraving that showed the house perfectly reflected in the azure water of its lake. "But I tell you, the worst part of it, Julie," he said shaking his head, "is that we've never even seen the house ourselves."

I glanced at him and our eyes met in a moment of confusion that quickly passed to something else. I leant forward:

"He did not say we couldn't go there, did he, Richard?" I demanded. "That we couldn't visit the house before it was destroyed."

"No, of course he didn't!" Richard said. The smile broke over his face easily. "After all, don't we owe it to the others, Julie? Uncle Baxter who spent the last of his fortune restoring the house, even this old Mrs. Blessington that has kept it all these years?"

"And what about the village itself?" I added quickly. "What will it mean to these people to see Rampling Gate destroyed? Of course we must go and see the place ourselves."

"Then it's settled. I'll write to Mrs. Blessington immediately. I'll tell her we're coming and that we can not say how long we will stay."

"Oh, Richard, that would be too marvelous!" I couldn't keep from hugging him, though it flustered him and he pulled on his pipe just exactly the way Father would have done. "Make it at least a fortnight," I said. "I want so to know the place, especially if . . ."

But it was too sad to think of Father's admonition. And much more fun to think of the journey itself. I'd pack my manuscripts, for who knew, maybe in that melancholy and exquisite setting I'd find exactly the inspiration I required. It was almost a wicked exhilaration I felt, breaking the gloom that had hung over us since the day that Father was laid to rest.

"It is the right thing to do, isn't it, Richard?" I asked uncertainly, a little disconcerted by how much I wanted to go. There was some illicit pleasure in it, going to Rampling Gate at last.

" 'Unspeakable horror,' " I repeated Father's words with a little grimace. What did it all mean? I thought again of the strange, almost exquisite young man I'd glimpsed in that railway carriage, gazing at us all with that wistful expression on his lean face. He had worn a black greatcoat with a red woollen cravat, and I could remember how pale he had been against that dash of red. Like bone china his complexion had been. Strange to remember it so vividly, even to the tilt of his head, and that long luxuriant brown hair. But he had been a blaze against that window. And I realized now that, in those few remarkable moments, he had created for me an ideal of masculine beauty which I had never questioned since. But Father had been so angry in those moments . . . I felt an unmistakable pang of guilt.

"Of course it's the right thing, Julie," Richard answered. He at the desk, already writing the letters, and I was at a loss to understand the full measure of my thoughts.

It was late afternoon when the wretched old trap carried us up the gentle slope from the little railway station, and we had at last our first real look at that magnificent house. I think I was holding my breath. The sky had paled to a deep rose hue beyond a bank of softly gilded clouds, and the last rays of the sun struck the uppermost panes of the leaded windows and filled them with solid gold.

"Oh, but it's too majestic," I whispered, "too like a great cathedral, and to think that it belongs to us." Richard gave me the smallest kiss on the cheek. I felt mad suddenly and eager somehow to be laid waste by it, through fear or enchantment I could not say, perhaps a sublime mingling of both.

I wanted with all my heart to jump down and draw near on foot, letting those towers grow larger and larger above me, but our old horse had picked up speed. And the little line of stiff starched servants had broken to come forward, the old withered housekeeper with her arms out, the men to take down the boxes and the trunks.

Richard and I were spirited into the great hall by the tiny, nimble figure of Mrs. Blessington, our footfalls echoing loudly on the marble tile, our eyes dazzled by the dusty shafts of light that fell on the long oak table and its heavily carved chairs, the sombre, heavy tapestries that stirred ever so slightly against the soaring walls.

"It is an enchanted place," I cried, unable to contain myself. Oh, Richard, we are home!" Mrs. Blessington laughed gaily, her dry hand closing tightly on mine.

Her small blue eyes regarded me with the most curiously vacant expression despite her smile. "Ramplings at Rampling Gate again, I can not tell you what a joyful day this is for me. And yes, my dear," she said as if

reading my mind that very second, "I am and have been for many years, quite blind. But if you spy a thing out of place in this house, you're to tell me at once, for it would be the exception, I assure you, and not the rule." And such warmth emanated from her wrinkled little face that I adored her at once.

We found our bedchambers, the very finest in the house, well aired with snow white linen and fires blazing cozily to dry out the damp that never left the thick walls. The small diamond pane windows opened on a glorious view of the water and the oaks that enclosed it and the few scattered lights that marked the village beyond.

That night, we laughed like children as we supped at the great oak table, our candles giving only a feeble light. And afterwards, it was a fierce battle of pocket billiards in the game room which had been Uncle Baxter's last renovation, and a little too much brandy, I fear.

It was just before I went to bed that I asked Mrs. Blessington if there had been anyone in this house since Uncle Baxter died. That had been the year 1838, almost fifty years ago, and she was already housekeeper then.

"No, my dear," she said quickly, fluffing the feather pillows. "Your father came that year as you know, but he stayed for no more than a month or two and then went on home."

"There was never a young man after that . . ." I pushed, but in truth I had little appetite for anything to disturb the happiness I felt. How I loved the Spartan cleanliness of this bedchamber, the stone walls bare of paper or ornament, the high luster of the walnut-paneled bed.

"A young man?" She gave an easy, almost hearty laugh as with unerring certainty of her surroundings, she lifted the poker and stirred the fire. "What a strange thing for you to ask."

I sat silent for a moment looking in the mirror, as I took the last of the pins from my hair. It fell down heavy and warm around my shoulders. It felt good, like a cloak under which I could hide. But she turned as if sensing some uneasiness in me, and drew near.

"Why do you say a young man, Miss?" she asked. Slowly, tentatively, her fingers examined the long tresses that lay over my shoulders. She took the brush from my hands.

I felt perfectly foolish telling her the story, but I managed a simplified version, somehow, our meeting unexpectedly a devilishly handsome young man whom my Father in anger had later called the master of Rampling Gate.

"Handsome, was he?" she asked as she brushed out the tangles in my hair gently. It seemed she hung upon every word as I described him again.

"There were no intruders in this house, then, Mrs. Blessington?" I asked. "No mysteries to be solved . . ."

She gave the sweetest laugh.

"Oh, no, darling, this house is the safest place in the world," she said quickly. "It is a happy house. No intruder would dare to trouble Rampling Gate!"

Nothing, in fact, troubled the serenity of the days that followed. The smoke and noise of London, and our Father's dying words, became a dream. What was real were our long walks together through the overgrown gardens, our trips in the little skiff to and fro across the lake. We had tea under the hot glass of the empty conservatory. And early evening found us on our way upstairs with the best of the books from Uncle Baxter's library to read by candlelight in the privacy of our rooms.

And all our discreet inquiries in the village met with more or less the same reply: the villagers loved the house and carried no old or disquieting tales. Repeatedly, in fact, we were told that Rampling was the most contented hamlet in all England, that no one dared—Mrs. Blessington's very words—to make trouble here.

"It's our guardian angel, that old house," said the old woman at the bookshop where Richard stopped for the London papers. "Was there ever the town of Rampling without the house called Rampling Gate?"

How were we going to tell them of Father's edict? How were we going to remind ourselves? But we spoke not one word about the proposed disaster, and Richard wrote to his firm to say that we should not be back in London till Fall.

He was finding a wealth of classical material in the old volumes that had belonged to Uncle Baxter, and I had set up my writing in the little study that opened off the library which I had all to myself.

Never had I known such peace and quiet. It seemed the atmosphere of Rampling Gate permeated my simplest written descriptions and wove its way richly into the plots and characters I created. The Monday after our arrival I had finished my first short story and went off to the village on foot to boldly post it to editors of *Blackwood's Magazine*.

It was glorious morning, and I took my time as I came back on foot.

What had disturbed our father so about this lovely corner of England, I wondered? What had so darkened his last hours that he laid upon this spot his curse?

My heart opened to this unearthly stillness, to an undeniable grandeur that caused me utterly to forget myself. There were times here when I felt I was a disembodied intellect drifting through a fathomless silence, up and down garden paths and stone corridors that had witnessed too much to take cognizance of one small and fragile young woman who in random moments actually talked aloud to the suits of armour around her, to the broken statues in the garden, the fountain cherubs who had had not water to pour from their conches for years and years.

But was there in this loveliness some malignant force that was eluding us still, some untold story to explain all? Unspeakable horror . . . In my mind's eye I saw that young man, and the strangest sensation crept over me, that some enrichment of the picture had taken place in my memory or imagination in the recent past. Perhaps in dream I had re-invented him, given a ruddy glow to his lips and his cheeks. Perhaps in my re-creation for Mrs. Blessington, I had allowed him to raise his hand to that red cravat and had seen the fingers long and delicate and suggestive of a musician's hand.

It was all very much on my mind when I entered the house again, soundlessly, and saw Richard in his favorite leather wing chair by the fire.

The air was warm coming through the open garden doors, and yet the blaze was cheerful, made the vast room with its towering shelves of leatherbound volumes appear inviting and almost small.

"Sit down," Richard said gravely, scarcely giving me a glance. "I want to read you something right now." He held a long narrow ledger in his hands. "This was Uncle Baxter's," he said, "and at first I thought it was only an account book he kept during the renovations, but I've found some actual diary entries made in the last weeks of his life. They're hasty, almost indecipherable, but I've managed to make them out."

"Well, do read them to me," I said, but I felt a little tug of fear. I didn't want to know anything terrible about this place. If we could have remained here forever . . . but that was out of the question, to be sure.

"Now listen to this," Richard said, turning the page carefully. " 'Fifth of May, 1838: He is here, I am sure of it. He is come back again.' And several days later: 'He thinks this is his house, he does, and he would drink my wine and smoke my cigars if only he could. He reads my books and my papers and I will not stand for it. I have given orders that everything is to be locked.' And finally, the last entry written the morning before he died: 'Weary, weary, unto death and he is no small cause of my weariness. Last night I beheld him with my own eyes. He stood in this very room. He moves and speaks exactly as a mortal man, and dares tell me his secrets, and he a demon wretch with the face of a seraph and I a mere mortal, how am I to bear with him!' "

"Good Lord," I whispered slowly. I rose from the chair where I had settled, and standing behind him, read the page for myself. It was the scrawl, the writing, the very last notation in the book. I knew that Uncle Baxter's heart had given out. He had not died by violence, but peacefully enough in this very room with his prayer book in his hand.

"Could it be the very same person Father spoke of that night?" Richard asked.

In spite of the sun pouring through the open doors, I experienced a violent chill. For the first time I felt wary of this house, wary of our boldness in coming here, heedful of our Father's words.

"But that was years before, Richard . . ." I said. "And what could this mean, this talk of a supernatural being! Surely the man was mad! It was no spirit I saw in that railway carriage!"

I sank down into the chair opposite and tried to quiet the beating of my heart.

"Julie," Richard said gently, shutting the ledger. "Mrs. Blessington has lived here contentedly for years. There are six servants asleep every night in the north wing. Surely there is nothing to all of this."

"It isn't very much fun, though, is it?" I said timidly, "not at all like swapping ghost stories the way we used to do, and peopling the dark with imaginary beings, and laughing at friends at school who were afraid."

"All my life," he said, his eyes fixing me steadily, "I've heard tales of spooks and spirits, some imagined, some supposedly true, and almost invariably there is some mention of the house in question feeling haunted, of having an atmosphere to it that fills one with foreboding, some sense of menace or alarm . . ."

"Yes, I know, and there is no such poisonous atmosphere here at all."

"On the contrary, I've never been more at ease in my life." He shoved his hand into his pocket to extract the inevitable match to light his pipe which had gone out. "As a matter of fact, Julie, I don't know how in the world I'm going to comply with Father's last wish to tear down this place."

I nodded sympathetically. The very same thing had been on my mind since we'd arrived. Even now, I felt so comfortable, natural, quite safe.

I was wishing suddenly, irrationally, that he had not found the entries in Uncle Baxter's book.

"I should talk to Mrs. Blessington again!" I said almost crossly, "I mean quite seriously . . ."

"But I have, Julie," he said. "I asked her about it all this morning when I first made the discovery, and she only laughed. She swears she's never seen anything unusual here, and that there's no one left alive in the village who can tell tales of this place. She said again how glad she was that we'd come home to Rampling Gate. I don't think she has an inkling we mean to destroy the house. Oh, it would destroy her heart if she did."

"Never seen anything unusual?" I asked. "That is what she said? But what strange words for her to use, Richard, when she can not see at all."

But he had not heard me. He had laid the ledger aside and risen slowly, almost sluggishly, and he was wandering out of the double doors into the little garden and was looking over the high hedge at the oaks that bent their heavy elbowed limbs almost to the surface of the lake. There wasn't a sound at this early hour of the day, save the soft rustle of the leaves in the morning air, the cry now and then of a distant bird.

"Maybe it's gone, Julie," Richard said, over his shoulder, his voice carrying clearly in the quiet, "if it was ever here. Maybe there is nothing any longer to frighten anyone at all. You don't suppose you could endure the winter in this house, do you? I suppose you'd want to be in London again by then." He seemed quite small against the towering trees, the sky broken into small gleaming fragments by the canopy of foliage that gently filtered the light.

Rampling Gate had him. And I understood perfectly, because it also had me. I could very well endure the winter here, no matter how bleak or cold. I never wanted to go home.

And the immediacy of the mystery only dimmed my sense of everything and every place else.

After a long moment, I rose and went out into the garden, and placed my hand gently on Richard's arm.

"I know this much, Julie," he said just as if we had been talking to each other all the while. "I swore to Father that I would do as he asked, and it is tearing me apart. Either way, it will be on my conscience for ever, obliterating this house or going against my own father and the charge he laid down to me with his dying breath."

"We must seek help, Richard. The advice of our lawyers, the advice of Father's clergymen. You must write to them and explain the whole thing. Father was feverish when he gave the order. If we could lay it out before them, they would help us decide."

It was three o'clock when I opened my eyes. But I had been awake for a long time. I had heard the dim chimes of the clock below hour by hour. And I felt not fear lying here alone in the dark but something else. Some vague and relentless agitation, some sense of emptiness and need that caused me finally to rise from my bed. What was required to dissolve this tension, I wondered. I stared at the simplest things in the shadows. The little arras that hung over the fireplace with its slim princes and princesses lost in fading fiber and thread. The portrait of an Elizabethan ancestor gazing with one almond-shaped eye from his small frame.

What was this house, really? Merely a place or a state of mind? What was it doing to my soul? Why didn't the entries in Uncle Baxter's book send us flying back to London? Why had we stayed so late in the great hall together after supper, speaking not a single word?

I felt overwhelmed suddenly, and yet shut out of some great and dazzling secret, and wasn't that the very word that Uncle Baxter had used?

Conscious only of an unbearable restlessness, I pulled on my woollen wrapper, buttoning the lace collar and tying the sash. And putting on my slippers, I went out into the hall.

The moon fell full on the oak stairway, and on the deeply recessed door to Richard's room. On tiptoe I approached and, peering in, saw the bed was empty, the covers completely undisturbed

So he was off on his own tonight the same as I. Oh, if only he had come to me, asked me to go with him.

I turned and made my way soundlessly down the long stairs.

The great hall gaped like a cavern before me, the moonlight here and there touching upon a pair of crossed swords, or a mounted shield. But far beyond the great hall, in the alcove just outside the library, I saw unmistakably a flickering light. And a breeze moved briskly through the room, carrying with it the sound and the scent of a wood fire.

I shuddered with relief. Richard was there. We could talk. Or perhaps we could go exploring together, guarding our fragile candle flames behind cupped fingers as we went from room to room? A sense of well-being pervaded me and quieted me, and yet the dark distance between us seemed endless, and I was desperate to cross it, hurrying suddenly past the long supper table with its massive candlesticks, and finally into the alcove before the library doors.

Yes, Richard was there. He sat with his eyes closed, dozing against the inside of the leather wing chair, the breeze from the garden blowing the fragile flames of the candles on the stone mantel and on the table at his side.

I was about to go to him, about to shut the doors, and kiss him gently and ask did he not want to go up to bed, when quite abruptly I saw in the corner of my eye that there was some one else in the room.

In the far left corner at the desk stood another figure, looking down at the clutter of Richard's papers, his pale hands resting on the wood.

I knew that it could not be so. I knew that I must be dreaming, that nothing in this room, least of all this figure, could be real. For it was the same young man I had seen fifteen years ago in the railway carriage and not a single aspect of that taut young face had been changed. There was the very same hair, thick and lustrous and only carelessly combed as it hung to the thick collar of his black coat, and the skin so pale it was almost luminous in the shadows, and those dark eyes looking up suddenly and fixing me with the most curious expression as I almost screamed.

We stared at one another across the dark vista of that room, I stranded in the doorway, he visibly and undeniably shaken that I had caught him unawares. My heart stopped.

And in a split second he moved towards me, closed the gap between us, towering over me, those slender white fingers gently closing on my arms.

"Julie!" he whispered, in a voice so low it seemed my own thoughts speaking to me. But this was no dream. He was real. He was holding to me and the scream had broken loose from me, deafening, uncontrollable and echoing from the four walls.

I saw Richard rising from the chair. I was alone. Clutching to the door frame, I staggered forward, and then again in a moment of perfect clarity I saw the young intruder, saw him standing in the garden, looking back over his shoulder, and then he was gone.

I could not stop screaming. I could not stop even as Richard held me and pleaded with me, and sat me down in the chair.

And I was still crying when Mrs. Blessington finally came.

She got a glass of cordial for me at once, as Richard begged me once more to tell what I had seen.

"But you know who it was!" I said to Richard almost hysterically. "It was he, the young man from the train. Only he wore a frockcoat years out of fashion and his silk tie was open at his throat. Richard, he was reading your papers, turning them over, reading them in the pitch dark."

"All right," Richard said, gesturing with his hand up for calm. "He was standing at the desk. And there was no light there so you could not see him well."

"Richard, it was he! Don't you understand? He touched me, he held my arms." I looked imploringly to Mrs. Blessington who was shaking her head, her little eyes like blue beads in the light. "He called me Julie," I whispered. "He knows my name!"

I rose, snatching up the candle, and all but pushing Richard out of the way went to the desk. "Oh, dear God," I said, "Don't you see what's happened? It's your letters to Dr. Partridge, and Mrs. Sellers, about tearing down the house!"

Mrs. Blessington gave a little cry and put her hand to her cheek. She looked like a withered child in her nightcap as she collapsed into the straight-backed chair by the door.

"Surely you don't believe it was the same man, Julie, after all these years . . ."

"But he had not changed, Richard, not in the smallest detail. There is no mistake, Richard, it was he, I tell you, the very same."

"Oh, dear, dear . . ." Mrs. Blessington whispered, "What will he do if you try to tear it down? What will he do now?"

"What will who do?" Richard asked carefully, narrowing his eyes. He took the candle from me and approached her. I was staring at her, only half realizing what I had heard.

"So you know who he is!" I whispered.

"Julie, stop it!" Richard said.

But her face had tightened, gone blank and her eyes had become distant and small.

"You knew he was here!" I insisted. "You must tell us at once!"

With an effort she climbed to her feet. "There is nothing in this house to hurt *you*," she said, "nor any of us." She turned, spurning Richard as he tried to help her, and wandered into the dark hallway alone. "You've no need of me here any longer," she said softly, "and if you should tear down this house built by your forefathers, then you should do it without need of me."

"Oh, but we don't mean to do it, Mrs. Blessington!" I insisted. But she was making her way through the gallery back towards the north wing. "Go after her, Richard. You heard what she said. She knows who he is."

"I've had quite enough of this tonight," Richard said almost angrily. "Both of us should go up to bed. By the light of day we will dissect this entire matter and search this house. Now come."

"But he should be told, shouldn't he?" I demanded.

"Told what? Of whom do you speak!"

"Told that we will not tear down this house!" I said clearly, loudly, listening to the echo of my own voice.

The next day was indeed the most trying since we had come. It took the better part of the morning to convince Mrs. Blessington that we had no intention of tearing down Rampling Gate. Richard posted his letters and resolved that we should do nothing until help came.

And together we commenced a search of the house. But darkness found us only half finished, having covered the south tower and the south wing, and the main portion of house itself. There remained still the north tower, in a dreadful state of disrepair, and some rooms beneath the ground which in former times might have served as dungeons and were now sealed off. And there were closets and private stairways everywhere that we had scarce looked into, and at times we lost all track of where precisely we had been.

But it was also quite clear by supper time that Richard was in a state of strain and exasperation, and that he did not believe that I had seen anyone in the study at all.

He was further convinced that Uncle Baxter had been mad before he died, or else his ravings were a code for some mundane happening that had him extraordinarily overwrought.

But I knew what I had seen. And as the day progressed, I became ever more quiet and withdrawn. A silence had fallen between me and Mrs. Blessington. And I understood only too well the anger I'd heard in my father's voice on that long ago night when we had come home from Victoria Station and my mother had accused him of imagining things.

Yet what obsessed me more than anything else was the gentle countenance of the mysterious man I had glimpsed, the dark almost innocent eyes that had fixed on me for one moment before I had screamed.

"Strange that Mrs. Blessington is not afraid of him," I said in a low distracted voice, not longer caring if Richard heard me. "And that no one here seems in fear of him at all . . ." The strangest fancies were coming to me. The careless words of the villagers were running through my head. "You would be wise to do one very important thing before you retire," I said. "Leave out in writing a note to the effect that you do not intend to tear down the house."

"Julie, you have created an impossible dilemma," Richard demanded. "You insist we reassure this apparition that the house will not be destroyed, when in fact you verify the existence of the very creature that drove our father to say what he did."

"Oh, I wish I had never come here!" I burst out suddenly.

"Then we should go, both of us, and decide this matter at home."

"No, that's just it. I could never go without knowing . . . 'his secrets' . . . 'the demon wretch.' I could never go on living without knowing now!"

Anger must be an excellent antidote to fear, for surely something worked to alleviate my natural alarm. I did not undress that night, nor even take off my shoes, but rather sat in that dark hollow bedroom gazing at the small square of diamond-paned window until I heard all of the house fall quiet. Richard's door at last closed. There came those distant echoing booms that meant other bolts had been put in place.

And when the grandfather clock in the great hall chimed the hour of eleven, Rampling Gate was as usual fast asleep.

I listened for my brother's step in the hall. And when I did not hear him stir from his room, I wondered at it, that curiosity would not impel him to come to me, to say that we must go together to discover the truth.

It was just as well. I did not want him to be with me. And I felt a dark exultation as I imagined myself going out of the room and down the stairs as I had the night before. I should wait one more hour, however, to be certain. I should let the night reach its pitch. Twelve, the witching hour. My heart was beating too fast at the thought of it, and dreamily I recollected the face I had seen, the voice that had said my name.

Ah, why did it seem in retrospect so intimate, that we had known each other, spoken together, that it was someone I recognized in the pit of my soul?

"What is your name?" I believe I whispered aloud. And then a spasm of fear startled me. Would I have the courage to go in search of him, to open the door to him? Was I losing my mind? Closing my eyes, I rested my head against the high back of the damask chair.

What was more empty than this rural night? What was more sweet?

I opened my eyes. I had been half dreaming or talking to myself, trying to explain to Father why it was necessary that we comprehend the reason ourselves. And I realized, quite fully realized—I think before I was even awake—that *he* was standing by the bed.

The door was open. And he was standing there, dressed exactly as he had been the night before, and his dark eyes were riveted on me with that same obvious curiosity, his mouth just a little slack like that of a school boy, and he was holding to the bedpost almost idly with his right hand. Why, he was lost in contemplating me. He did not seem to know that I was looking at him.

But when I sat forward, he raised his finger as if to quiet me, and gave a little nod of his head.

"Ah, it is you!" I whispered.

"Yes," he said in the softest, most unobtrusive voice.

But we had been talking to each other, hadn't we, I had been asking him questions, no, telling him things. And I felt suddenly I was losing my equilibrium or slipping back into a dream.

No. Rather I had all but caught the fragment of some dream from the past. That rush of atmosphere that can engulf one at any moment of the day following when something evokes the universe that absorbed one utterly in sleep. I mean I heard our voices for an instant, almost in argument, and I saw Father in his top hat and black overcoat rushing alone through the streets of the West End, peering into one door after another, and then, rising from the marble-top table in the dim smoky music hall you . . . your face.

"Yes . . ."

Go back, Julie! It was Father's voice.

". . . to penetrate the soul of it," I insisted, picking up the lost thread. But did my lips move? "To understand what it is that frightened him, enraged him. He said, 'Tear it down!' "

". . . you must never, never, can't do that." His face was stricken, like that of a schoolboy about to cry.

"No, absolutely, we don't want to, either of us, you know it . . . and you are not a spirit!" I looked at his mud-spattered boots, the faintest smear of dust on that perfect white cheek.

"A spirit?" he asked almost mournfully, almost bitterly. "Would that I were."

Mesmerized I watched him come toward me and the room darkened, and I felt his cool silken hands on my face. I had risen. I was standing before him, and I looked up into his eyes.

I heard my own heartbeat. I heard it as I had the night before, right at the moment I had screamed. Dear God, I was talking to him! He was in my room and I was talking to him! And I was in his arms.

"Real, absolutely real!" I whispered, and a low zinging sensation coursed through me so that I had to steady myself against the bed.

He was peering at me as if trying to comprehend something terribly important to him, and he didn't respond. His lips did have a ruddy look to them, a soft look for all his handsomeness, as if he had never been kissed. And a slight dizziness had come over me, a slight confusion in which I was not at all sure that he was even there.

"Oh, but I am," he said softly. I felt his breath against my cheek, and it was almost sweet. "I am here, and you are with me, Julie . . ."

"Yes . . ."

My eyes were closing. Uncle Baxter sat hunched over his desk and I could hear the furious scratch of his pen. "Demon wretch!" he said to the night air coming in the open doors.

"No!" I said. Father turned in the door of the music hall and cried my name.

"Love me, Julie," came that voice in my ear. I felt his lips against my neck. "Only a little kiss, Julie, no harm . . ." And the core of my being, that secret place where all desires and all commandments are nurtured, opened to him without a struggle or a sound. I would have fallen if he had not held me. My arms closed about him, my hands slipping in the soft silken mass of his hair.

I was floating, and there was as there had always been at Rampling Gate an endless peace. It was Rampling Gate I felt around me, it was that timeless and impenetrable soul that had opened itself at last. . . . A power within me of enormous ken . . . To see as a god sees, and take the depth of things as nimbly as the outward eyes can size and shape pervade . . . Yes, I whispered aloud, those words from Keats, those words . . . To cease upon the midnight without pain . . .

No. In a violent instant we had parted, he drawing back as surely as I.

I went reeling across the bedroom floor and caught hold of the frame of the window, and rested my forehead against the stone wall.

For a long moment I stood with my eyes closed. There was a tingling pain in my throat that was almost pleasurable where his lips had touched me, a delicious throbbing that would not stop.

Then I turned, and I saw all the room clearly, the bed, the fireplace, the chair. And he stood still exactly as I'd left him and there was the most appalling distress in his face.

"What have they done to me?" he whispered. "Have they played the cruelest trick of all?"

"Something of menace, unspeakable menace," I whispered.

"Something ancient, Julie, something that defies understanding, something that can and will go on."

"But why, what are you?" I touched that pulsing pain with the tips of my fingers and, looking down at them, gasped. "And you suffer so, and you are so seemingly innocent, and it is as if you can love!"

His face was rent as if by a violent conflict within. And he turned to go. With my whole will, I stood fast not to follow him, not to beg him to turn back. But he did turn, bewildered, struggling and then bent upon his purpose as he reached for my hand. "Come with me," he said.

He drew me to him ever so gently, and slipping his arm around me guided me to the door.

Through the long upstairs corridor we passed hurriedly, and through a small wooden doorway to a screw stairs that I had never seen before.

I soon realized we were ascending the north tower of the house, the ruined portion of the structure that Richard and I had not investigated before.

Through one tiny window after another I saw the gently rolling landscape moving out from the forest that surrounded us, and the small cluster of dim lights that marked the village of Rampling and the pale streak of white that was the London road.

Up and up we climbed until we had reached the topmost chamber, and this he opened with an iron key. He held back the door for me to enter and I found myself in a spacious room whose high narrow windows contained no glass. A flood of moonlight revealed the most curious mixture of furnishings and objects, the clutter that suggests an attic and a sort of den. There was a writing table, a great shelf of books, soft leather chairs and scores of old yellowed and curling maps and framed pictures affixed to the walls. Candles were everywhere stuck in the bare stone niches or to the tables and the shelves. Here and there a barrel served as a table, right alongside the finest old Elizabethan chair. Wax had dripped over everything, it seemed, and in the very midst of the clutter lay rumpled copies of the most recent papers, the *Mercure de Paris,* the London *Times.*

There was no place for sleeping in this room.

And when I thought of that, where he must lie when he went to rest, a shudder passed over me and I felt, quite vividly, his lips touching my throat again, and I felt the sudden urge to cry.

But he was holding me in his arms, he was kissing my cheeks and my lips again ever so softly, and then he guided me to a chair. He lighted the candles about us one by one.

I shuddered, my eyes watering slightly in the light. I saw more unusual objects: telescopes and magnifying glasses and a violin in its open case, and a handful of gleaming and exquisitely shaped sea shells. There were jewels lying about, and a black silk top hat and a walking stick, and a bouquet of withered flowers, dry as straw, and daguerreotypes and tintypes in their little velvet cases, and opened books.

But I was too distracted now by the sight of him in the light, the gloss of his large black eyes, and the gleam of his hair. Not even in the railway station had I seen him so clearly as I did now amid the radiance of the candles. He broke my heart.

And yet he looked at me as though I were the feast for his eyes, and he said my name again and I felt the blood rush to my face. But there seemed a great break suddenly in the passage of time. I had been thinking, yes, what are you, how long have you existed . . . And I felt dizzy again.

I realized that I had risen and I was standing beside him at the window and he was turning me to look down and the countryside below had unaccountably changed. The lights of Rampling had been subtracted from the darkness that lay like a vapor over the land. A great wood, far older and denser than the forest of Rampling Gate, shrouded the hills, and I was afraid suddenly, as if I were slipping into a maelstrom from which I could never, of my own will, return.

There was that sense of us talking together, talking and talking in low agitated voices and I was saying that I should not give in.

"Bear witness, that is all I ask of you . . ."

And there was in me some dim certainty that by knowledge alone I should be fatally changed. It was the reading of a forbidden book, the chanting of a forbidden charm.

"No, only what was," he whispered.

And then even the shape of the land itself eluded me. And the very room had lost its substance, as if a soundless wind of terrific force had entered this place and was blowing it apart.

We were riding in a carriage through the night. We had long long ago left the tower, and it was late afternoon and the sky was the color of blood. And we rode into a forest whose trees were so high and so thick that scarcely any sun at all broke to the soft leafstrewn ground.

We had no time to linger in this magical place. We had come to the open country, to the small patches of tilled earth that surrounded the ancient village of Knorwood with its gabled roofs and its tiny crooked streets. We saw the walls of the monastery of Knorwood and the little church with the bell chiming Vespers under the lowering sky. A great bustling life resided in Knorwood, a thousand hearts beat in Knorwood, a thousand voices gave forth their common prayer.

But far beyond the village on the rise above the forest stood the rounded tower of a truly ancient castle, and to that ruined castle, no more than a shell of itself anymore, as darkness fell in earnest, we rode. Through its empty chambers we roamed, impetuous children, the horse and the road quite forgotten, and to the Lord of the Castle, a gaunt and white-skinned creature standing before the roaring fire of the roofless hall, we came. He turned and fixed us with his narrow and glittering eyes. A dead thing he was, I understood, but he carried within himself a priceless magic. And my young companion, my innocent young man passed by me into the Lord's arms. I saw the kiss. I saw the young man grow pale and struggle to turn away. It was as I had done this very night, beyond this dream, in my own bedchamber; and from the Lord he retreated, clutching to the sharp pain in his throat.

I understood. I knew. But the castle was dissolving as surely as anything in this dream might dissolve, and we were in some damp and close place.

The stench was unbearable to me, it was that most terrible of all stenches, the stench of death. And I heard my steps on the cobblestones and I reached to steady myself against the wall. The tiny square was deserted; the doors and windows gaped open to the vagrant wind. Up one side and down the other of the crooked street I saw the marks on the houses. And I knew what the marks meant. The Black Death had come to the village of Knorwood. The Black Death had laid it waste. And in a moment of suffocating horror I realized that no one, not a single person, was left alive.

But this was not quite right. There was some one walking in fits and starts up the narrow alleyway. Staggering he was, almost falling, as he pushed in one door after another, and at last came to a hot, stinking place where a child screamed on the floor. Mother and Father lay dead in the bed. And the great fat cat of the household, unharmed, played with the screaming infant, whose eyes bulged from its tiny sunken face.

"Stop it," I heard myself gasp. I knew that I was holding my head with both hands. "Stop it, stop it please!" I was screaming and my screams would surely pierce the vision and this small crude little room should collapse around me, and I should rouse the household of Rampling Gate to me, but I did not. The young man turned and stared at me, and in the close stinking room, I could not see his face.

But I knew it was he, my companion, and I could smell his fever and his sickness, and the stink of the dying infant, and see the sleek, gleaming body of the cat as it pawed at the child's outstretched hand.

"Stop it, you've lost control of it!" I screamed surely with all my strength, but the infant screamed louder. "Make it stop!"

"I can not . . ." he whispered. "It goes on forever! It will never stop!"

And with a great piercing shriek I kicked at the cat and sent it flying out of the filthy room, overturning the milk pail as it went, jetting like a witch's familiar over the stones.

Blanched and feverish, the sweat soaking his crude jerkin, my companion took me by the hand. He forced me back out of the house and away from the crying child and into the street.

Death in the parlor, death in the bedroom, death in the cloister, death before the high altar, death in the open fields. It seemed the Judgment of God that a thousand souls had died in the village of Knorwood—I was sobbing, begging to be released—it seemed the very end of Creation itself.

And at last night came down over the dead village and he was alive still, stumbling up the slopes, through the forest, toward that rounded tower where the Lord stood with his hand on the stone frame of the broken window waiting for him to come.

"Don't go!" I begged him. I ran alongside him crying, but he didn't hear. Try as I might, I could not affect these things.

The Lord stood over him smiling almost sadly as he watched him fall, watched the chest heave with its last breaths. Finally the lips moved, calling out for salvation when it was damnation the Lord offered, when it was damnation that the Lord would give.

"Yes, damned then, but living, breathing!" the young man cried, rising in a last spasmodic movement. And the Lord, who had remained still until that instant, bent to drink.

The kiss again, the lethal kiss, the blood drawn out of the dying body, and then the Lord lifting the heavy head of the young man to take the blood back again from the body of the Lord himself.

I was screaming again, *Do not, do not drink*. He turned and looked at me. His face was now so perfectly the visage of death that I couldn't believe there was animation left in him, yet he asked: What would you do? Would you go back to Knorwood, would you open those doors one after another, would you ring the bell in the empty church, and if you did would the dead rise?

He didn't wait for my answer. And I had none now to give. He had turned again to the Lord who waited for him, locked his innocent mouth to that vein that pulsed with every semblance of life beneath the Lord's cold and translucent flesh. And the blood jetted into the young body, vanquishing in one great burst the fever and the sickness that had wracked it, driving it out with the mortal life.

He stood now in the hall of the Lord alone. Immortality was his and the blood thirst he would need to sustain it, and that thirst I could feel with my whole soul. He stared at the broken walls around him, at the fire licking the blackened stones of the giant fireplace, at the night sky over the broken roof, throwing out its endless net of stars.

And each and every thing was transfigured in his vision, and in my vision—the vision he gave now to me—to the exquisite essence of itself. A wordless and eternal voice spoke from the starry veil of heaven, it sang in the wind that rushed through the broken timbers; it sighed in the flames that ate the sooted stones of the hearth.

It was the fathomless rhythm of the universe that played beneath every surface, as the last living creature—that tiny child—fell silent in the village below.

A soft wind sifted and scattered the soil from the new-turned furrows in the empty fields. The rain fell from the black and endless sky.

Years and years passed. And all that had been Knorwood melted into the very earth. The forest sent out its silent sentinels, and mighty trunks rose where there had been huts and houses, where there had been monastery walls.

Finally nothing of Knorwood remained: not the little cemetery, not the little church, not even the name of Knorwood lived still in the world. And it seemed the horror beyond all horrors that no one anymore should know of a thousand souls who had lived and died in that small and insignificant village, that not anywhere in the great archives in which all history is recorded should a mention of that town remain.

Yet one being remained who knew, one being who had witnessed, and stood now looking down upon the very spot where his mortal life had ended, he who had scrambled up on his hands and knees from the pit of Hell that had been that disaster; it was the young man who stood beside me, the master of Rampling Gate.

And all through the walls of his old house were the stones of the ruined castle, and all through the ceilings and floors the branches of those ancient trees.

What was solid and majestic here, and safe within the minds of those who slept tonight in the village of Rampling, was only the most fragile citadel against horror, the house to which he clung now.

A great sorrow swept over me. Somewhere in the drift of images I had relinquished myself, lost all sense of the point in space from which I saw. And in a great rush of lights and noise I was enlivened now and made whole as I had been when we rode together through the forest, only it was into the world of now, this hour, that we passed. We were flying it seemed through the rural darkness along the railway toward London where the nighttime city burst like an enormous bubble in a shower of laughter, and motion, and glaring light. He was walking with me under the gas lamps, his face all but shimmering with that same dark innocence, that same irresistible warmth. And it seemed we were holding tight to one another in the very midst of a crowd. And the crowd was a living thing, a writhing thing, and everywhere there came a dark rich aroma from it, the aroma of fresh blood. Women in white fur and gentlemen in opera capes swept into the brightly lighted doors of the theater; the blare of the music hall inundated us, then faded away. Only a thin soprano voice was left, singing a high, plaintive song. I was in his arms, and his lips were covering mine, and there came that dull zinging sensation again, that great uncontrollable opening within myself. Thirst, and the promise of satiation measured only by the intensity of that thirst. Up stairs we fled together, into high-ceilinged bedrooms papered in red damask where the loveliest women reclined on brass bedsteads, and the aroma was so strong now I could not bear it, and before me they offered themselves, they opened their arms. "Drink," he whispered, yes, drink. And I felt the warmth filling me, charging me, blurring my vision, until we broke again, free and light and invisible it seemed as we moved over the rooftops and down again through rain drenched streets. But the rain did not touch us; the falling snow did not chill us; we had within ourselves a great and indissoluble heat. And together in the carriage, we talked to each other in low, exuberant rushes of language; we were lovers; we were constant; we were immortal. We were as enduring as Rampling Gate.

I tried to speak; I tried to end the spell. I felt his arms around me and I knew we were in the tower room together, and some terrible miscalculation had been made.

"Do not leave me," he whispered. "Don't you understand what I am offering you; I have told you everything; and all the rest is but the weariness, the fever and the fret, those old words from the poem. Kiss me, Julie, open to me. Against your will I will not take you . . ." Again I heard my own scream. My hands were on his cool white skin, his lips were gentle yet hungry, his eyes yielding and ever young. Father turned in the rain-drenched London street and cried out: "Julie!" I saw Richard lost in the crowd as if searching for some one, his hat shadowing his dark eyes, his face haggard, old. Old!

I moved away. I was free. And I was crying softly and we were in this strange and cluttered tower room. He stood against the backdrop of the window, against the distant drift of pale clouds. The candle-light glimmered in his eyes. Immense and sad and wise they seemed, and oh, yes, innocent as I have said again and again. "I revealed myself to them," he said. "Yes, I told my secret. In rage or bitterness, I know not which, I made them my dark co-conspirators and always I won. They could not move against me, and neither will you. But they would triumph still. For they torment me now with their fairest flower. Don't turn away from me, Julie. You are mine, Julie, as Rampling Gate is mine. Let me gather the flower to my heart."

Nights of argument. But finally Richard had come round. He would sign over to me his share of Rampling Gate, and I should absolutely refuse to allow the place torn down. There would be nothing he could do then to obey Father's command. I had given him the legal impediment he needed, and of course I should leave the house to him and his children. It should always be in Rampling hands.

A clever solution, it seemed to me, as Father had not told *me* to destroy the place, and I had no scruples in the matter now at all.

And what remained was for him to take me to the little train station and see me off for London, and not worry about me going home to Mayfair on my own.

"You stay here as long as you wish, and do not worry," I said. I felt more tenderly towards him than I could ever express. "You knew as soon as you set foot in the place that Father was all wrong. Uncle Baxter put it in his mind, undoubtedly, and Mrs. Blessington has always been right. There is nothing to harm there, Richard. Stay, and work or study as you please."

The great black engine was roaring past us, the carriages slowing to a stop. "Must go now, darling, kiss me," I said.

"But what came over you, Julie, what convinced you so quickly . . ."

"We've been through all, Richard," I said. "What matters is that we are all happy, my dear." And we held each other close.

I waved until I couldn't see him anymore. The flickering lamps of the town were lost in the deep lavender light of the early evening, and the dark hulk of Rampling Gate appeared for one uncertain moment like the ghost of itself on the nearby rise.

I sat back and closed my eyes. Then I opened them slowly, savoring this moment for which I had waited too long.

He was smiling, seated there as he had been all along, in the far corner of the leather seat opposite, and now he rose with a swift, almost delicate movement and sat beside me and enfolded me in his arms.

"It's five hours to London," he whispered in my ear.

"I can wait," I said, feeling the thirst like a fever as I held tight to him, feeling his lips against my eyelids and my hair. "I want to hunt the London streets tonight," I confessed, a little shyly, but I saw only approbation in his eyes.

"Beautiful Julie, my Julie . . ." he whispered.

"You'll love the house in Mayfair," I said.

"Yes . . ." he said.

"And when Richard finally tires of Rampling Gate, we shall go home."

EDWARD BRYANT
(b. 1945)

Born and raised in Wyoming, Edward Bryant received his college education at the University of Wyoming. That state is the setting for several of his short stories, collected as Wyoming Sun (1980).

Bryant has written primarily short stories, beginning with "They Come Only in Dreams" (1970). His first collection of short stories, Among the Dead and Other Events Leading up to the Apocalypse, was published in 1973, and his second, Cinnabar, in 1976—the latter being a collection of related short works about a future California city. His work is complex and sometimes dark, as illustrated by the story "Shark" (1973), in which an unhappy young woman wants to have her brain transplanted into a shark. His novels include The Man of the Future (1990), The Cutter (1988), Fetish (1991), and The Thermals of August (1992). He is a contributor to the Wild Cards series of superhero shared-universe novels; edited the anthology 2076: The American Tricentennial (1977); and is one of the regular book reviewers for Locus magazine. Bryant sometimes writes under the pseudonym Lawrence Talbot.

"Good Kids" is a cocky tale of streetwise children old beyond their years. The children's snappy dialogue is suave and fluent and sounds authentic. The story's climax is at once surprising, bloody, and satisfying. A pleasant surprise tucked into the text that follows is just how much, and how deftly, Bryant has borrowed from the story of the king vampire, Stoker's Dracula.

GOOD KIDS

"That blood?" said Donnie, appalled. "That's grossss."

Angelique was peeking over her shoulder at the lurid paperback vampire novel. "Don't draw out your consonants. You sound like a geek."

"I'm not a geek," said Donnie. "I'm only eleven years old, you jerk. I get to draw out my esses if I want to."

"We're all too goddamned bright," said Camelia gloomily. "The last place I went to school, everybody just played with dolls or talked all day about crack."

"Public schools," Angelique snorted.

Donnie flipped the page and squinted. "Yep, he's lapping up her menstrual blood, all right. This vampire's a real gink."

"Wonderful. So her arching, lily-white swan throat wasn't enough," said Cammie. "Oh boy. I can hardly wait till *I* start having my period."

The lights flashed and the four of us involuntarily glanced up. Ms. Yukoshi, one of the Center's three night supervisors, stood framed in the doorway. "Okay, girls, lights out in three. Put away the book. Hit those bunks. Good night, now." She started to exit, but then apparently changed her mind. "I suppose I ought to mention that this is my last night taking care of you."

Were we supposed to clap? I wondered. Maybe give her a four-part harmony chorus of "Thank you, Ms. Yukoshi"? What was appropriate behavior?

"No thanks are necessary," said Ms. Yukoshi. "I just know I need a long, long vacation. Lots of R and R." We could all see her sharp, white teeth gleaming in the light from the overhead. "You'll have a new person to bedevil tomorrow night. His name is Mr. Vladisov."

"So why don't we ever get a good WASP?" Cammie whispered.

The other two giggled. I guess I did too. It's easy to forget that Camelia is black.

Ms. Yukoshi looked at us sharply. Donnie giggled again and dog-eared a page before setting the vampire book down. "Good night, girls." Ms. Yukoshi retreated into the hall. We listened to the click and echo of her stylish heels moving on to the next room, the next island of kids. Boys in that one.

"I wonder what Mr. Vladisov will be like," Donnie said.

Angelique smiled. "At least he's a guy."

"Good night, girls." Donnie mimicked Ms. Yukoshi.

I snapped off the lamp. And that was it for another fun evening at the renovated brownstone that was the Work-at-Night Child Care Center and

Parenting Service. Wick Pus, we called it, all of us who had night-shift parents with no other place to put their kids.

"Good night," I said to everybody in general. I lay back in the bunk and pulled the covers up to my chin. The wool blanket scratched my neck.

"I'm hungry," said Angelique plaintively. "Cookies and milk aren't enough."

"Perhaps you want some blooood?" said Donnie, snickering.

"Good night," I said again. But I was hungry too.

The next day was Wednesday. Hump day. Didn't matter. No big plans for the week—or for the weekend. It wasn't one of the court-set times for my dad to visit, so I figured probably I'd be spending the time reading. That was okay too. I like to read. Maybe I'd finish the last thousand pages of Stephen King's new novel and get on to some of the stuff I needed to read for school.

We were studying urban legends and old wives' tales—a side issue was the class figuring out a nonsexist term for the latter.

We'd gone through a lot of the stuff that most of us had heard—and even believed at one time—like the hook killer and the Kentucky Fried Rat and the expensive car that was on sale unbelievably cheap because nobody could get the smell out of the upholstery after the former owner killed himself and the body wasn't discovered for three hot days. Then there was the rattlesnake in the K-Mart jeans and the killer spiders in the bouffant. Most of that didn't interest me. What I liked were the older myths, things like keeping cats out of the nursery and forbidding adults to sleep in the presence of children.

Now I've always liked cats, so I know where my sympathy lies with that one. Kitties love to snuggle up to warm little faces on chilly nights. No surprise, right? But the bit about sucking the breath from babies' lungs is a load of crap. Well, most of the time. As for the idea that adults syphon energy from children, that's probably just a cleaner way of talking about the incest taboo.

It's a way of speaking metaphorically. That's what the teacher said.

I can see why adults would want to steal kids' energy. Then they could rule the world, live forever, win all the Olympics. See what I mean? So maybe some adults do. You ever feel just how much energy is generated by a roomful of hyper kids? I know. But then, I'm a kid. I expect I'll lose it all when I grow up. I'm not looking forward to that. It'll be like death. Or maybe undeath.

It all sounds sort of dull gray and drab, just like living in the book *1984*.

The thing about energy is that what goes out has to come in first. Another lesson. First Law of Thermodynamics. Or maybe the Second. I didn't pay much attention that day. I guess I was too busy daydreaming about horses, or maybe sneaking a few pages of the paperback hidden in my vinyl binder.

Don't even ask what I'm going to do when I grow up. I've got lots of time to figure it out.

Mr. Vladisov had done his homework. He addressed us all by name. Evidently he'd sucked Ms. Yukoshi dry of all the necessary information.

"And you would be Shauna-Laurel Andersen," he said to me, smiling faintly.

I felt like I ought to curtsy at least. Mr. Vladisov was tall and courtly, just like characters in any number of books I'd read. His hair was jet-black and fixed in one of those widow's peaks. Just like a novel. His eyes were sharp and black too, though the whites were all bloodshot. They didn't look comfortable. He spoke with some kind of Slavic accent. Good English, but the kind of accent I've heard actors working in restaurants goofing around with.

Shauna-Laurel, I thought. "My friends call me SL," I said.

"Then I hope we shall be friends," said Mr. Vladisov.

"Do we have to call you 'sir'?" said Angelique. I knew she was just being funny. I wondered if Mr. Vladisov knew that.

"No." His gaze flickered from one of us to the next. "I know we shall *all* be very close. Ms. Yukoshi told me you were all . . ." he seemed to be searching for the correct phrase. ". . . good kids."

"Sure," said Donnie, giggling just a little.

"I believe," said Mr. Vladisov, "that it is customary to devour milk and cookies before your bedtime."

"Oh, that's not for a while yet," said Angelique.

"Hours," chimed in Donnie.

Our new guardian consulted his watch. "Perhaps twenty-three minutes?"

We slowly nodded.

"SL," he said to me, "will you help me distribute the snacks?"

I followed Mr. Vladisov out the door.

"Be careful," said Angelique so softly that only I could hear. I wondered if I really knew what she meant.

Mr. Vladisov preceded me down the corridor leading to the playroom and then to the adjacent kitchenette. Other inmates looked at us through the doorways as we passed. I didn't know most of their names. There were about three dozen of them. Our crowd—the four of us—was pretty tight.

He slowed so I could catch up to his side. "Your friends seem very nice," he said. "Well behaved."

"Uh, yes," I answered. "They're great. Smart too."

"And healthy."

"As horses."

"My carriage," mused Mr. Vladisov, "used to be pulled by a fine black team."

"Beg pardon?"

"Nothing," he said sharply. His tone moderated. "I sometimes slip into the past, SL. It's nothing."

"Me," I said. "I love horses. My dad says he'll get me a colt for my graduation from middle school. We'll have to stable it out in Long Island."

Mr. Vladisov didn't comment. We had reached the closetlike kitchenette. He didn't bother to turn on the light. When he opened the refrigerator and took out a carton of milk, I could see well enough to open the cabinet where I knew the cookies were stored.

"Chocolate chip?" I said. "Double Stuf Oreos?"

Mr. Vladisov said, "I never eat . . . cookies. Choose what you like."

I took both packages. Mr. Vladisov hovered over the milk, assembling quartets of napkins and glasses. "Don't bother with a straw for Donnie," I said. "She's not supposed to drink through a straw. Doctor's orders."

Mr. Vladisov nodded. "Do these things help you sleep more soundly?"

I shrugged. "I 'spose so. The nurse told me once that a high-carb snack before bed would drug us out. It's okay. Cookies taste better than Ritalin anyway."

"Ritalin?"

"An upper that works like a downer for the hypers."

"I beg your pardon?"

I decided to drop it. "The cookies help us all sleep."

"Good," said Mr. Vladisov. "I want everyone to have a good night's rest. I take my responsibility here quite seriously. It would be unfortunate were anyone to be so disturbed she woke up in the early morning with nightmares."

"We all sleep very soundly," I said.

Mr. Vladisov smiled down at me. In the dim light from the hall, it seemed to me that his eyes gleamed a dusky red.

I passed around the Double Stuf Oreos and the chocolate-chip cookies. Mr. Vladisov poured and distributed the glasses of milk as solemnly as if he were setting out communion wine.

Cammie held up her milk in a toast. "We enjoyed Ms. Yukoshi, but we know we'll like you much better."

Mr. Vladisov smiled without parting his teeth and raised an empty hand as though holding a wine glass. "A toast to you as well. To life everlasting, and to the dreams which make it bearable."

Angelique and I exchanged glances. I looked at Donnie. Her face was saying nothing at all. We all raised our glasses and then drank. The milk was cold and good, but it wasn't the taste I wished. I wanted chocolate.

Mr. Vladisov wished us a more conventional good night, then smoothly excused himself from the room to see to his other charges. We listened hard but couldn't hear his heels click on the hallway tile.

"Slick," said Angelique, nibbling delicately around the edge of her chocolate-chip cookie.

"Who's he remind me of?" mused Cammie. "That old guy—I saw him in a play once. Frank Langella."

"I don't know about this," said Donnie.

"What don't you know?" I said.

"I don't know whether maybe one of us ought to stay up all night on watch." Her words came out slowly. Then more eagerly, "Maybe we could take turns."

"We all need our rest," I said. "It's a school night."

"I sure need all the energy *I* can get," said Cammie. "I've got a geography test tomorrow. We're supposed to know all the capitals of those weird little states west of New Jersey."

I said, "I don't think we have anything to worry about for a while. Mr. Vladisov's new. It'll take him a little while to settle in and get used to us."

Cammie cocked her head. "So you think we got ourselves a live one?"

"So to speak." I nodded. "Metaphorically speaking . . ."

So I was wrong. Not about what Mr. Vladisov was. Rather that he would wait to get accustomed to how things ran at Wick Pus. He must have been very hungry.

In the morning, it took Donnie forever to get up. She groaned when Cammie shook her, but didn't seem to want to move. "I feel shitty," she said, when her eyes finally opened and started to focus. "I think I've got the flu."

"Only if bats got viruses in their spit," said Cammie grimly. She gestured at Donnie's neck, gingerly zeroing in with her index finger.

Angelique and I leaned forward, inspecting the throat.

Donnie's brown eyes widened in alarm. "What's wrong?" she said weakly.

"What's wrong ain't pimples," said Cammie. "And there's two of them."

"Damn," said Angelique.

"Shit," said Donnie.

I disagreed with nobody.

The four of us agreed to try not to get too upset about all of this until we'd had time to confer tonight after our parents dropped us off at the Center. Donnie was the hardest to convince. But then, it was her throat that showed the pair of matched red marks.

Mrs. Maloney was the morning shift lady who saw us off to our various buses and subways to school. Mr. Vladisov had gone off duty sometime before dawn. Naturally. He would return after dark. Double naturally.

"I'm gonna tell my mom I don't want to come back to the Center tonight," Donnie had said.

"Don't be such a little kid," said Cammie. "We'll take care of things."

"It'll be all right," Angelique chimed in.

Donnie looked at me as though begging silently for permission to chicken out. "SL?"

"It'll be okay," I said as reassuringly as I could. I wasn't so sure it would be that okay. Why was everyone staring at me as though I were the leader?

"I trust you," Donnie said softly.

I knew I was blushing. "It'll be all right." I wished I knew whether I was telling the truth.

At school, I couldn't concentrate. I didn't even sneak reads from my Stephen King paperback. I guess I sort of just sat there like a wooden dummy while lessons were talked about and assignments handed out.

I started waking up in the afternoon during my folklore class.

"The thing you should all remember," said Mrs. Dancey, my teacher, "is that myths never really change. Sometimes they're garbled and they certainly appear in different guises to different generations who recount them. But the basic lessons don't alter. We're talking about truths."

The truth was, I thought, I didn't know what we were all going to do about Mr. Vladisov. That was the long and short of it, and no urban myth Mrs. Dancey tempted me with was going to take my mind off that.

Time. Things like Mr. Vladisov, they figured they had all the time in the world, so they usually seemed to take things easy. Given time, we'd figure something out. Cammie, Donnie, Angelique, and me. We could handle anything. Always had.

"Shauna-Laurel?" It was Mrs. Dancey. Talking to me.

I didn't know what she had asked. "Ma'am?" I said. "Sorry."

But it was too late. I'd lost my chance. Too much daydreaming. I hoped it wouldn't be too late tonight.

Donnie's twin red marks had started to fade when the four of us huddled in our room at the Center to talk.

"So maybe they *are* zits," said Cammie hopefully.

Donnie irritably scratched at them. "They itch."

I sat on the edge of the bunk and swung my legs back and forth. "Don't scratch. They'll get infected."

"You sound like my mother."

"Good evening, my good kids." Mr. Vladisov filled the doorway. He was all dark clothing and angular shadows. "I hope you are all feeling well tonight?"

"Aren't you a little early?" said Angelique.

Mr. Vladisov made a show of consulting his watch. It was the old-fashioned kind, round and gold, on a chain. It had hands. I glanced out the window toward the street. The light had gone while we were talking. I wondered where Mr. Vladisov spent his days.

"Early? No. Perhaps just a bit," he corrected himself. "I find my position here at the Center so pleasant, I don't wish to be late." He smiled at us. We stared back at him. "What? You're not all glad to see me?"

"I have the flu," said Donnie dully.

"The rest of us will probably get it too," Angelique said.

Cammie and I nodded agreement.

"Oh, I'm sorry," said Mr. Vladisov. "I see why this should trouble you. Perhaps I can obtain for you an elixir?"

"Huh?" That was Cammie.

"For your blood," he said. "Something to strengthen your resistance. Tomato juice, perhaps? or V-8? Some other healthful beverage?"

"No," said Donnie. "No thank you. I don't think so. No." She hiccupped.

"Oh, you poor child." Mr. Vladisov started forward. Donnie drew back. "Is there something I can do?" he said, checking himself in midstride. "Perhaps I should call for a doctor?" His voice sounded *so* solicitous. "Your parent?"

"No!" Donnie came close to shouting.

"She'll be okay," said Cammie.

Mr. Vladisov looked indecisive. "I don't know . . ."

"We do," I said. "Everything will be fine. Donnie just needs a good night's sleep."

"I'm sure she will get that," said Mr. Vladisov. "The night is quiet." Then he excused himself to fetch our milk and cookies. This time he didn't ask for volunteer help.

Cammie was stroking Donnie's hair. "We'll see nothin' happens. You'll be just fine."

"That's right," said Angelique. "We'll all stay up."

"No need," I said. "We can take turns. No use everybody killing themselves."

"Bad phrasing," said Cammie. "Taking turns sounds good to me."

I volunteered, "I'll take the first watch."

"Yeah." Cammie grinned. "That way the rest of us got to stay up in the scariest part of the night."

"Okay, so you go first and wake me up later."

"Naw, Just kidding."

I liked being friends with Cammie and the others. But then we were so much alike. More than you might think.

The daughter of a widowed Harlem mortician.

The daughter of the divorced assistant French consul.

The daughter of an ambitious off-Broadway director.

The daughter of a divorced famous novelist.

All of us denied latchkeys and dumped at Wick Pus. Handier than boarding school if a parent wanted us. But still out of their hair.

One of us used to love drugs. One of us was thinking about loving God. Another was afraid of being the baby of the group. And another just wanted peace and a horse. I smiled.

Donnie actually did look reassured.

After a while, Mr. Vladisov came back with our nightly snacks. He seemed less exuberant. Maybe he was catching on to the fact that we were on to him. Maybe not. It's hard to tell with adults.

At any rate, he bid us all a good evening and that was the last we saw of him until he came around to deliver a soft, "Lights out, girls. Sleep well. Sleep well, indeed."

We listened for his footsteps, didn't hear any, heard him repeating his message to the boys down the hall. Finally we started to relax just a little.

Through the darkness, Cammie whispered, "Three hours, SL. That's it. Don't knock yourself out, okay? Wake me up in three hours."

"Okay."

I heard Donnie's younger, softer whisper. "Thanks, guys. I'm glad you're all here. I'm even going to try to sleep."

"Want a ghost story first?" That was Angelique.

"No!" Donnie giggled.

We were all silent.

I listened for steady, regular breathing. I waited for anything strange. I eventually heard the sounds of the others sleeping.

I guess I really hadn't expected them to drift off like that.

And then I went to sleep.

I hadn't expected that either.

I woke up sweaty, dreaming someone was slapping me with big slabs of lunch meat. Someone *was* slapping me. Cammie.

"Wake up, you gink! She's gone!"

"Who's gone?" The lamp was on and I tried to focus on Cammie's angry face.

"Donnie! The honky bloodsucker stole her."

I struggled free of the tangled sheet. I didn't remember lying down in my bed. The last thing I recalled was sitting bolt upright, listening for anything that sounded like Mr. Vladisov skulking around. "I think he— he put me to sleep." I felt terrible.

"He put us all to sleep," said Angelique. "No time to worry about that. We've got to find Donnie before he drains her down to those cute little slippers." Donnie had been wearing a pair of plush Felix the Cat foot warmers.

"Where we gonna look?" Cammie looked about ready to pull Mr. Vladisov apart with her bare fingers with their crimson painted nails.

"Follow running blood downhill," I said.

"Jeez," Cammie said disgustedly.

"I mean it. Try the basement. I bet he's got his coffin down there."

"Traditionalist, huh?"

"Maybe. I hope so." I pulled on one Adidas, wound the laces around my ankle, reached for the other. "What time is it, anyway?"

"Not quite midnight. Sucker didn't even wait for the witching hour." I stood up. "Come on."

"What about the others?" Angelique paused by the door to the hall.

I quickly thought about that. We'd always been pretty self-sufficient. But this wasn't your ordinary situation. "Wake 'em up," I said. "We can use the help." Cammie started for the door. "But be quiet. Don't wake up the supervisors."

On the way to the door, I grabbed two Oreos I'd saved from my bedtime snack. I figured I'd need the energy.

I realized there were thirty or thirty-five kids trailing just behind as my roommates and I found one of Donnie's Felix slippers on the landing in the fire stairs. It was just before the final flight down to the dark rooms where the furnace and all the pipes were. The white eyes stared up at me. The whiskers didn't twitch.

"Okay," I said unnecessarily, "come on. Hurry!"

Both of them were in a storage room, just up the corridor from the place where the furnace roared like some giant dinosaur. Mr. Vladisov sat on a case of toilet paper. It was like he was waiting for us. He expected us. He sat there with Donnie cradled in his arms and was already looking up at the doorway when we burst through.

"SL . . ." Donnie's voice was weak. She tried to reach out toward me, but Mr. Vladisov held her tightly. "I don't want to be here."

"Me neither," muttered Cammie from beside me.

"Ah, my good kids," said Mr. Vladisov. "My lambs, my fat little calves. I am sorry that you found me."

It didn't sound like he was sorry. I had the feeling he'd expected it, maybe even wanted it to happen. I began to wonder if this one was totally crazy. A psychotic. "Let Donnie go," I said, trying for a firmness I don't think was really showing in my voice.

"No." That was simple enough.

"Let her go," I repeated.

"I'm not . . . done," he said, baring his fangs in a jolly grin.

I said, "Please?"

"You really don't understand." Mr. Vladisov sighed theatrically. "There are two dozen or more of you and only one of me; but I am a man of some power. When I finish snacking on this one, I will kill most of the rest of you. Perhaps all. I'll kill you and I will drink you."

"Horseshit," said Cammie.

"You will be first," said Mr. Vladisov, "after your friend." He stared directly at me, his eyes shining like rubies.

"Get fucked." I surprised myself by saying that. I don't usually talk that way.

Mr. Vladisov looked shocked. "Shauna-Laurel, my dear, you are not a child of *my* generation."

I definitely wasn't. "Let. Her. Loose," I said distinctly.

"Don't be tiresome, my child. Now be patient. I'll be with you in just a moment." He lowered his mouth toward Donnie's throat.

"You're dead," I told him.

He paused, smiling horribly. "No news to me."

"I mean *really* dead. For keeps."

"I doubt that. Others have tried. Rather more mature specimens than all of you." He returned his attention to Donnie's neck.

Though I didn't turn away from Mr. Vladisov, I sensed the presence of the other kids behind me. We had all crowded into the storage room, and now the thirty-odd of us spread in a sort of semicircle. If Mr. Vladisov wondered why none of us was trying to run away, he didn't show it. I guess maybe like most adults, he figured he controlled us all.

I took Cammie's hand with my right, Angelique's with my left. All our fingers felt very warm. I could sense us starting to relax into that fuzzy-feeling receptive state that we usually only feel when we're asleep. I knew we were teaming up with the other kids in the room.

It's funny sometimes about old folktales (we'd finally come up in class with a nonsexist term). Like the one forbidding adults to sleep in the same room with a child. They had it right. They just had it backwards. It's *us* who suck up the energy like batteries charging . . .

Mr. Vladisov must have felt it start. He hesitated, teeth just a little ways from Donnie's skin. He looked at us from the corners of his eyes without raising his head. "I feel . . ." he started to say, and then trailed off. "You're taking something. You're feeding—"

"Let her go." I shouldn't even have said that. It was too late for making bargains.

"My . . . blood?" Mr. Vladisov whispered.

"Don't be gross," said Cammie.

I thought I could see Donnie smile wanly.

"I'm sorry," said Angelique. "I thought you were going to work out okay. We wouldn't have taken much. Just enough. You wouldn't have suspected a thing. Finally you would have moved on and someone else would have taken your place."

Mr. Vladisov didn't look well. "Perhaps—" he started to say. He looked like he was struggling against quicksand. Weakly.

"No," I said. "Not on your life."

And then we fed.

Laura Anne Gilman
(b. 1967)

Born and raised in New Jersey, Laura Anne Gilman received her bachelor's degree from Skidmore College in Saratoga Springs, and then went into publishing. She has worked in the science fiction and mystery genres for the past decade as an editor for variety of talented writers, ranging from award-winning mystery author Dana L. Stabenow to cyberpunk writer Wilhelmina Baird.

Gilman's short fiction has varied widely within the fantasy/science fiction genres, from a quiet but charming character study in The Day the Magic Stopped (1995) to an intense story about love and magic in Lammas Night (1995) to a hilarious look at artificial intelligence in Don't Forget Your Spacesuit, Dear (1996) to a straightforward adventure tale involving a telepath in Highwaymen: Robbers and Rogues (1997). Gilman also co-edited a critically acclaimed alternate were-creature anthology entitled OtherWere: Stories of Transformation with Keith R. A. DeCandido (1996).

"Exposure," written for an anthology called Blood Muse (1995), is a very modern vampire tale. In it, the vampire, a professional photographer whose daily work involves him in decisions about light and dark, faces a challenge unique to his situation. Despite the story's whimsical tone, the serious nature of Westin's artistic problem is never lost sight of in the story. Anyone who has ever taken photography seriously will feel for him.

EXPOSURE

The timer clicked, a cicada in the dark. Lifting the tongs off their rest, he swirled the paper gently; watching, deeming Good to go by the rules, better to work by instinct. Finally deeming it complete, he lifted the sheet out of its bath, placing it in another shallow tub and turning the water on, cold, over it.

The music played, one cd after another, continuous shuffle so that he never knew what would come up next: Melissa Etheridge, Vivaldi, the exotic noises of a rain forest. It suited his mood, prepped him for the evening's work. For now the lilting strains of *The Four Seasons* kept him company. Tugging at his ear where it itched, he studied the image floating face-up at him. Satisfied, he lifted it between two fingertips, shaking some of the wetness off. Turning off the water, he transferred the print to his right hand and reached out to flick the toggle switch on the wall next to the room's exit. Stepping into the revolving door, he pushed the heavy plastic with one shoulder and emerged from the darkroom.

Blinking in the sudden fluorescent lighting, he cast a glance over his shoulder to make sure that the warning light had gone off, then carried the print over to the line strung across the far end of the studio. Clipping it to the line, he stepped back to examine the other prints already there. Several, most notably the three shots of the hookers talking over coffee, leaning intently across the table to get in each other's faces, pleased him. Others were less successful, but overall he was satisfied. Checking his watch once again, he took off the stained apron he wore, hung it on a hook beside the door, shut off the stereo, and went to take a shower. Time to go to work.

"Hey, Westin!"

He slung the bag more comfortably over his shoulder, and stopped to wait for the overweight Latino cop who chugged up alongside him. "Going out again tonight, huh?"

"As I've done every night this week," Westin replied. "And the week before that."

"But not the week before that," the cop said.

"But the entire month before that I didn't miss a single night. So why are you asking now?"

The cop ignored the slight edge to Westin's voice. "There's some weirdo out there, past few nights. Scared the hell out of a couple slits Tuesday, cut into their business too. Guy's wearing Pampers and some kinda bonnet, according to reports. If you happen to run into him . . ."

"I should take his picture for your album?"

"The brass'd be thankful. And ya gotta know the *Post*'d pay for that picture. Anyway, keep your eyes out."

"I always do," Westin said, holding up his camera. He watched with detached affection as the cop loped back to his post, holding up a wall in the upper hall of the Port Authority. Swaddling and a bonnet. That was a new one. He could certainly understand johns keeping away, but why were the hookers afraid of him? Westin thought briefly about following up on it, then put those thoughts away. If he came into the viewfinder, then would be the time to wonder. For now, there was the rent to pay. He stepped into the men's room to moisten his contact lenses, darkened to protect his hypersensitive eyes. Another thing to bless technology for. Even he couldn't take photographs through sunglasses.

Leaving the bustling noise of the terminal, he exited into the sharp cold night of Eighth Avenue and paused. Where to go? Where were the pictures, the images waiting for him to capture? He turned in a slow half-circle, ignoring the line of dinner-hour cabs waiting in front of him, letting his instinct pick a direction. There. The hot white lights were calling him.

Walking briskly, he cut crosstown, one hand on his camera, the other hanging loosely by his side. The sidewalk hustlers and gutter sharks watched him pass, recognizing a stronger predator. But the hookers, ah, the hookers were another story. They swarmed to him, offered him deals, enticements. He did love women so, their softness hiding such strong, willful blood. But he was not feeding tonight. At least, not of that. Tonight was for a different passion. Bypassing Times Square itself, he wandered the side streets, catching the occasional sideways stare from well-dressed theatergoers on their way from dinner to their entertainment. Only the expensive Konica hanging by his side kept them from assuming he was a panhandler. The long trench had seen better decades, and not even the Salvation Army had been able to find anything nice to say about his boots except for the fact that they had once been sturdy. And the less said about his once-white turtleneck, the better. But he preferred these clothes, using them the same way wildlife photographers hid within camouflaged blinds. He was stalking wildlife as well, a form that was more easily spooked than any herd of gazelles or a solitary fox.

For the next seven hours he took shot after shot of the ebb and flow of humanity around him, occasionally moving to a new spot when people became too aware of him or, more accurately, of the camera. His choices satisfied him. The elderly woman in rags stepping over a crack in the sidewalk with graceful poise. The businesswoman striding along, topcoat open to the bracing wind. Two too-young figures doing a deal with brazen indifference to the mounted policeman just yards away, and the cop's equal indifference to their infractions. The hooker holding a Styrofoam cup in her hands, allowing the steam to rise to her face, taking delicate sips. He loved them all, carefully, surreptitiously, with each click of the shutter, every zoom of the lens to catch their expressions, the curve of their hands, the play of neon across their skin. He could feel the beat of their blood, pulling him all unwilling, and he blessed the cold which kept their scents from him. He couldn't afford the distractions.

Stopping in a Dunkin' Donuts to pick up a cup of coffee, he dug in his trench pocket for a crumpled dollar bill to pay for it. "Why can't you carry a wallet?" he could hear Sasha complain. "That way when someone finally puts you out of your misery I'll know to collect the body." Lovely, long-suffering Sasha. But she forgot her complaints when he had a show ready for her pale white walls, secure in her status as Michael Westin's only gallery. For three long, hungry years she had supported him, and for the last eleven he had returned the favor. He understood obligation, and needing, and the paying of debts.

Finally he came to the last roll of film he had prepared for the night. He took it out of the pouch hanging from his belt and looked at it, black plastic against the black of his thin leather gloves. High-speed black and white, perfect for catching moments silhouetted against the darkness, sudden bursts of light and action. His trademark. One roll left. He still had time to shoot this roll before heading home, still subjects to capture.

Or he could try again, a little voice whispered inside his head. There was time.

Shaking his head to silence the unwanted voice, he removed the used film from the camera, marked it with the date, location, and an identifying number, then replaced it in the pouch. Still the unused film sat in his palm. He could reload the camera, finish the evening out. Or he could save it for the next trip, cutting the session short and going home. At the thought his lips curled in a faint smile. Home to where Danielle slept in their bed, her hair fanned out against the flannel sheets. She would be surprised to see him, surprised and pleased, if he knew his Dani.

Or you could try again.

"Damnit, enough!" He would be a fool to listen to that voice, a fool to even consider it. Hadn't the three attempts been enough to teach him that? If the third time wasn't a charm, then certainly the fourth was for fools. And his kind didn't survive by being fools.

But still the thought lingered, caressing his ego, his artist's conceit. He could picture the shot, frame it perfectly in his mind. The conditions were ideal tonight, the location tailor-made. It would be the perfect finish to this show, the final page of the book he knew Sasha would want to do.

Stuffing the thought back into the darkness of his mind, he deftly inserted the black cartridge, advancing the shutter until the camera was primed. He cast one practiced eye skyward. Four A.M., give or take fifteen minutes. He had another hour, at most, before he would have to head home, wrap his head under a pillow, and get the few hours of sleep he still required before locking himself in the darkroom to develop this night's work. Then dinner with Dani, and perhaps he would take tomorrow night off. Fridays were too busy to get really good photos. Better to spend it at home, in front of a roaring fire, and his smooth-necked, sweet-smelling wife and a bottle of her favorite wine.

You work too hard, she had fussed at him just last month, rubbing a minty-smelling oil into his aching muscles after a particularly grueling night hunched over the lightboard, choosing negatives. *Always pushing, always proving. You don't have anything to prove.* But he did. Had to take better photos, find the most haunting expressions, the perfect lighting. All to prove to himself that he was the photographer his press made him out to be, and not just some freak from a family of freaks, that his work was the result of talent and dedication, not some genetic mutation, a parasite on human existence.

Shh, my love, he could hear Dani whisper. *I'm here, and I love you.* She would whisper that, baring her neck so that he might graze along that smooth dark column, feel the pulsing of her blood . . .

He swore, cutting off those thoughts before his body reacted to the thought of her strength, her warmth. Jamming his hands into the pockets of his trench, he watched the street theater, looking for something that would finish the evening on a positive note, leave him anxious to see the proof page. But the street was empty for the moment, leaving him with the little voice, which had crept back the moment his attention was distracted. *The perfect photograph,* it coaxed him. *Something so heartbreakingly perfect that only you could create. Otherwise this exhibit is going to end on a downer, and there's enough of that in this world, isn't there?*

Cursing under his breath, he scared off a ragged teen who had sidled up next to him. Westin watched the kid's disappearing backside with wry amusement. It had been a long time since anyone had tried to mug him, and he would have given the boy the twenty or so bucks he had in his pocket, just to reward such *chutzpa.*

Checking the street one last time, he sighed and gave up. Time to call it a good haul, and head on home. *To bed, perchance to screw, and then to sleep.* Hanging the camera strap around his shoulder, he adjusted the nylon webbing until the shoulder patch fit snugly against his coat. *There's still film left,* the little voice said, sliding and seducing like a televangelist. *Can't go home with film left.*

"I'll take shots of some of New York's Finest," he told himself. Fragile humans, holding back the night. It would be a good image, and it would please Miguel to be included. And Tonio, his partner. Kid was so green his uniform squeaked when he walked. Veteran and rook, side by side, against the squalor of the bus terminal. Maybe he'd catch them in an argument. He could see that, frame it in his head. The possibilities grew, flicking across the screen in his head fast enough to wipe all thoughts of That Shot out of his head. By the time he reached the corner of Seventh Avenue, he had it all planned out. Stopping to look up at the still-dark sky, he thought he could see just the faintest hint of light creeping skyward

from the east. False dawn. At home, he would be watching the deer come down from the wooded area to eat his bushes. He had done an essay on them for National Wildlife which paid well enough to replace the rose-bushes the hoofed terrorists had devoured the spring before.

Waiting at the light on the corner of Forty-first and Eighth, something made him tilt his head to the right. There. By the chain-link fence protecting an empty lot. A shadow that wasn't a shadow. His soothing thoughts broke like mirror shards, and he turned his head to stare straight across the street. Live and let live. The fact that he chose not to hunt—did not, in fact, have to—did not mean others might not. Only once had he made it his concern, when a kinswoman had gotten messy, leaving corpses over the city—*his city*. His mouth tightened as he remembered the confrontation that had followed. He hadn't wanted to destroy her—but he wasn't ready to end his existence yet either. And letting her continue was out of the question. Only fools saw humans as fodder. They were kin, higher in some ways, lesser in others, but in the balance of time, equal. He believed that, as his father had believed that, raising his children to live alongside the daylight-driven world as best they could, encouraging them to build support groups, humans—companions—that would offer so that they need not take. It was possible, his father had lectured them, to exist without violence. And so they had. And the daylight world had given him good friends, a loving wife—and the means to express the visions which only his eyes could see.

With that thought in mind, he turned slowly, looking up at the sky behind him. False dawn. It was almost upon him.

The perfect photograph. It would only take one shot. One exposure, and then it's done.

A scrap of memory came over him. "If 't were done, 't were best done quickly . . ." *Damn. Damn damn damn damn.*

It seemed almost as though another person took control; moved his body across the street, dodged the overanxious cabs turning corners to pick up the last fare of the night. Someone else walked across the bare floor of the terminal that even at this hour still hosted a number of grubby souls wandering, some slumped over knapsacks, asleep, some reading newspapers or staring down into their coffee as though it held some terrible answer. His hand powered by someone else reached for the camera, holding it like a talisman, a fetish. Standing on the escalator, he watched out of habit, his mind already on what he was going to do. He could feel it pulling him, a siren's song, and he cursed himself. But he couldn't stop, no more than the first three times he had tried. Tried, and failed.

Crossing over to the next level of escalators, he paused at the first step, willing his body to stop, turn around, get on the bus that would take him home. Only a fool would continue, only a madman. Looking down, he saw first one boot, then the other, move on to the metal steps, his left hand grasping the railing. With his right hand he fingered the camera's casing, stroking his thumb over the shutter button.

At the end of this escalator he stopped, hitting his free hand against the sign that thanked him in Spanish and English for not giving money to panhandlers. The pain made him wince. At least in that they were equal, humans and he. Pain was a bitch. He hit his hand again, then gave up. The siren call, as strong as blood, had him again, and he had no choice but to give in. If it was to be done, it had to be done fast. Get in, get out, go home. Punching the up button, he waited for the elevator that would take him to the rooftop parking lot.

He adjusted the camera in his hand, barely aware of the sweat that ran down the back of his neck and down the front of his shirt. Shifting closer to the roof edge, he leaned against the ornate masonry, bracing himself. A glint of light caught his attention and he squinted, the hair along his arm rising in protest. "One minute more," he told himself. "Just one damn more minute, you bitch, and I'll have you. Come on, come on, do it for me!" He swallowed with difficulty, wishing for the water bottle at arms' reach, as impossible as if it were on another planet.

Another flicker of light caught the first building, fracturing against the wall of windows. "Come on," he said under his breath, unaware of anything except the oncoming moment. He could feel it, a sexual thrill waiting to shoot through his body, better than anything, even the flush of the first draw of blood. This was why he was alive. This was it, this was the perfect moment . . . He drew the camera to his face, focusing on primal instinct. The light rose a fraction higher, and he was dropping the camera, running for the maintenance door, aware only of the screaming animal need to hide, survive, get away from that damn mocking bitch. The camera lay where it fell: abandoned, broken.

"Goddamn," Westin swore, shaking himself free of the memory. "Go home, Westin. It's a fucking picture. Not worth dying for." The woman exiting the elevator glanced at him, pulling her coat closer around her body as she swept past him, eyes forward in a ten-point exhibition of New York street sense. The first rule: never let them see you seeing them. He moved past her on instinct, not realizing until the doors had closed that he passed the Rubicon. "Well goddamn," he said again, but he was grinning. A predator's flash of too-white teeth, a grin of hungry anticipation. His fangs tingled, the veins underneath them widening in response to the rush of adrenaline coursing through his body.

The parking lot was mostly deserted—the late-night partiers having headed home, and the Jersey commuters not yet in. There were a handful of cars parked in the back for monthly storage, and one beat-up blue Dart pulled in as he stood there. He waited in the shadows until the driver, a heavy-set man wearing workboots and carrying a leather briefcase, passed by him into the elevator.

Going to the edge of the lot, he sat on the cold metal railing, hooking one foot under the longest rung to keep himself from slipping five stories to the pavement waiting below. The air was noticeably colder here, the wind coming at him without buffer. Dawn was coming, damn her. He could feel it in every sinew of his body, every instinct-driven muscle screaming for him to find a dark cave in which to wait the daylight hours out.

Forcing himself to breathe evenly, he took control of those instincts, forcing them back under the layers of civilization and experience. There would be plenty of time to find a bolthole somewhere in the massive bulk of the Port Authority. He had done it before, here and elsewhere. It was all timing. Timing, he reminded himself, and not panicking.

Squinting against the wind, he swung his body into better position, facing eastward, toward the East River. Toward the rising sun.

Idiot, a new, more rational voice said in tones of foreboding. *Do the words crispy critter mean anything to you?* He shrugged off the voice, lifting the camera to his eye. There was only the moment, and the shot. His entire universe narrowed down to that one instant, his entire existence nothing more than the diameter of the lens. His fingers moved with a sure steadiness, adjusting the focus minutely, his body tense.

A particularly aggressive gust of wind shook the rooftop, making him lose the frame. Swearing, he fought to regain it, all the while conscious of seconds ticking by, each moment more deadly than the last. A taloned claw clenched in his gut, and sweat ran along his hairline and down under his collar. "Damn, damn, damn," he chanted under his breath, a mantra. The muscles in his back tightened, his legs spasming. But his arms, his hands, remained still, the muscles cording from the strain.

The first ray of light touched the rooftops, glinting deadly against empty windows. He swore again, his finger hovering over the shutter button.

"Come on, baby," he coaxed it, a tentative lover. "Come here. That's it, you're so perfect."

Another ray joined the first, the faintest hint of yellow in the pure light. The hairs along his arms stirred underneath the turtleneck, his heart agitating with the screaming in his head to *get out get away you dumb fuck get OUT.* His hands remained steady, his eyes frozen, unblinking: waiting, just waiting. He could smell it now, that perfect moment, with more certainty than he'd ever known. Everything slowed, his breathing louder than the wind still pushing the building beneath him, his body quivering under the need for release.

A third ray sprang across the sky, then a fourth and fifth too fast to discern. Suddenly the rooftops were lit by a glorious burst of prism-scattered light, heart-stopping, agonizing, indelible. A ray flashed toward him, reflected by a wall of glass, and glanced off the brick barely a foot to the left. His forefinger oh so slowly pressed toward the shutter button while every muscle twisted in imagined agony. "Come on come on come on . . ." he whispered, holding himself back for the perfect second.

The smooth metal was underneath his fingertip when the first light caught him, slashing against his cheek, his chest, reaching through the skin into his vital organs.

He screamed, falling backwards in a desperate attempt to keep the deadly light from him, slamming to the cold cement floor even as his finger pushed, even as his ears heard the click of the shutter closing underneath the sound of his own primal voice.

His skin was burning, the blood seeping from the pores of his face and arms. The pain was everywhere, searing him, branding him. Tears tinctured with red washed a track down his narrow nose.

Crawling to his feet, Westin barely retained the presence of mind to shove the camera back into its padded carry-bag before dragging himself to the elevator and slamming his fist against the Down button. Blood dripped down his arm and onto the fabric.

The elevator opened in front of him. Westin pushed himself into the empty space, shaking. He leaned against the back wall and drew a deep breath, knowledge of his own stupidity battling with the sheer exhilaration of a different sort of hunt.

All too soon, the rush was over, and he was himself again, drenched in sweat and drying blood. In his memory, the sun rose like some killer angel, and he knew his actions for what they were—vanity.

But he would do it again.

ACKNOWLEDGMENTS

Allen, Woody: "Count Dracula." Copyright © 1971 by Woody Allen. Reprinted by permission of Random House, Inc.

Beaumont, Charles: "Blood Brother." Copyright © 1961 by HMH Pub. Co., renewed 1989 by Christopher Beaumont.

Brown, Frederic: "Blood." Copyright © 1955 by Frederic Brown.

Bryant, Edward: "Good Kids." Copyright © 1989 by Edward Bryant. First appeared in *Blood is Not Enough,* edited by Ellen Datlow.

Carter, Leslie Roy: "Vanishing Breed." Copyright © 1970 by Leslie Roy Carter. First published in *Curse of the Undead,* edited by Margaret L. Carter.

Casper, Susan: "A Child of Darkness." Copyright © 1989 by Susan Casper.

Charnas, Suzy McKee: "Unicorn Tapestry." Copyright © 1988 by Suzy McKee Charnas.

Cheever, John: "Torch Song." From *The Stories of John Cheever* by John Cheever. Copyright © 1947 by John Cheever. Reprinted by permission of Alfred A. Knopf Inc.

Derleth, August: "The Drifting Snow." Copyright © 1997 by Arkham House Publishers.

Ewers, Hanns Heinz: "The Spider." Copyright © 1921 by Hanns Heinz Ewers.

Gilman, Laura Anne: "Exposure." Copyright © 1995 by Laura Anne Gilman.

King, Stephen: *Salem's Lot.* Reprinted with permission. Copyright © 1976 Stephen King. All rights reserved. Originally published in *Playboy* magazine.

Lee, Tanith: "Bite-Me-Not or Fleur de Feu." Copyright © 1984 by Tanith Lee.

Leiber, Fritz: "The Girl With the Hungry Eyes." Copyright © 1989 by Fritz Leiber.

Matheson, Richard: *I Am Legend.* Copyright © 1954, renewed 1982 by Richard Matheson. Reprinted by permission of Don Congdon Associates, Inc.

Moore, C. L.: "Shambleau." Copyright © 1933 by Popular Fiction Publishing Co., renewed 1961 by C. L. Moore. Reprinted by permission of Don Congdon Associates, Inc.

Oates, Joyce Carol: *Bellefleur.* Copyright © 1980 by Ontario Review Press. Reprinted by permission of John Hawkins & Associates, Inc.

Rice, Anne: "The Master of Rampling Gate." Copyright © 1983 by Anne O'Brien Rice. Originally published in *Redbook.* Reprinted by permission of author.

Strieber, Whitley: "The Hunger." Copyright © 1981 by Andrew Strieber.

Yarbro, Chelsea Quinn: *Hôtel Transylvania.* Copyright © 1978, 1988 by Chelsea Quinn Yarbro.

Zelazny, Roger: "The Stainless Steel Leech." Copyright © 1963 by Roger Zelazny.